UNDERSTANDING LANGUAGE CHOICES

A Guide to Sociolinguistic Assessment

SIL International®

Series Editor
Mike Cahill

Volume Editor
Bonnie Brown

Production Staff
Bonnie Brown, Managing Editor
Barbara Alber, Compositor
Barbara Alber, Cover design

Cover Photo
John Grummitt

UNDERSTANDING LANGUAGE CHOICES

A Guide to Sociolinguistic Assessment

Ken Decker
John Grummitt

SIL International®
Dallas, Texas

Copies of this and other publications of SIL International® may be obtained from

SIL International Publications
7500 W. Camp Wisdom Road
Dallas, TX 75236-5629

Voice: 972-708-7404
Fax: 972-708-7363
publications_intl@sil.org
www.ethnologue.com/bookstore.asp

CONTENTS

CASE STUDIES

PREFACE

In sociolinguistics today, language vitality is the most current topic of research and concern. Fifty years ago there were still many speech communities throughout the world that existed in isolation. For them, language choice was just not an issue, nor was language vitality. Even communities that had some contact with other languages often limited their interaction. But today there are only a handful of isolated groups that are considered 'uncontacted'. Hundreds of languages are considered endangered and many are no longer spoken. There are a great many marginalized speech communities that are choosing to shift to the use of languages of wider communication. Every day, hundreds of millions of people must make choices as to which language they will use as they encounter people from other speech communities, or even people from their own. This prevalence of language choice is unprecedented in human history.

Most people in the world are living in multilingual environments. Through the last several decades numerous theories have been proposed to describe how people make language use choices. These theories have focused on choices motivated by identity, economic pressures, prestige, social mobility and other factors. However, most of these studies are based on research conducted in major world cities or dealing with major European languages. There is still much urgent research needed in less urban environments in which non-European languages are threatened. Therefore, this textbook has been designed to focus on research in multilingual communities confronted by language use choices that threaten their very existence.

It is in this environment of threatened lesser-known languages that I have worked for over 25 years. I was blessed in the beginning with gracious teachers and as the years went by I gave more effort to passing on my experience to new young people. This book builds on earlier generations of related publications. Those most familiar to me are: *Dialect Intelligibility Testing* (1974) by Eugene Casad, *Language Variation and Limits to Communication* (1983) by Gary Simons, *The Survey Reference Manual* (1989) compiled by Ted Bergman, *Survey on a Shoestring* (1990) by Frank Blair, the *Language Survey Reference Guide* (1995) by Joseph Grimes, and *Assessing Ethnolinguistic Vitality* (2000) edited by Gloria Kindell and Paul Lewis; I am grateful to all of these authors as mentors.

In recent years I have become aware of a need for a textbook that expresses new attitudes towards collaborative research and the application of such research to language planning and development. To this end, *Understanding Language Choices* was written with the novice researcher in mind. While an introductory knowledge of sociolinguistics may be helpful to understanding the issues, this book should be easily accessible to someone without previous exposure to the topics.

This textbook will help novice researchers understand the choices that confront speakers of lesser-known languages who live in multilingual environments. It also covers methods that can be used to study the sociolinguistic environments of these speech communities. While the book is titled *Understanding Language Choices*, it is not limited to an academic understanding of the sociolinguistic factors that drive the choices people make, but goes on to describe the impact of these choices.

This is not a general sociolinguistics textbook. The speech communities and environments described here are predominantly those with lesser-known languages in the Third World. This is not a book that will teach all types of research methods. We have focused on those methods with which we are most familiar and most applicable to the Third World environment in which we do this research.

This book was created through a collaborative process. First, I invited John Grummitt to help me. John was a student of mine who I quickly saw had very good writing skills. Although he was new to language assessment, he had an ability to comprehend the concepts quickly. He was also able to look at the material through the eyes of a novice, which helped us to keep focus as together we wrote this textbook. Next, we invited reviews from a number of colleagues, whom we would like to thank: Ted Bergman, Douglas Boone, Leoni Bouwer, Ed Brye, Lynn Landweer, Paul Lewis, Dan Paul, and Wilma Parker. Finally, the book was used in several language assessment training courses. We would like to thank the instructors: Karl Anderbeck, John Clifton and Randy Lebold, and their students, who gave us feedback. My apologies to any whom I have not mentioned by name.

I would like to thank my wife, Sandy, and daughter, Tirzah, for their love and encouragement. Lastly, we would like to thank all our friends and colleagues who have supported us in this project and our heavenly Father in whom we find life.

Ken Decker

Dallas, March 2012

"Choice is the pivotal notion of sociolinguistics."

Florian Coulmas

1 INTRODUCTION

In this chapter, we introduce you to the book and the field of **LANGUAGE ASSESSMENT.** We will:

- define some essential vocabulary,
- describe the context of language assessment within the larger study of **LANGUAGE DEVELOPMENT**,
- explain the layout of the book, and
- explain how it can be used as an aid to study and a reference.

Let's start by introducing language assessment through two case studies of situations that are good examples of what's involved.

CASE STUDY 1A
MORE THAN MEETS THE EYE
PAKISTAN

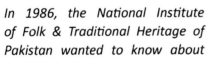

In 1986, the National Institute of Folk & Traditional Heritage of Pakistan wanted to know about and preserve knowledge of the languages and cultures in the north of their country. The Northern Pakistan survey team was formed to respond to this request and I was part of that team. When we began, we thought there were 14 languages in the northern portion of the country.

We found quite a mix of situations. Our linguistic research showed that some communities spoke the same language varieties, even

DEFINITION ▸ LANGUAGE ASSESSMENT is the process of regularly monitoring and studying language use.

DEFINITION ▸ LANGUAGE DEVELOPMENT is a result of a series of on-going, planned actions that a community takes to ensure that their LANGUAGE REPERTOIRE continues to serve their changing social, cultural, political, economic, and spiritual needs and goals.

DEFINITION ▸ LANGUAGE REPERTOIRE is the range of languages or varieties of a language that are available to an individual or community to meet their needs and goals.

CASE STUDY 1A SOURCE ▸ Ken Decker, International Language Assessment Coordinator, SIL International.

NOTE ▸ The team included expatriates and nationals who were advised by consultant professors from several local universities.

though the people told us that they spoke different languages. And in other communities, when we identified languages as being different, the people insisted that they were the same! People in some communities we visited were using only one language. People in other communities used several languages. Some groups were very motivated to develop writing for their language. Then, others were shifting away from using their parents' language altogether, and there was little interest in developing it.

In another complex situation we found very little difference between one village and the next, but we found that with each village we visited further from the first village, the difference would become greater and greater. Eventually, we'd arrive in a place where the people could not understand the language of the first place we'd surveyed, and they called it by another name. Looking at our maps, we realized that there was nowhere obvious that we could draw a boundary between one language and another. How could each village speak different languages if everyone understood their neighbors? But how could they speak the same language if they couldn't understand their neighbors' neighbors? It seemed that everywhere we went we found information that only made our task more complex. By the time we'd finished studying the ethnic identities, language use, language attitudes, and language variation of northern Pakistan, instead of the 14 languages we'd thought we had, we ended up describing 26— nearly double we'd what anticipated.

_____

CASE STUDY 1B
MARA CLUSTER
TANZANIA

The Mara Cluster is a coordinated language development effort in Central Tanzania, Africa. This effort is led by a **PARTNERSHIP** *including Tanzanian church leaders, and local and regional representatives of* **SIL INTERNATIONAL® (SIL).** *An advisory committee consisting of representatives of over 20 church denominations had created a list of languages in the area with the SIL survey team leader. The partnership determined that more information was needed about the variation between these languages in need of vernacular Bible translation. The survey team developed a plan*

DEFINITION ‣ PARTNERSHIP is a relationship where parties commit to share complementary resources to achieve mutually agreeable goals, working together at each stage of planning, implementation, and evaluation.

DEFINITION ‣ SIL INTERNATIONAL is a faith-based, not-for-profit language development organization, formerly known as the *Summer Institute of Linguistics.*

to collect wordlists and other information from a large number of locations.

During a one-month trip, the team visited 30 villages, conducting group and village leaders' interviews and collecting 15 word lists. The interviews gave valuable information about language attitudes and speech community boundaries. The wordlist data was analyzed to identify consistent phonological patterns that identified variation between languages and **DIALECTS.** *The findings were described in a report presented to the program manager and members of the partnership. The final choice of languages to be included in the Mara Cluster Program was made on the basis of this report.*

This book is the next generation in a series of books that have guided and provided resources for the kinds of work described in Case Study 1A and Case Study 1B. In both, we see that there is a partnership of organizations that are collaborating on the guidance of language development work. Local community leaders may already be involved, and each partner is offering its expertise to meeting the needs of the program. As the partners assess what they know and what they need to know, they identify gaps in their knowledge. The partners ask a team of **LANGUAGE SURVEYORS** to collect information. The team:

- assesses what they know of the situation,
- conducts background research,
- formulates research questions,
- modifies or designs research instruments for the survey,
- takes survey trips to gather information,
- documents and analyzes the data, and
- presents their findings to the partners.

The partners then use the findings from the survey to inform the ongoing development work.

What has just been described here is an idealized process. There is a range of situations around the world where language development takes place, and in each of these, the assessment process will vary in some way. Although surveyors aim to follow a clearly defined process as they work, it is quite common to encounter unexpected events and situations. This means the processes, as well as the surveyors, have to be flexible to adapt to these. Generally though, the description above and our first two case studies

DEFINITION ▸ A **DIALECT** is regionally or socially distinctive variety of a language.

NOTE ▸ The authors believe that social research and development is best done in partnership with those who will be influenced by it. However, in some cases, research may be conducted for purely academic reasons or requested by someone external to the community.

DEFINITION ▸ **LANGUAGE SURVEYORS** are people who do the secondary and primary research, including data collection, analysis, and reporting activities for language assessment.

NOTE ▸ We use the term *surveyor* rather than *researcher* because we want to describe a particular kind of research work that is more specific than general language use research, which we call language assessment.

CROSS-REFERENCE ▸ See **Chapter 7** on page 167 for a thorough description of the complete assessment process.

illustrate the typical processes and experiences a person can expect from language assessment work.

DEFINITION ▸ SOCIOLINGUISTICS is the study of how languages are used in different social situations and how social and cultural factors affect linguistic interaction.

We have written this book as a guide to students who are learning about language assessment for the first time. We did not set out to write a textbook about **SOCIOLINGUISTICS**, but in the course of explaining language assessment we needed to explain many sociolinguistic principles. We hope the book will be useful to others though, even if they have more experience in sociolinguistics or language assessment itself. Throughout the book, we try to make as much use as possible of the pronoun "we." This is to make those new to assessment feel welcome: you have joined a global team doing some amazing work. We also want to use "we" to indicate that, just like students, even those of us with a great deal of experience are learning new things about language assessment each time we do it. The information in this book is just as important to the experienced surveyor as it is to the newest member of our community.

CROSS-REFERENCE ▸ See Case Study 3H on page 87 and Section 4.2.5 on page 129.

QUOTE ▸ *A greeting is not simply a greeting; it is a forum in which to enact through linguistic practices the cultural ideologies of equality in Australia or inequality in West Africa. The communicated meaning is radically different. The way language is used... reflects different beliefs about human nature and how truth and social harmony can be most advantageously arrived at.* (Foley 1997:259)

We have chosen "Understanding Language Choices" as our title for a number of reasons. First of all, it is a *desire to understand* that fuels everything we do in assessment. We do not do our work simply for the sake of data collection, language documentation, or report writing. Instead, we want our data and documentation to inform our understanding so that our report writing is a reflection of what we understand and a vehicle to help others reach understanding. There are *language choices* that we want to understand. We want to understand why it is that a speech community would decide one day to abandon its language and start using another or why parents would use a different language only when talking to their children about school. Society is constantly changing all around us. For the people we work with in language assessment, this change is often large and rapid, and language users are thus faced with serious choices about whether they adapt their language capacities to cope and, if so, how (Coste and Simon 2009:171). Understanding these kinds of choices will help us to understand how language development can be of most help to the communities we work with.

1.1   Some Distinctions

We need to start out with some definitions to ensure that you, the reader, know what we mean when we use terms which you may have seen used differently elsewhere.

1.1.1   Distinguishing Survey and Assessment

From the start, we want to highlight a distinction in the use of the terms **SURVEY** and assessment. In the past, *language survey* was described as an attempt "to uncover and present a broad overview of the linguistic and sociolinguistic facts" that relate to a particular community (Blair 1990:1). This 'uncovering' and "broad overview" reflected the fact that surveys were done before any other language development activities and were considered superficial. In this book, we describe survey as an activity that can be done at any time in the life of a language development effort and may address very specific research questions. A survey is the activity of doing secondary and primary research, data collection, analysis, and reporting. This data-collection often involves travel somewhere, so we also say *going on a language survey* when we mean a data collection trip.

Language survey activities need to be conducted as part of a long-term process of assessment. *Assessment* is therefore the process of regularly monitoring and studying language use. Regular assessment is an important part of any intentional effort to maintain the sustainability of a language. We make this distinction to emphasize that the study of a sociolinguistic environment may take more forms than a simple data collection trip, and that ideally assessment should be an ongoing part of the life of any language development program. Having defined *assessment* and distinguished it from *survey*, we now turn to the much more problematic definitions of *language* and *dialect*.

DEFINITION ‣ LANGUAGE SURVEY is the activity of doing the secondary and primary research, data collection, analysis, and reporting activities for language assessment. A LANGUAGE SURVEY may refer to the data collection trip.

1.1.2   Distinguishing Language and Dialect

Crystal (1985) has defined dialect as "a regionally or socially distinctive variety of a language" and says that "dialects are subdivisions of language." Linguists consider all varieties of a language to be dialects. A **LANGUAGE** can be defined as the sum total of all the varieties that are used by the people who consider that they all speak the same language. However, people use the terms dialect and language to mean different things. And sociolinguists have identified many cases of complex relationships that make these distinctions difficult.

Between linguists there are disagreements that illustrate the huge variety of situations in which scholars have attempted to define language. At one extreme, Chomsky's transformational grammar (2002) describes language as a pure linguistic code studied in isolation from people or communication.

DEFINITION ‣ A LANGUAGE is the sum total of all the linguistic varieties that are used by the people who consider that they all use the same language.

QUOTE ‣ *Unless we want to postpone working on language… until the probably never arriving day when all the conceptual problems of defining language in all of its different senses are resolved… we need a pragmatic approach to dealing with this problem.* (Himmelmann 2006:2)

At the other extreme, Makoni and Pennycook (2006) view language as a human behavior that cannot be described artificially as a distinct code in dictionaries, grammars, and with arbitrary writing systems. Wandruszka gives us a pretty clear description of reality when he says,

> *For humans there exists neither a complete control of language nor a completely homogeneous* **SPEECH COMMUNITY**. *Never and nowhere will we find a perfect, homogeneous monosystem; always and everywhere we will just find imperfect heterogeneous polysystems. The relationship of humans towards their language is not one of perfect monolingualism, but just the opposite, it is one of imperfect polylingualism and one of polylingual imperfection. (Wandruszka 1979 cited in Hinnenkamp 2005 and translated from the original German, bolding ours)*

DEFINITION ‣ **A SPEECH COMMUNITY** is a hypothetical group of people who do not necessarily share the same **HERITAGE LANGUAGE**, but do share common normative socio-behavioral rules concerning when different language forms are used with one another. This can include multilingual, diglossic, and monolingual communities. People are members of many speech communities at the same time. The term includes forms of language that are not spoken such as literature and also communities that do not use speech such as the Deaf.

DEFINITION ‣ **HERITAGE LANGUAGE** is a language that has been used in the home for multiple generations.

These definitions vary because "how one chooses to define a language depends on the purposes one has in identifying that language as distinct from another" (Lewis 2009:9). Thus, the speakers of a language, language developers, and linguists have different purposes for and ways of looking at language.

A language development program needs to begin with understanding the perspective of the speakers of the language. When they think of "their language," who do they include or exclude as speakers? Often people will include speakers who use their language with some slight phonological or lexical differences as speakers of their language. Sometimes, there is a great deal of linguistic variation in the speech of a people who consider that they all speak the same language. Of course, while we can't assume that everyone in a group will have the same opinion, within a particular speech community, there will be generally shared agreement about the rules and norms of using language. In fact, where this agreement is in question will indicate the sociolinguistic boundaries between speech communities.

To some people, a speech variety is only a language if it is written, everything else is a dialect. In some countries, the language variety used by the politically dominant people is a language and the other varieties are dialects. Sometimes people use the term dialect to refer to speech varieties that are considered less prestigious. Sometimes the term language is synonymous with the ethnic identity, so it could be beneficial to include more people in the group to make the group more powerful. In a case such as Sweden and Norway, spoken forms of Norwegian and

Swedish are so similar that people usually use their own language when they meet (Gooskens 2007:445). Yet, they still prefer to consider them different languages for reasons of national identity. Sanskrit is an ancient language of India from which the modern Indo-Aryan languages have diverged. Rajasthani is the name given by linguists to a cluster of Indo-Aryan varieties (such as Marwari, Malvi, Dhundhari, and others) spoken in the Indian state of Rajasthan. People from the same area, speaking essentially the same way, will identify either as Dhundhari, Marwari, Rajasthani, or Sanskrit speakers (Lockwood 1972:195–199). We can see that definitions of speech communities are therefore dependent on perspective and not absolute. People may choose those they want to identify with for all sorts of reasons, and they may also be placed in them or excluded from them by socially dominant groups.

Thus, an understanding of the sociolinguistic perspectives of a speech community is essential if language development activities are to succeed. If the linguistic needs of a certain group are ignored, then there will be less impact, and the people in that group will be needlessly marginalized. If people are grouped together who don't see themselves as members of the same speech community, one group may reject the efforts for language development.

Surveyors also need to consider a more measureable definition of language. Language is used for the purpose of communication. If two people cannot understand one another, then they aren't communicating, and some would say that they aren't using the same language. But how much a loss of **COMPREHENSION** is acceptable before two varieties are considered different languages? Sometimes, simply a change in stress or intonation can create misunderstanding. Surveyors can establish somewhat artificial thresholds to establish the difference between languages. For example, SIL surveys consider that lexical similarity that is less than 70 percent indicates two different languages (Kindell 1991:28). However, Romaine (2000:22) reminds us that "boundaries between speech communities are essentially social rather than linguistic." Thus, a focus on linguistic features such as lexical similarity alone cannot help us to understand the speech communities we work with.

DEFINITION ▸ COMPREHENSION is what is understood when communication takes place.

CROSS-REFERENCE ▸ See **Chapter 4** on page 113 for more about measuring linguistic differences and **Section 4.4.2** on page 141 specifically for lexical similarity.

Members of a language development team have to work with different definitions for language. They must be aware of the perception of the people, but they must also deal with the linguistic realities of the variation found in the dialects that are being grouped for development. One of the major goals of many language development efforts is the production

QUOTE ▸ *...for the linguist then, spatial delimitation of dialects cannot be an efficient parameter in the study of dynamic linguistics.* (Canut 2002:39)

DEFINITION ‣ **AN ORTHOGRAPHY** is a standardized writing system. It consists of the rules of using the script and also describes the script itself. The script alone is not an orthography. Languages can have more than one orthography. Serbian, for example, is digraphic and uses both Latin and Cyrillic orthographies.

of literature. In most cases, we cannot develop an **ORTHOGRAPHY** for varieties that don't understand one another. However, there is a certain amount of variation that can be handled with a standardized orthography.

As we consider different definitions for *language* and *dialect*, we define these terms here primarily on the basis of their suitability as language varieties for development programs and the production of literature. Grimes (1995:17) defines a language as "a cluster of regional or social speech varieties ("dialects"), at least one of which can be understood adequately by everyone who speaks any of the varieties in the cluster natively." This definition recognizes that members of a speech community may include differing speech varieties into their definition of their language, and it also recognizes the need for there to be comprehension that unites the group.

There are two important points to make about Grimes' definition. Firstly, we need to define the word adequately for the particular situation we are involved in. In many situations there is measureable difference between two varieties, but if two speakers are allowed a short time of interaction, they are able to adapt their expectations and gain better comprehension. Among users of signed languages there is a considerable ability to adapt to significant differences in signing systems and have adequate comprehension. We must also realize that comprehension of oral speech isn't always required for communication of ideas. For example, in China, comprehension based on literacy alone may be adequate as many languages in China share the same equally comprehensible script, but there is not comprehension between the spoken forms. On this basis, when people see a written text from a different speech variety they might not think of it as a different language.

Secondly, Grimes' definition implies that comprehension is not only a linguistic factor but rather depends heavily on social factors such as favorable attitudes and motivation. These factors are themselves extremely complex, and for these reasons Grimes adds a caveat to his definition:

> *The linguistically central dialect of a cluster does not always coincide with the cultural or economic or political perception of a center. The actual paths of best communication may place the boundaries of the cluster where the political view might refuse to recognize them for reasons that have nothing to do with language. It is therefore important both for linguistics and for language policy that we understand the differences. (1995:17)*

We will investigate the reasons for these differences in later chapters.

Variation exists within any language. In fact, for languages that have not been standardized, the people may not recognize a central variety. When asked about the speech of others, the language users may not be able to describe differences other than to simply say that some speech is more similar or more different from their own. There is therefore a spectrum of variation within any language and these varieties are often referred to as dialects.

QUOTE ‣ *...closed communities and unified identities no longer exist; neither do homogeneous linguistic areas.* (Canut 2002:38)

The introduction to *Ethnologue™*, SIL International's database of the world's languages, contains three important criteria for a pragmatic distinction between the terms language and dialect and variety:

- Two related varieties are normally considered varieties of the same language if speakers of each variety have inherent understanding of the other variety at a functional level (that is, can understand based on knowledge of their own variety without needing to learn the other variety).
- Where spoken **INTELLIGIBILITY** between varieties is marginal, the existence of a common literature or of a common ethnolinguistic identity with a central variety that both understand can be a strong indicator that they should nevertheless be considered varieties of the same language.
- Where there is enough intelligibility between varieties to enable communication, the existence of well-established distinct ethnolinguistic identities can be a strong indicator that they should nevertheless be considered to be different languages. (Lewis 2009:9)

DEFINITION ‣ **INTELLIGIBILITY** is the quality of being able to be understood in communication. It differs from comprehension, which is what is understood in communication.

CROSS-REFERENCE ‣ See **Section 4.3.1** on page 133 for more on intelligibility.

So we see that there are many different ways to define language and dialect. We will use the perspective of the members of the speech community as the beginning point for deciding how to define a specific language situation being studied. With the communities we work with, we also seek to identify a common speech community which can use one form of literature.

1.1.3   Distinguishing Different Kinds of Language

There are complexities when choosing an appropriate reference to the language spoken by someone as their dominant or original language. For years people have used the term mother tongue, but what if someone's language is not the same as that spoken by their mother? Another term used by some people is first language. But what if the language best controlled by the person is not the first language that had been learned? Other terms have been proposed such as vernacular, native language, cradle language, or others. Often, the reason for referencing this primal language is the assumption that it is the language best controlled or most identified with. However, people learn their languages in different ways, from different people, at different ages, and for different purposes. Some people use certain languages for certain topics, for example, such as one language for reading, another language for religious purposes, and another language in the marketplace.

QUOTE ‣ *People choose their linguistic systems so as to resemble those of the group or groups they wish from time to time to be identified with, or so as to distinguish themselves from those they wish to distance themselves from.* (Le Page 1997:29)

DEFINITION ‣ **A NATIONAL LANGUAGE** is a language that has gained prominence for communication between ethnolinguistic groups throughout a country.

Consider a mother and father who didn't come from the same speech community and in this culture the wife adopts the language of the husband. They have a daughter who begins learning her father's language, but sometimes hears the mother's language. Neither of these languages are the **NATIONAL LANGUAGE**. Before gaining proficiency in the mother's or father's language, the unfortunate child is orphaned and raised by people in a third speech community outside of her home country. As an adult she returns to her home country and learns her national language, which she chooses to identify with and prefers to use in all situations. This fourth language is not her *mother tongue, first language,* or *native language,* and for a time as an adult, it was not her **DOMINANT LANGUAGE** in terms of proficiency. But this fourth language is the one she chooses for her identity. While this would be a rare situation, it reveals the challenge to choosing a term of reference.

DEFINITION ‣ **DOMINANT LANGUAGE** is the language that a person has their best competency in. It may or may not be their heritage language.

Another aspect to this conundrum is the competency of a person in a language. Even in large, predominantly monolingual communities, like those we find in many western nations, we recognize that some individuals have better control of their language than other people, for example, an educated poet versus an uneducated laborer. Furthermore, as in the example above, people can gain greater competency in a language learned later in life, and people can also choose a language other than their childhood language as a language of identity later in life.

DEFINITION ‣ **L1** is commonly understood to be the first language that a child acquires. In this book, we consider L1 to be the same as heritage language.

In this book, we use the term **HERITAGE LANGUAGE** when referring to the language that has been used in the home for multiple generations, without specifying the person's competency in that language. We will use the term dominant language to refer to a person's language of best competency, with no reference to any cultural significance. Sometimes we will use the notation **L1** to refer to the heritage language when it contrasts with another language that has been learned, designated as **L2**, or **L3**, etc.

1.2   Assessment's Contribution to Language Development

People are always changing the way they use their language or languages. These changes are a response to their changing world and help them adapt to the changes. Generally, this is a natural process, but sometimes the social or environmental changes occur so rapidly that intentional action is required to attain sustainability. In such cases, international and local organizations work with local communities to develop languages for specific purposes, that is, to help communities to do new things with their languages in order to promote the community's own welfare. Since many of the world's languages are unwritten, language development often includes developing writing systems and producing written materials. But there can be many other kinds of interim and final development goals, such as developing new indigenous terminology, **MULTILINGUAL EDUCATION**, and the promotion of traditional language practices.

DEFINITION ▸ MULTILINGUAL EDUCATION attempts to help children first learn reading, writing, and other subjects in their L1, then at some later stage they shift to an L2 as either the medium of instruction or as a subject.

Language assessment has a critical role in the planning and evaluation aspects of language development. Language assessment gathers information to help with

- determining appropriate language development goals,
- planning language development activities, and
- ongoing evaluation of development activities.

If development efforts such as creating written materials are to be effective, they must be applied in the right places and implemented in the most suitable ways for maximum sustainability. A particularly important consideration for this sustainability is ensuring that research is conducted in collaboration with the local community from the start. Apart from ensuring that development programs start out correctly, they also need to be monitored to assess their progress and to be sensitive to any changes in the social environment. We can also carry out assessment once programs have finished, and this benefits future programs by evaluating reasons for success and failure.

In previous books, the focus has been on identifying where new writing systems need to be developed and to determine how many communities will potentially be able to use this writing system. However, languages can also be developed for sustainable **ORALITY**, or even maintaining the language as a symbol of a people's identity and heritage. In this book, we

DEFINITION ▸ ORALITY is expression through non-written speech.

will continually emphasize that the key to making decisions is to respond to the reality of the sociolinguistic situation of the people we work with. They are the ones who will make the choices, through their behavior, that will determine the effectiveness of the language development efforts.

1.2.1   Our Focus of Study

It is crucial that as surveyors, we are clear about the purpose of language assessment. In broad terms, we can define our purpose in language assessment as being to

- determine, either by ourselves or with others, "whether or not a language development project should be undertaken in a given speech" variety, "and what the nature and scope of such projects should be" (Kindell 1991:21),
- gain a greater knowledge of sociolinguistic issues relevant to scholars and official entities, and
- monitor the progress and success of ongoing language development activities.

Clarity about the purpose of what the surveyors will do comes at the start of each language assessment project because those who initiate the assessment do so with particular goals in mind. When language development is central to their purposes, it is important that the language assessment **STAKEHOLDERS** define the parameters of the research.

In light of our desire to understand sociolinguistic reality, one of the major goals of language assessment is to identify what language varieties are most favored by a community for a particular purpose. This book is therefore limited to helping us learn how people use languages for different purposes. We are interested in the things that influence variation in the language repertoire as well as variation in the features of the languages themselves. We focus on these areas because they are the most influential in determining the success of language development.

We combine sociolinguistic, linguistic, and **ETHNOGRAPHIC** research, because if we studied society or languages separately from each other, we'd only discover a limited amount of the information needed for the success of development efforts. At all points in the assessment process, even if we're considering linguistic data such as phonetic forms, we need to keep in mind the connections with the social environment the language is part of. And these social environments can vary widely.

DEFINITION ▸ A STAKEHOLDER is an individual or group that is affected by and/or influences the outcomes of a development program.

QUOTE ▸ *Language issues are political and social and must be considered in their contexts...the view that it is linguistic attributes that account for language dominance or subordination is now a very dated one.* (Edwards 2002:40)

DEFINITION ▸ ETHNOGRAPHY is a branch of anthropology that studies human cultures and their behavior.

Aspects of this kind of research have been described as the *ethnography of communication* (Hymes 1968; Saville-Troike 1982).

The context where social interaction happens may be on an international scale or simply between two people. For example, we might study how governments choose an official language or we could look at how parents talk to their children at home. By emphasizing the primacy of social factors, this book is different from others that have preceded it. In each chapter, we begin our focus not at the linguistic level, nor by describing data collection **TOOLS** that we use. Instead, we begin by describing the social factors that influence language choices and move on from there.

1.2.2   Our Research

The research approach we describe in this book is cyclic, as shown in Figure 1. The first step in any research is to identify the purpose of the research. The purpose may be determined by some authority who commissions the assessment, or by a student who is doing research for a university degree. From this point we carry out a number of steps: we observe, form our research questions, decide what we'll study and how we will gather new data, gather the data, analyze the data, draw conclusions from the analysis, and attempt to answer the research questions. Research generally results in raising new questions, so we can then begin again by forming new research questions. The process is actually more spiral than cyclic in that each time around we know more about what we are studying.

CROSS-REFERENCE ‣ See **Section 4.2.2** on page 120 for more on the ethnography of communication.

QUOTE ‣ *...naturally, the factors influencing social cohesion or the more or less harmonious future of all beings on planet earth may under no circumstances be reduced to questions of language only.* (Coste and Simon 2009:69)

DEFINITION ‣ **TOOLS** are instruments for collecting information that involve established procedures, for example, a questionnaire or a language proficiency test.

FIGURE 1 ‣ The research cycle.

DEFINITION ‣ SECONDARY RESEARCH involves collecting information from research which has already been carried out.

DEFINITION ‣ PRIMARY RESEARCH involves collecting new, previously unknown information.

DEFINITION ‣ An **NGO** is a non-governmental Organization. UNICEF is an NGO.

DEFINITION ‣ TRIANGULATION involves using more than one methodology and more than one tool to collect data so that results can be confirmed through more than one data source (Rubin and Babbie 2010:139).

CROSS-REFERENCE ‣ See **Section 5.2.6** on page 187 for more about triangulation.

DEFINITION ‣ A test has **VALIDITY** if it produces the data it was designed to produce and not something else.

DEFINITION ‣ BILINGUALISM is the learned ability by an individual to use two different languages.

There are two types of research: **SECONDARY** and **PRIMARY**. All assessment should begin with secondary research, reviewing what is already known. When we do secondary research, we collect information from sources like libraries, reports from knowledgeable **NGO**s, interviews with knowledgeable outsiders, the work of previous researchers, and the Internet. Primary research is done through three methodologies which we describe as *observing, asking,* and *measuring.* We can observe how people are using languages, we can ask people about how they use languages and feel about them, and we can measure how languages differ, how many people use the language a certain way or feel a certain way about languages. Throughout this process, we attempt to use **TRIANGULATION** to increase the **VALIDITY** of our data. For example, if we

- hear people from different dialects communicating with little difficulty, and
- they tell us that they understand people from the other dialect, and
- we measure very little difference in linguistic features between the dialects,

then we can be fairly certain that the two varieties are similar.

As we start to gain knowledge about the apparent sociolinguistic characteristics which define a speech community, we begin to ask questions about different aspects of it. For example, we may read in a book that a language is reported to have two dialects. That leads us to question how different or similar these dialects are or even whether they exist in the perception of the members of the speech community or only in the research of linguists. We might next talk to knowledgeable people from the area, and they tell us that people from the two dialects don't understand each other. Now we have two more questions: are they different languages, and do the people still consider that they are two dialects of the same language? This reflects a typical pattern of research at the initial stages of an assessment project.

We then use tools to study these questions. Some of the typical tools we use are questionnaires, observation schedules, wordlists, comprehension tests, and **BILINGUALISM** tests. Usually, we use tools that we have used before to answer similar research questions. As we work through the book, we'll be introducing these typical tools to you. Often, we will adapt these tools for specific situations. Sometimes though, we may need to design new tools that are more appropriately matched to the situations we're working in. Importantly, we do not conduct the same kind of research every time in every place. The way we conduct our research is guided by what we know about the specific situation. Because of this, we need to be flexible in our approach to research and this means being ready to adapt tools and procedures as necessary. However, maintaining some consistency across studies, by using the same tools and following accepted protocols, has the benefit of making the results more comparable.

1.3   Book Organization

1.3.1   A Conceptual Approach to Organizing the Book

In order to help us understand the context of sociolinguistic assessment, we focus on the choices that the communities we work with make when they communicate. Working with the people in a community, we want our research to result in an understanding of their perspective of their own speech community.

We focus on communities, not individuals, for the fundamental reason that language is a social phenomenon; language change is societal, not individual. As Coulmas (2005:11, 14) says,

> [t]he principle task of sociolinguistics is to uncover, describe and interpret the socially motivated restrictions on linguistic choices.... For, while every speaker's speech act is the manifestation of choice, the individual act of choice does not reveal the social nature of language. That only becomes apparent if we can show how individual choices add up to form collective choices...every language and language variety is the result of collective choice, that is, cooperative creation.

We also investigate language choices at the level of the speech community and not the individual because it is at this level that decisions about language development are made. We talk to individuals to gather data. But we do so in a way that helps us to get an accurate picture of the larger community they are part of. And while we may work with individuals in a community to make decisions, they will ideally have been chosen to represent all the community stakeholders.

NOTE ▸ What we are talking about here is sampling, and you can find out more about sampling in **Section 5.4.2** on page 195.

Our third reason for working at the level of the community is a little more difficult to describe: it is only at the level of community that true freedom of language choice is possible. For the individual, there are always restrictions on language choice. One set of restrictions is imposed on us by the physical constraints within which language takes place. Our ability to produce and interpret sounds is limited by the ranges of pitch we can speak and hear, for example. Another set of restrictions is imposed by the structural rules of the languages we speak. For instance, word order restrictions mean that we cannot simply order words randomly. And this hints at the biggest set of restrictions as far as our focus is concerned: "Social norms are restrictions on individual choices making deviations that imperil communication unacceptable, if not impossible" (Coulmas 2005:7).

These "social norms" are so deeply ingrained in us that they are subconscious and don't seem like choices at all. We hardly notice them. However, they do come to our attention when we are faced with someone discovering what they are such as the toddler, the language learner, or by someone abusing them in some way such as the drunk on the train or comedians playing on words. Changing these social norms is the privilege not of the individual but the community as a whole. We know this because in each of the examples we've just mentioned, society will tend to conform each speaker to the norms that are commonly accepted. Mothers, teachers, the sober, and the serious: these are the guardians of sociolinguistic norms.

Whereas individuals are bound to conform to social norms or risk losing their membership of the speech communities they are part of, society as a whole offers constant challenges to these very norms that are so deeply ingrained. A whole host of factors contribute to society's challenge on language, eroding and reshaping the linguistic world around us. New technologies require new terminology, immigrant communities apply new and innovative meanings to traditional terms while introducing new ones from their original cultures, and sub-groups within communities, such as the young, purposefully break norms to reflect their social status as different from the crowd. Each of these forces is created by social factors that influence the speech community, and if we are familiar with the influence of these factors on language, we are more likely to be able to accurately describe and possibly predict language choices.

So, our task is clear. In order to understand the language choices that people make, we must first of all be able to describe the language that they use, helping people to make its norms explicit. In addition, we need to consider a range of social factors and how their impact on the community is revealed through conscious or unconscious adjustments to language norms. Having done this, we are then in a much stronger position to help the community make conscious proactive adjustments to these norms as we partner with them through the process of language development.

In an ideal world, a speech community as a whole is free to adapt the social norms of its language whenever it is in the interest of the community to do so. However, as we shall see, not all speech communities enjoy this freedom. Social factors not only impart change, they can also resist it. And when a community faces the influence of social factors that originate from outside it but which are greater than those within, conflict can arise between imposed norms and desired norms.

1.3.2   How the Book is Organized

Our book thus begins here, at what we will call the **Level of Restricted Language Choice**. At this level the people we work with are members of a very large speech community, and their membership and identity within that community have been imposed on them by more dominant social groups. In effect, this leaves them no sociolinguistic voice. The social influences at this level originate outside their ethnic community and are so strong that language choices are effectively made for them. Differences in the scale of power make it impossible for the people we work with to engage at this level with the social factors that influence language. Figure 2 illustrates this.

CROSS-REFERENCE ▸ See **Section 2.2** on page 25 for further description of the Restricted Level.

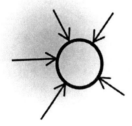

FIGURE 2 ▸ The Restricted Level showing the forces acting on the ethnic group from the socially dominant speech community of which they are members.

Not all communities have so little freedom. The most common situation we will encounter in language assessment is where speech communities live in interdependence with others as shown in Figure 3. At this level, interaction between a community and those they define as others create social factors

CROSS-REFERENCE ‣ See **Section 3.1** on page 47 for further description of the Negotiated Level.

DEFINITION ‣ **SOCIAL NETWORK:** a pattern of social associations or relationships.

CROSS-REFERENCE ‣ See **Section 3.2.1.1** on page 54 for more about social networks.

which impact language choices. We will call this the **Level of Negotiated Language Choice.** As interaction takes place at this level, members of different speech communities negotiate the language they use through the **SOCIAL NETWORKS** people establish. The key distinction between this and the Restricted Level is the inclusion of this interactive element. The community does have a voice although it must compete with others to make it heard. Thus, the people can control the impact of social factors on their language at this level because they have a certain amount of freedom to choose other speech communities they are members of. How much freedom they have and how much influence they have on language choice in those they join will vary widely with each scenario we study. A major aspect of our work is to describe the extent of this freedom and influence.

FIGURE 3 ‣ The Negotiated Level showing the impact of social forces that come about through the interaction of speech communities.

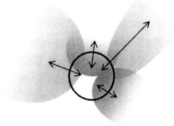

CROSS-REFERENCE ‣ See **Section 4.1** on page 115 for further description of the Free Level.

Where a community has the liberty to make their own choices about how they communicate, the focus lies within the speech community that the people most identify with as in Figure 4. We will call this the **Level of Free Language Choice.** It is the introspective nature of this situation which makes it different from the Negotiated Level where language users have to give consideration to those in other speech communities. In contrast to the Restricted Level, the social factors that influence language choices come from within the speech community itself. The people are therefore free to vary the amount of influence these social factors have on the language they use. One interesting aspect of the Free Level is that while the people have considerable control of language choices, their membership of the speech community is largely a matter of fate. This is in stark contrast to the Restricted Level where membership of larger speech communities is often a matter of politics.

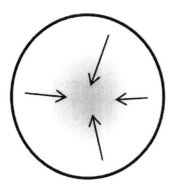

FIGURE 4 ▸ The Free Level showing that social factors which influence language choices come from within the community which the people we work with identify most strongly with.

In reality, of course, these levels exist on a continuum and they occur simultaneously as Figure 5 shows. Although our choice of these levels is artificial and the model does have limitations, we hope that by providing this framework, we can better organize and understand the large number of factors that influence language use choices in a speech community. Each of these levels is directly related to the other two, and any attempts at language development that only take into account data from one level will have little chance of success if there is no support for it at the other two levels. Providing this framework is our attempt to help guide assessment so that all aspects of the sociolinguistic environment are considered.

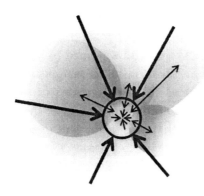

FIGURE 5 ▸ The reality of the communities we work with experiencing the influence of social factors at all three of our levels simultaneously.

1.3.3   Chapter Outlines

In **Chapter 1**, we discussed the world of assessment and some of what it involves. We have looked at the development context in which sociolinguistic assessment happens including both who asks for the assessment and who the research is done with.

Chapters 2 to 4 look in turn at each of the Restricted, Negotiated, and Free levels of language choice. In each chapter, we begin by looking at the relevant social factors and describing how these affect language and language use. We then go on to consider typical research questions that language assessment teams investigate. In the final section at each level, we introduce you to a number of data collection tools that have been used to collect data in numerous studies worldwide over many years.

Chapter 5 gives you an introduction to academic research and writing. You probably bring important academic skills to your survey work already. This section will help you to make sure you are carrying out assessment ethically and with academic rigor. Finally, we will give you advice on how to write for the academic community.

Chapter 6 concludes the book with a practical guide to planning a survey trip. We talk about the personal qualities a surveyor needs to be a successful member of an assessment team and discuss some of the ethical issues involved. We also provide information on roles and resources to help you prepare for both the expected and the unexpected!

1.3.4   Other Features

You will also find some other features in this book that we hope will be helpful. Each page has a large margin on one side where we give definitions of key terms that you will need to know to understand the assessment world. You can also use the margins to take notes. We have included cross-references to other sections of the book to help you make connections between different parts of the assessment process and to other resources that you might find useful. We have included a range of quotations from leading researchers in each field to inspire you, and we recommend that you follow up the sources we quote from. For more guidance in developing your assessment skills beyond this book, we have included a selection for further reading at the end of each chapter. Finally, we have placed a glossary and an index at the end of the book for reference.

1.3.5   Companion Website

We considered writing this book in two volumes: a first volume that presents the conceptual approaches and practical methodologies and a second volume with the data collection tools. However, the tools require detailed lists of procedures for precise use, and there are frequent developments and refinements of tools. To help meet this challenge, we have created a website at **WWW.SURVEYWIKI.INFO** to provide resources for language assessment which registered users can edit and update as changes occur.

WWW.SURVEYWIKI.INFO ‣ Whenever there are resources to support the textbook on our companion website SurveyWiki, you will see a note like this in the margin. Why not visit Survey-Wiki and register now? You don't need to register to read content, but if you register, you can contribute to content and help improve the site.

1.4   Further Reading

1.4.1   Introductions to Sociolinguistics

An Introduction to Sociolinguistics by Ronald Wardhaugh (2009)

The sixth edition of this ever-popular textbook is written in a very informal style which makes it a great introduction for anyone completely new to the world of sociolinguistics. The book includes very useful further reading sections, discussion sections, and exercises.

An Introduction to Sociolinguistics by Janet Holmes (2008)

Now in its third edition, this has become a standard introductory textbook useful for understanding basic sociolinguistic topics and terminology. One of the book's strengths is that you can use it to teach yourself as it has plenty of examples for discussion and exercises to help you develop sociolinguistic awareness of the world around you. The book is divided into three sections focusing on varying patterns of use in multilingual communities, the social reasons for language change, and how attitudes affect language. All of these are essential to understand in order to carry out language assessment.

Sociolinguistics: The Study of Speaker's Choices by Florian Coulmas (2005)

This is a rare book because its focus on choice, which is similar to this book, is not often found in this field. Very readable with discussion questions and further reading suggestions throughout, it also includes a chapter focused on written language choices.

Language in Society by Suzanne Romaine (2000)

This classic brief introduction to the main issues we need to consider in sociolinguistics is now in its second edition. The strength of Romaine's approach is her constant reference to the influence of social factors on language choices, a theme we echo in this book.

1.4.2   Introductions to Language Survey

Survey on a Shoestring by Frank Blair (1990)

This book describes itself as "a manual for small-scale language survey" and has been a standard book for language surveyors for over 20 years. Although it deals with many issues too briefly, like the Survey Reference Manual below, it provides a good understanding as to where language assessment has come from.

Survey Reference Manual by Ted Bergman (1989)

This is a binder of short papers and articles related to sociolinguistic survey and, although they are dated now, this collection provides a good idea of where language assessment has come from and what has made it what it is today. Many of the articles in this manual are foundational for understanding the value of key issues such as considerations when carrying out intelligibility testing and the importance of assessing attitudes.

The Steps of Language Survey by Ramzi Nahhas (2007)

WWW.SURVEYWIKI.INFO ‣ *Steps of Language Survey* is available on SurveyWiki.

This is a very readable basic manual in pdf form which provides step-by-step instructions for conducting language assessment. Although the guide is designed primarily for training Southeast Asian university students, the materials are easily transferable to other regions of the world.

Language Variation and Survey Techniques edited by Richard Loving and Gary Simons (1977)

An early, foundational collection of papers on the basic tools and procedures of language surveys.

2 RESTRICTED LANGUAGE CHOICE

In this chapter we introduce you to language assessment at the level of restricted choice. In the first part of the chapter, we will discuss the social factors which influence language use choices at this level. These include

- how international and national economic policies and trends affect speech communities,
- the impact of government language policies on local speech communities, and
- the influence of socio-political conflicts and environmental disasters on speech communities.

We will then go on to consider typical research questions that assessment projects usually deal with at this level. In particular, we focus on ways in which **MULTILINGUALISM** and language **VITALITY** may be affected. We conclude this chapter with a look at a number of tools that we often use to answer typical research questions at this level.

2.1 Introduction

When language choices are restricted, the people we work with typically have little or no ability to control the impact of the sociolinguistic factors affecting the norms of their language. This is due to differences in the scale of power which makes it impossible for them to engage with the forces behind these factors. These factors may include a wide range of government, economic, or environmental factors. For example, national language policies and multi-national trade agreements are as non-negotiable as earthquakes to most minority communities. Even if we are studying a language group that is dominant in the country and their

DEFINITION ▸ MULTILINGUALISM refers to the ability of a person to use more than one language. Use of the term makes no claim as to how proficient the person may be in any of the languages, nor, when referring to a community, does it imply that everyone has equal proficiency. See **Section 2.3.1** on page 32 for a more thorough discussion of multilingualism.

DEFINITION ▸ THE VITALITY of a language refers to the commitment and availability of resources to the users of a heritage language to maintain their language.

language is the national language, there are national and international economic and political factors that most of the people will not have any ability to influence, yet those factors influence their lives and language use choices.

Study of the Restricted Level could begin at the global scale with factors such as climate change and political and economic networks. But the outer boundary is determined by what factors have a particular influence on the speech community concerned. Often, the outer boundary will be issues at the national or regional level and involve governmental policies, the work of NGOs, or the influence of such factors as international conflict or natural disasters.

Research at the Restricted Level does not need to include all the possible issues at the national or international level. We need to be flexible and apply this concept at the level most appropriate for the community and language repertoire in focus. If a country has a particularly large and diverse population, we might begin at the state or regional level. India has a population of over one billion people with 22 official languages, and some minority languages have more than one million speakers. Clearly, with situations like India, investigating things from the national level down would be overwhelming. It is better to look for issues on a scale that more nearly reflects the scale we are working with.

One of the key factors in defining the scope of the Restricted Level is where the initiation of the assessment comes from and therefore, the purpose of an assessment effort. If the focus of those who initiate the assessment is multinational, then it makes sense to begin there.

One assessment project (S. Showalter 2001) with the aim to "explore attitudes toward the language variation that permeates rural West African life," began with an overview of sociolinguistic issues in West Africa before focusing on Burkina Faso. In this case, the Restricted Level covered no fewer than 19 countries over thousands of miles. Languages often cross political boundaries, and trans-national language groups are common.

Showalter's approach therefore indicates the importance of defining the expanse of the Restricted Level relative to the research we are focused on. Even though Showalter started with such a broad scale of research, he maintained his focus on the communities he was interested in by singling out those issues which are "relevant to the research reported" (p. 5). At the Restricted Level, it is particularly important for us to use the community we are focused on to determine what is relevant from the start and not simply secondary research which may contain data that did not actually take the reality of the community into account.

2.2   Social Factors at the Restricted Level

This section will explore three factors that are typically relevant for surveyors doing assessment at the Restricted Level and the kinds of research questions that arise from these situations. These three factors are: economic, political, and conflict/disaster. We will then look at some typical data collection tools at the Restricted Level that can help us answer those questions.

2.2.1   Economic Factors

We must not underestimate the influence that macroeconomic factors have on the language choices of the people in minority communities. There is a long history of dominant peoples taking the lands and resources of less powerful people. This may result in major changes to the cultures and languages of the minority peoples. These changes may not be the result of any significant contact with outsiders, but simply the destruction of their traditional environment, which forces the people to alter their lifestyles. In Case Study 2A below we see how the global demand for lumber has affected one minority group in the Philippines. The expansion of agriculture, logging, mining, and oil drilling are four major activities that have impacted small language groups around the world.

Economic factors may be the result of intentional government policy or the result of changes in the culture and society. Language policies initiated by governments will often be motivated by budgetary concerns. It can be very costly for a government to give equality to all the languages spoken within their borders. Educational programs need to be developed for each language, multilingual civil servants need to be trained to deal with their tasks in a multilingual environment, and official documents need to be produced in every language. Governments may choose to create language policies that limit official recognition to one or a few languages to limit the cost of dealing with a multilingual population. A government may favor one language over others to maintain the political and economic dominance of speakers of that language. Governments may be pressured by large global organizations like the World Bank or United Nations to develop inclusive language policies if they want to receive financial aid.

Aside from intentional government policies, social and technological development creates a major motivation for economic change. It is a basic human instinct to maintain or improve the quality of our lives. Parents want to raise their children in a safe environment, to provide for their needs, and prepare them for adulthood. However, different cultures see different ways to do these things. Some surveyors may come from cultures that equate material goods and market economies with development, progress, and an improved lifestyle. Because of this, we should be careful not to assume that all cultures hold the same values as the cultures we come from. Many cultures around the world value subsistence and the ability to derive life's necessities from their immediate environment. However, because they hold these values, communities can often find themselves in a dilemma if the resources that they traditionally use to maintain their lifestyles are threatened in any way. When this happens, they are often left with no choice but to adopt alternatives and, in most cases, this means adapting to dominant economic systems.

The exploitation of natural resources is another cause for immigration. This can happen either through the depletion of resources necessary for living or through migration in search of employment where resources are being exploited. These natural resources could be anything from farm land and timber to gems and minerals. People move from many different places to find work. This not only puts people from different places together, it can also bring new people onto land that has traditionally belonged to other speech communities.

CASE STUDY 2A
LOGGING AND THE AGTA
THE PHILIPPINES

CASE STUDY 2A SOURCE ‣ Dr. Thomas N. Headland, Adjunct Professor of Linguistics, University of Texas at Arlington (Headland 2004).

Until the 1960s, the Agta of the Philippines lived a nomadic, hunter-gatherer lifestyle largely untouched by the outside world.

Then, driven by a worldwide demand for more lumber, logging operations began in the traditional Agta lands. By the end of the 1970s, with the destruction of their rainforest homelands and loss of wild game, the Agta had become dependent on the national economy. Nowadays, they wear commercially manufactured clothes and buy cheap packaged food. With the loss of most vestiges of their traditional culture their language has also become endangered.

We should also bear in mind that changes such as these have been going on worldwide for at least 200 years. The Industrial Revolution that began in eighteenth-century Britain had profound effects on culture and society at that time. The establishment of factories offering large amounts of paid employment in towns and cities meant that workers in rural communities had the opportunity to increase their economic status often by working fewer hours. But by choosing to do so, they had to abandon their subsistence lifestyles. As they became increasingly dependent on new economic sources, they lost the skills and traditions that were necessary for subsistence. This basic pattern of industrialization has been repeated worldwide since that time, with the only difference being an increased pace of change.

The impact of the social factors involved in industrialization on language is very important because, from an economic viewpoint, language contains the keys to well-being and status (Grin 1999:22). The force of industrialization can create strong motivational urges that make language secondary to well-being. Such motivation drives a full range of social choices affecting language from migration and education to parental choices about languages used to socialize children. As people make these choices, it is often necessary to replace their heritage language with one that enables them to function in their new social networks. Even if changed situations result in a determination to maintain their heritage language, enforced contact with others who communicate differently will certainly influence them in some way and we will need to know how.

> QUOTE ▸ *Language practices are bound up in the creation, exercise, maintenance or change of relationships of power...using language is tied to the ability to gain access to, and exercise power. (Heller 2006:164)*

> CROSS-REFERENCE ▸ See **Section 1.1.3** on page 10 for more about heritage language.

> CROSS-REFERENCE ▸ See **Sections 2.3.2** on page 34, 3.3.3 on page 88 and 4.2.4 on page 128 for more about language vitality. See **Section 3.2.3** on page 73 for more on language shift.

In this way, choices influenced by macro-economic factors can have profound effects on language vitality and **LANGUAGE SHIFT** for two reasons: they are based on what people feel provide them with the best options for status and well-being (Myers-Scotton 2002:46), and even if it were possible to resist such factors, it would likely result in extreme hardship.

> DEFINITON ▸ **LANGUAGE SHIFT** is the process by which a speech community transitions from the use of their heritage language to the predominant use of another language.

2.2.2   Political Factors

One of the most fundamental ways that we can study the Restricted Level is by looking at the relevant political system of the nation or region. Political systems exist at every level of society and are simply ways people decide to administer authority. Because minority communities typically lack authority, they can often be politically isolated. Political factors are very influential because they determine policies, formal or otherwise, that can range from education to clothing.

DEFINITION ▸ LANGUAGE PLANNING is the process of a governing body choosing specific languages for specific purposes and implementing those choices.

LANGUAGE PLANNING is one of the direct ways that the political system exerts influence on the language of the community surveyed. The process of establishing certain languages as official and selecting them for education means, by default, that other languages are not recognized for these purposes. The consequences of such decisions can be seen in Case Study 2B.

CASE STUDY 2B
THE STRUGGLE FOR
LINGUISTIC EQUALITY
BANGLADESH

CASE STUDY 2B SOURCE ▸ Based on an article by Amena Mohsin, Chair-person, International Relations, University of Dhaka (Mohsin 2003).

In 1947 when Pakistan separated from India the country was divided into West and East Pakistan. The choice of Urdu as the sole national language sparked riots in East Bengal where Bengali was the language of the majority.

QUOTE ▸ If a majority language is endowed with a symbolic status which asserts its superiority over minority languages, there are issues of social justice, as linguistic minority speakers may be excluded from access to, or membership in, the more powerful group. (Blackledge 2004:68)

This legislation essentially barred all Bengalis from political or military leadership. Students who began organizing the opposition were eventually joined by Bengali political leaders to form a movement to establish Bengali as a second official language for the country. The 21st of February marks the anniversary of the death of four students killed by Pakistani police who opened fire on a crowd of demonstrators demanding recognition of Bengali as one of the national languages of Pakistan.

Although the constitution was eventually amended in 1954, a political and economic imbalance continued to favor West Pakistan. Eventually, after the outbreak of war in 1971, Bangladesh declared independence. Hundreds of thousands, possibly millions, of Bengalis died in their 24-year struggle for language equality.

With tragic irony, however, the right of linguistic equality has not been extended to the linguistic minorities of present-day Bangladesh who continue to be marginalized from the Bengali mainstream.

CROSS-REFERENCE ▸ See **Section 3.2.2** on page 68 for more about the sentimental attitudes being described here.

The links between language and group identity in the form of nationalism have often fueled decisions about language planning. These links are often stronger when a speech community has appeared at risk from another more dominant group in the past. This is the case of Irish which has been adopted as the first official language of the Republic of Ireland despite less than a tenth of the population using it. In this example, there was a large group of people who identified with the language. Even though few of them used it, they still considered themselves part of the Irish speech community.

The opposite can also be true. Case Study 2B is related to an example of a powerful minority imposing their language on larger, less powerful groups. In 1947, when Pakistan separated from India, the leaders of the Pakistan separatist movement came from a region of India where people spoke Urdu. They made Urdu the national language of Pakistan even though it wasn't a language used within the boundaries of the new nation. However, it is most frequently the dominant group in a nation that lobbies to make their language official with the intent of imposing it on all less-powerful language groups.

The example of Welsh in the UK demonstrates the importance of considering Restricted Level concepts to get accurate information about the reality that a speech community faces. An observation of life in the homes of many Welsh families would indicate a monolingual community of either Welsh or English. However, it is government policy that local schools use Welsh and/or English as the medium of instruction, and this means that the language of education could well differ from that of the home (Baker 1985). Surveyors who didn't collect data on education policies in this situation would be unaware of this possibility.

CASE STUDY 2C
DECIDING TO DIE
PAPUA NEW GUINEA

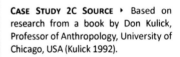

Over 800 languages are spoken in Papua New Guinea. Tok Pisin is one of only three languages with official status and has gained prestige in the country as a result.

Representative of the many small language groups in Papua New Guinea, Taiap speakers form a small community of only a few hundred people. The Taiap adults believe that, for their children, using Tok Pisin will raise their status and open doors to education and, therefore, economic opportunity. As of 1992, no child under the age of 10 in this community used Taiap; preferring to use Tok Pisin instead.

CASE STUDY 2C SOURCE ▸ Based on research from a book by Don Kulick, Professor of Anthropology, University of Chicago, USA (Kulick 1992).

CROSS-REFERENCE ▸ Partnerships can use participatory methods for interaction and planning. See **Section 4.4.5** on page 161 for a description of participatory methods and the rationale for talking with partners at the same level.

Language planning decisions can have tremendous social implications for people whose languages have no official representation. Taiap, as described in Case Study 2C, represents a typical situation worldwide and shows how influential Restricted Level factors can be. In this example, language planning decisions made by a government 400 miles away in 1975 had an impact on the language of a small community of people 20 years later. Since the influence occurs at the Restricted Level, where the people have no say in their membership of the speech community, unless there is a change at this level the people may find resisting these influences difficult even if they should want to.

Finally, political systems may also determine what partnerships we will form as we carry out assessment, and we should consider the potential of these when we begin projects. Most governments have departments whose responsibility involves language planning, and there may be NGOs who work closely with these. We can form partnerships with both government and NGO agencies. Likewise, dominant religious groups may have influence on our collaboration with religious organizations.

2.2.3   Conflict and Disaster

Sometimes political policies are only a secondary factor at this level. While a war is a political issue, the migration that occurs as people flee the conflict is not always a result of political policy. Whether it is tribal or international warfare, people desire peace and security for their families. As they flee their homelands, there are several possible outcomes for communities. They may

- be forced into contact with speakers of other languages,
- be dispersed,
- lose their means of livelihood, or
- be forced to learn other languages to find employment.

In Southeast Asia, conflict has caused millions of people to flee from neighboring countries into Thailand. The Thai government houses these people in refugee camps to better meet their needs. In Thailand, as in some other cases, this has made education more available to people who come from remote rural areas. However, in such situations where thousands of people are forced together, there needs to be one language for communication. This works against the maintenance of the languages of those from minority language groups. Recently, the Thai government has repatriated Lao refugees who have lived for years in these camps, no doubt learning more Thai in the process. These repatriated refugees must choose between continuing to use Thai or returning to use languages that perhaps have lower status in the region.

In a similar way to conflict, natural or environmental disasters can cause people to flee devastated areas. A drought may cause an agricultural culture to become dependent on an urban society. A volcano may force a speech community to move to a new island. A disease that decimates cattle herds may destroy the livelihood of a pastoralist culture, forcing them to become dependent on another group. In light of the potential for global climate change, some people are concerned about the impact of rising sea levels on coastal communities. The depletion of natural resources is another kind of disaster that can cause immigration. The migrations and changes to lifestyles involved with these crises often influence the language choices of people as they struggle to cope with their new situations after disaster has struck.

It is important to realize, however, that these kinds of chaotic factors don't always have to have a long-term negative impact on the use of the heritage language. In July 1998, a tsunami hit the north coast of Papua New Guinea killing over 3000 people including a significant portion of several ethnolinguistic groups. As a result, the resolve of the people has been to put more effort into development efforts. Today the Aitape West language development program includes 11 language groups working together to preserve their languages and cultures.

As surveyors, we want to discover the sociolinguistic reality of the people. We must be attentive; the assessment of such a speech community can be very complex with variation occurring simultaneously across time, geography, status, age, and gender, and people within a group have differing values and goals. Some surveyors come from communities with strong ties to only one language. They need to take the time and care necessary to understand the Restricted Level factors involved in such a situation because they may underestimate the complexities or oversimplify the issues.

In summary, our research at the Restricted Level needs to examine the history and present situation of the people we focus on for each of these social factors: economic, political, and conflict/disaster. Rather than assuming that the presence of these forces will always have negative effects on the communication of the people, we need to remain open and look at the sociolinguistic reality of the people's situation. In the next section, we will look at the kind of research questions that usually concern assessment projects at the Restricted Level.

2.3   Typical Research Questions at the Restricted Level

Due to the importance of the three factors (economic, political, and conflict/disaster) discussed in the previous section there are several typical questions to be answered when doing research at the Restricted Level.

- Are there international or national economic forces that may impact the language choice decisions of minority speech communities?
- Are there national government policies that may impact the language choice decisions of minority speech communities?
- Have there been historical events, conflicts, or disasters that may have had an impact on the language choice decisions of minority speech communities?

From the perspective of the Restricted Level, there are two primary ways in which these forces may have an impact on the language choices: multilingualism and language vitality. In this section we will describe the relevance of understanding multilingualism and language vitality as language use choice outcomes. When doing research at the Restricted Level, surveyors may become familiar with certain people or institutions that could have an impact on further language development activities. Therefore, we will also discuss the relevance of understanding partnerships in this section.

2.3.1   Multilingualism

CROSS-REFERENCE ▸ See **Section 3.3.1** on page 74 for more on bilingualism and multilingualism.

The impact of factors at the Restricted Level may be felt at both the Negotiated and Free levels. One possible impact is that there will be contact with new groups. This contact may be forced or it may be that the people have a new opportunity for contact. Contact creates new networks with new people. These new networks may include the use of new languages. For there to be communication between these groups, some people from one of the groups must learn some of the language of the other group. To describe these situations, we will be using the term *multilingualism*. When we do so, it does not necessarily imply more than two languages, but we prefer it to the term bilingualism because this would limit us to talking about speech communities that only use two languages.

There is specialized terminology to refer to a number of different types of multilingual relationships. First, there is a distinction between whether the society we are working with uses multiple languages in commonly accepted ways. The term **DIGLOSSIA** is used to describe a social situation in which two or more languages, or language varieties, co-occur in a speech community, each with a distinct social function. In diglossic speech communities there are social norms that people follow which determine the language, or variety, used in specific **DOMAINS**. For example, in Paraguay, people use Guaraní for informal conversation but Spanish for formal exchanges. In parts of Switzerland people use Swiss-German for informal functions and High German for formal functions.

In other situations, there are not social norms for the use of the different languages or varieties that are available. In such situations different individuals gain varying proficiency in the other languages or varieties; there should be no expectation that everyone has some proficiency in another language or variety.

At the Restricted Level, we are describing speech communities that have been forced into contact with other communities due to politics, economics, or some conflict or disaster. Often one language will emerge as the default means of communication between language groups. When one language gains dominance for communication in a region of a country, this language is sometimes called a **REGIONAL LANGUAGE**. A national language is a language that has gained prominence in an entire nation as the typical means of communication between ethno-linguistic groups. An **OFFICIAL LANGUAGE** is a language that is given official status and support by the government. An official language is not necessarily a language spoken by a majority of people. For example, Maori is an official language in New Zealand spoken by a small ethnic minority, but it is supported by government mandate. Some regional languages are given official status. For example, in India languages that are dominant in a particular state are also given official status in that state. Some national languages become de facto official languages because they so completely dominate the political domain, such as English in the United States.

Some languages become important for multi-ethnic communication throughout a multinational region. These languages are known as **LANGUAGES OF WIDER COMMUNICATION** (LWC). However, LWC is frequently used to refer to regional and national languages when the context is simply multi-ethnic communication.

DEFINITION ‣ DIGLOSSIA is a social situation in which two or more languages, or language varieties, co-occur in a speech community, each with a distinct social function. See **Section 3.3.1.4** on page 83 for more on diglossia.

DEFINITION ‣ A DOMAIN is a cluster of features including speakers, location, topic, and a speech form associated with these other features. See **Section 3.3.2** on page 84 for more on domains of language use.

DEFINITION ‣ A REGIONAL LANGUAGE is a language that has gained prominence for communication between ethno-linguistic groups in a region of a country.

DEFINITION ‣ AN OFFICIAL LANGUAGE is a language that is given official status and support by a government.

DEFINITION ‣ A LANGUAGE OF WIDER COMMUNICATION (LWC) is a language that crosses national boundaries for use between different ethnolinguistic groups. Arabic is an LWC.

NOTE ‣ There is some inconsistency in the literature in the use of these terms. Some other terms, like trade language and lingua franca are also used to describe something similar to an LWC.

Governments often have the intent of using the national language as a non-partisan medium of communication whose neutrality stems from having roots in none of the nation's ethnic groups. The official statuses of English in Nigeria and French in Mali are examples of this. It is a direct consequence of the neutrality of these languages that they are used for mediating the social arenas of power such as government and law. They are also viewed as the pragmatic choice for higher education, academic research, and nationwide communication. Regardless of benign intentions, the speech communities that are not members of an LWC speech community are prevented from sharing in any of these social arenas and the power that is mediated there. This can create strong motivation to learn these LWCs as minority groups seek to establish their own voice and provide improved access to this power for future generations. For these reasons, on surveys we often hear people say that they are shifting to an LWC because that is the language they need for education and employment.

The use of an official or national language in the schools does not necessarily mean that it is having significant impact on all speech communities in the country. However, the presence and effectiveness of schools in which an LWC is used will give some indication of the immediacy of the pressures on the minority languages. During their research from 1986 to 1990, the Sociolinguistic Survey of Northern Pakistan found that the presence of schools, the length of time schools had been available, and the availability of teachers from the local languages all played a part in determining whether or not there was much bilingualism in Urdu, the national language. If a school had not been present for at least five years, there was very little likelihood of finding more than a few men with any bilingual proficiency in Urdu.

2.3.2   Vitality

Sometimes there may be reasons for another language to become more useful to an ethno-linguistic group than their heritage language. The speakers of the heritage language may lose their commitment and resources to maintain their language, as in Case Study 2C's example of Taiap earlier. In many minority communities, there are strong ties to heritage languages and these ties can conflict with the necessity to learn an LWC. Successful language development depends on the resolution of these conflicts to the satisfaction of the community. As surveyors, we therefore need to understand where people use the various languages

CROSS-REFERENCE ▸ See **Case Study 2C** on page 29 for more about Taiap.

involved both in geographic terms and by domain of language use. To best serve the interests of the people themselves, we need to be sensitive to the practical necessity of learning new languages. We must also be attentive to vitality issues such as maintaining heritage languages in domains that the community feels are essential. One example of success in this area comes from Thailand where the Pwo Karen people have managed to develop literacy simultaneously in Thai and Siltragool, their heritage language.

WWW.SURVEYWIKI.INFO ▸ See the **Multilingual Education** page for more examples of successful development like that with the Pwo Karen.

At the Restricted Level, another aspect of vitality involves the attitudes of the dominant population towards minority groups. If dominant groups accept minorities as part of the nation and appreciate diversity, this can help the maintenance of the minority languages. However, if there is no support for a minority language at the Restricted Level, then endangerment may only be a matter of time. Equally, if a government ignores some languages while developing others, this may negatively affect the vitality of those ignored. These situations illustrate how important knowledge of government policies and actions towards the minority languages is for accurate language assessment.

CROSS-REFERENCE ▸ We explore the important issues of language attitudes in **Sections 3.2.2** on page 68 and **4.2.4** on page 128.

2.3.3   Partnership

Individuals in smaller speech communities are not often in a position to interact with many organizations and institutions at the Restricted Level. Yet those institutions, through their policies and actions, influence everyday life in those very communities. Foremost is the government, but more specifically departments of internal policy, education, health, and culture. Universities, whether government-affiliated or not, are often interested in the study of and developmental efforts among minority speech communities. There are also large international non-governmental agencies, such as the United Nations Educational, Scientific, and Cultural Organization (UNESCO), World Bank, and the World Health Organization (WHO). There may be faith-based organizations interested in the well-being of minority speech communities and ethno-linguistic groups. By working with these agencies while carrying out assessment, language surveyors can help open up channels of interaction for communities, help ensure that needed resources are directed toward them, and help mediate the impact of these resources on the community.

For a development organization, partnerships are relevant to all levels, and the formation of important relationships may begin at the Restricted Level. Without partnership, development efforts will be unsustainable, unsupported, uninformed, and therefore, ultimately, unsuccessful. It is important to realize the distinction between partners and stakeholders. There may be some person or group that is opposed to the development efforts. Because the development affects them, they are stakeholders, but their opposition means that they are not going to be partners unless their objections are resolved.

Remember that social forces at the Restricted Level can only be mediated here, the very level where minority speech communities are relatively powerless. Thus, if Restricted Level forces need to be counteracted or redirected in some way for the sake of the speech communities we work with, development programs will need to have advocates at the Restricted Level. Otherwise, it is unlikely that the development efforts will be successful in bringing about change. For this reason, influential partnerships need to be formed in the early stages of a language development effort.

CROSS-REFERENCE ▸ See **Section 4.4.5** on page 161 for a description of participatory methods that can be used for partnership discussions.

It may take some time to identify appropriate partners and form relationships with them by gaining insight into their goals and ways of working. There needs to be an awareness of who has similar goals as well as who has resources that are available for the effort, who stands to benefit or may suffer loss, and who may be opposed to the development. Often a survey team has the opportunity to meet and learn about the different groups in a country. As survey teams are often involved at the inception of programs, they may be able to make a significant contribution to the facilitation of partnerships by identifying who those potential partners are.

2.4   Typical Restricted-Level Research Tools

It is important to understand some of the dynamics of multilingualism and language vitality issues as outcomes of economic, political, and conflict/disaster forces at the Restricted Level. However, we will discuss research tools for studying multilingualism and language vitality in chapters 3 and 4. In this section we will discuss background research, interviews, stakeholder identification, and engagement as important research tools.

2.4.1   Background Research

Research at the Restricted Level involves interacting with the agents behind the economic and political factors that we described above. On the one hand, the scale of these socioeconomic and political forces can make this stage of the research seem daunting. On the other, there are usually concrete sources of reference we can use to build up our knowledge. Unlike research at the Negotiated and Free levels, the Restricted Level is likely to hold a large body of publicly available information such as policy documents, histories, and previous research material. There may be a lot we can learn simply by spending some time in libraries or on the Internet. There is usually only a need for a survey team to do this kind of research once, or only when those who commission the research lack the necessary information to pursue their objectives in development. As a result, research at the Restricted Level begins with secondary research, accessing information that is available to others. There will probably be gaps in the information that we can gather through background research. If we learn everything we need through the background research, there is no need for any further primary research. Often, in order to complete the survey, it will also be necessary to fill in any gaps with our own primary research at the Negotiated and Free levels.

As secondary research is compiled, a picture begins to emerge of the significant issues that are likely to influence both the primary data we collect and the ways in which we collect and analyze it. Sources for secondary research include the Internet, libraries, bookstores, maps, newspapers, government documents, personal correspondence of informed individuals, and archives. We look for information about government policy, history, geography, immigration, emigration, education, census data, media, relevant anthropological and linguistic research, dominant religions, and tourism.

The time available and the type of research the survey team will conduct should determine the amount and sources of secondary research needed. For example, if the survey team aims to collect samples of phonological variation between language varieties that are already known to be closely related, there isn't as much need for background knowledge on the history of the country. It is important to learn to limit the amount of information that is gathered to only that which is necessary. *We only need to know what we need to know; we don't need to know **every**thing before we can do **any**thing.*

Judging the amount of information we really need is a key skill in assessment. If we gather information that is unnecessary instead of what we need, we waste precious resources and do not benefit those we serve. Therefore, we need to maintain a very clear understanding of the goals and purpose of the assessment from the start and always consider our research decisions in light of these. Being able to judge the optimum amount of necessary data is a valuable skill, but we need not limit ourselves only to this, particularly if reaching the survey location has been costly and/or the required information has not taken long to collect. If we have more resources available, we can then judge whether it would be worthwhile to gather more information that may be helpful in the future or conduct some other activity that might benefit the community.

Knowing the right information to collect also depends on our theories on factors that influence language vitality. These include things like the importance of socioeconomic and political forces. The skills and trades that are common to a minority speech community may have some relevance to their ability to access another culture and affect their multilingualism. But the way that they plant their crops or the tools they use for woodworking, probably don't have any significant impact on their multilingualism. Therefore, we don't spend time collecting data on such things. However, a researcher should always keep their mind open to consider a change to their theory. In the early days of the North Pakistan Survey, information on a person's khel, understood to be a somewhat mythical family grouping, was disregarded as irrelevant. However, the surveyors later learned that this was an indicator of an important social network revealing who they socialized and talked with. Thus, it became important to gather information on a person's khel.

CROSS-REFERENCE ▸ See **Section 5.6** on page 204 for more about writing proposals and reports.

In addition, the survey team needs to have good systems for organizing information. Later, we will discuss more about writing proposals and reports. Usually, survey teams use templates to begin writing their survey reports. It is important to note here that we can use these outlines from the start of an assessment project as a place to collect information and keep it organized and referenced. It is very frustrating to have to search for days for a citation to back up some fact that has not been properly referenced.

2.4.2   Interviews

We have already mentioned how partnerships at the Restricted Level can benefit the community. Partnerships and research at the Restricted Level can be initiated by the use of interviews. By engaging with knowledgeable people at an early stage, partnerships may form which could be of ongoing benefit to the development program even after the task of language assessment has been completed. So-called "knowledgeable outsiders" may come from partnering agencies and institutions. They may also include migrants or displaced persons who have firsthand experience of the speech communities we work with. The principles presented here are applicable to interviews both with knowledgeable outsiders at the Restricted Level and with insiders at the Negotiated and Free levels.

CROSS-REFERENCE ‣ See **Section 4.4.5** on page 161 for a description of participatory methods that can be used as an alternate method to interviewing.

WWW.SURVEYWIKI.INFO ‣ See Survey Wiki for more guidance on carrying out interviews. We strongly recommended you read these details and, as you develop experience in assessment, to contribute to SurveyWiki there.

CASE STUDY 2D
POLITICAL INFLUENCE
SOUTHEAST ASIA

What do you do when the region you are surveying is a political hotbed? On one survey, language development was such a hot topic that local propaganda officers went around to all the villages the survey team would visit before they got there, instructing all the villagers on how to answer the questions. In one village, the propaganda officer had not quite finished before the survey team started interviews, such that one subject was interviewed in the morning (pre-propagandized) and again in the afternoon (post-propagandized) with completely conflicting answers!

CASE STUDY 2D SOURCE ‣ SIL International's Mainland Southeast Asia Group survey team.

Bear in mind that our definition of partnership earlier involves sharing of complementary resources at each stage of the project. Therefore, if a partnership develops out of interviews there will be an appropriate expectation for the sharing of research findings. The relationship may also require the survey team to gather information of interest to a partner that would have otherwise not been part of the research. The survey team should be intentional about providing reports to the partners as well as discussing planning, depending on the relationship and context of the partnership.

When surveyors meet with officials, academics or potential partners, the mere fact that interest is being shown in a minority speech community may have an impact on the individuals being interviewed. They may have never thought about the special needs of these minority groups. They may have never heard of the speech community. As surveyors speak respectfully about the minority people they have the opportunity to present them in a favorable light, to consider their humanity. This is advocacy.

FIGURE 6 ▸ Mariela, a surveyor working in Mexico, records a Mixe speaker's tale of a near-death experience.

Secondary research is done before meeting with people for interviews. This is respectful of their time because we don't want to ask them about information that is readily available elsewhere. Previous secondary research should help us come with some established ideas in mind as to what we want to learn. It is important to document the interview accurately. Sometimes people are able to record interviews. However, in some cultural contexts, it may be inappropriate to have a notebook out and to be documenting responses. If it is inappropriate to be writing things during an interview, we will want to write them down as soon as possible afterward before we forget the facts. It may be worthwhile to make more than one visit to some people and build a relationship with them. Someone like a university professor can give special guidance on appropriate ways to do research in the country.

CROSS-REFERENCE ▸ See **Section 5.1.3** on page 170 for discussion concerning ethical issues for respecting privacy and confidentiality.

An interview differs from a questionnaire. An interview allows the person being interviewed to talk at length about a subject. An interviewee can shift the conversation to other topics. This can be very helpful when the interviewee brings things to light that the interviewer had not considered. It also allows the interviewer to explore other issues that arise during the conversation. A questionnaire attempts to limit responses to a specific context or to a limited set of potential answers.

Ethnographers often use an informal interviewing technique called ethnographic interviews. These involve writing down a series of topics or research questions that the researcher wants to focus on in advance. Then, during a normal conversational opportunity, the interviewer uses these notes, naturally and as appropriate, to guide the conversation into topic areas where, hopefully, the interviewee will provide relevant information. Particularly if the interviewer does not record or take notes of the conversation while it is going on, it can provide a very relaxed environment for people who would otherwise find the interview format difficult. We must be aware though that recording and publishing data collected without the respondent's awareness or agreement raises ethical concerns. If we are conducting an ethnographic interview, it is advisable after collecting the data to return to the respondent with our findings and agree with them regarding the extent of their use.

We should be aware that reactions to our questions in an interview will vary according to a number of factors depending on whether the interview is with a knowledgeable outsider or an insider. Firstly, a one-on-one interview itself may not be a familiar way of gaining information in the interviewee's culture. Because of this, what may seem straightforward questions to us may be difficult for the interviewee to answer. In cultures such as Melanesia where reciprocity is highly valued, a speech event where informants respond to question after question while the interviewer gives no information themselves may be uncomfortable. In addition, we must consider that the language that a respondent produces in an interview might be very different from language they normally use in other situations.

Secondly, the *observer paradox* states that the very presence of an outsider may skew the data being provided. Thus, data gathered through interviews must be balanced by observations made when there is less awareness of the observer. At the Restricted Level, we may interview an official about policy, later get a copy of the policy, and observe its implementation.

A third consideration is that the subject matter of some of the questions may pose problems. The language assistant may simply not know the answer to the questions and, wanting to be helpful, may provide information which differs from what we are looking for, as in Case Study 2E. Some areas of knowledge have taboos associated with them either because they are generally avoided topics in that culture or because access to such knowledge is restricted to certain groups of people. In Samoa, for example, questioning about motivations is unacceptable and doing so will result in generic declarations of ignorance (Duranti 1997:104). Asking

CROSS-REFERENCE ▸ See **Section 5.1** on page 168 for more about the ethical implications of our research.

about such topic areas might be seen as a violation of trust, especially if the interviewee is unclear as to what will be done with the data. The topic of a question may be difficult to answer because the interviewee has never thought about the issue before. In some egalitarian societies, the interviewee may be uncomfortable with the expectation that he/she is representing the whole speech community.

CASE STUDY 2E
MAKING THE BEST IMPRESSION
TANZANIA

CASE STUDY 2E SOURCE ▸ Susanne Krüger, Language Assessment Coordinator, SIL Uganda-Tanzania Branch.

On one survey we had difficulty with individual interviews. Previously, we sampled fifty participants and had now come back to actually talk to them in more depth. The village leader was bringing the people one after the other and introduced each one to us by name checking the name off his list. We had noted some information while sampling: name, age, and education. I was a bit surprised when I interviewed one person, who on my list was described as having limited education, but now told me that he was teaching at the local secondary school.

Some of the other surveyors had similar experiences with their information seemingly not fitting with what people told us when they came the second time. Of course, we could not confront people about this, and there are no such things like identity cards or driver's licenses we could use to verify identity. We just carried on. What we think happened is that people in this area know very little Swahili (the national language of Tanzania) and have very little education. But as people with little Swahili were not that keen on talking to us, and the village leader was very eager to present his village in the best possible light, he sent us the "best" people from his location instead of the names we had sampled. We could not use the information from the village in our analysis but it still told us a lot!

CROSS-REFERENCE ▸ See **Section 4.4.5** on page 161 for a description of participatory methods that can be used with partners for stakeholder analysis and for discussions with stakeholders.

Finally, bear in mind this advice about knowledgeable outsiders:

> *They are often people who have lived and worked outside of the community for a certain period of time or have relatives from another area or country. This means that they are more capable*

of taking the point of view of the researcher and understanding his needs, but at the same time, that they are probably not the most typical individuals in the community. This is one of the paradoxes that field researchers must live with, namely, that the people who understand us the best and are most easily understood by us are usually the ones who are the closest to the way we are.
(Duranti 1997:112)

2.4.3   Stakeholder Identification

There is much that can be said about how to work in a collaborative relationship with stakeholders. We will only mention a few basic aspects here and recommend further reading. There are two important parts of beginning to work with stakeholders: the identification of stakeholders and the engagement process. There can be different stakeholders at each of the three levels of Restricted, Negotiated, and Free language choice. At each level, there needs to be identification of all the possible stakeholders, as well as other potential partners, and each needs to be given consideration as to their potential interest and influence. This step is referred to as stakeholder analysis.

WWW.SURVEYWIKI.INFO ‣ See our page on Stakeholder Analysis on SurveyWiki for detailed methodology of how to identify stakeholders.

There are four categories of stakeholders:
1. Those who have *positive attitudes* towards the goals of development *and have influence* over others,
2. Those who have *negative attitudes* towards the goals of development *and have influence* over others,
3. Those who have *positive attitudes* towards the goals of development *but have little influence* over others, and
4. Those who have *negative attitudes* towards the goals of development *but have little influence* over others.

Consideration needs to be given as to how stakeholders in each category will be approached. People in the first category may be the easiest to talk with, but we should not take their attitudes for granted. We should not ignore people in the second category and we should assume that they have good reasons for their attitudes. We shouldn't ignore the people in the third and fourth categories just because they do not have much influence; we need to be respectful to all of these people.

2.4.4   Stakeholder Engagement

To engage with stakeholders means finding ways to build relationships, to become more familiar with one another, to identify shared values and goals, and in general learn how to work together in mutually beneficial ways. However, it is not possible to build relationships with everyone, so we need to find a way to engage with the most crucial people.

There are many ways to engage with stakeholders. Basically, engaging with stakeholders is similar to building any other relationships in life. It involves spending time together, listening to one another, and building trust. When organizations are engaging with one another, it is still people who are relating. The success of the efforts will probably be more dependent on the ability of the people to relate together rather than the perceived benefits of the collaboration of the organizations. One difference between friendships and the collaboration of organizations is that people from organizations can be more intentional about formal ways of interacting. Organizations can have meetings to get to know one another; individuals usually don't have formal meetings to build a relationship. Organizations also have a greater potential for maintaining relationships beyond the connections of specific individuals. However, members of minority groups may not be familiar with working with an organization and may be more comfortable building relationships with specific individuals. In such cases, an organization should not assume that the people have the same feelings toward the organization as they do towards people they have already learned to trust.

2.5   Further Reading

Learning How to Ask: A Sociolinguistic Appraisal of the Role of the Interview in Social Science Research **by Charles Briggs (1986)**

> Based on his own mistakes in his early research in Mexico, Briggs outlines how to avoid common pitfalls when carrying out interviews through carefully understanding the context you are working in when you design your research tools. This book is particularly useful because it shows how we can only carry out valid assessment using interviews if we understand what they mean to the people we are working with.

When Languages Collide: Perspectives on Language Conflict, Competition, and Language Coexistence **by Brian D. Joseph et al. (2003)**

This volume is a collection of papers, many of which deal with the impact of politics on languages and speech communities.

Whose Reality Counts?: Putting the First Last by Robert Chambers (1997)

Based on participatory rural appraisal, Chambers analyzes the relationship between professionals and the poor with a challenge to re-evaluate our approaches to those we might work with in language assessment. This book would be a good foundation for understanding participatory methods which we introduce later in this book.

Getting What You Asked For: A Study of Sociolinguistic Survey Questionnaires by Catherine J. Showalter (1991)

Showalter challenges surveyors' tendencies to re-use questionnaire items repeatedly without evaluating their effectiveness and improving them. The paper's appendix is a long annotated list of survey questions. You might want to find this and then evaluate her suggestions for suitability to a context you are familiar with. This article can be found on pages 302–325 in *Proceedings of the Summer Institute of Linguistics International Language Assessment Conference* edited by Gloria E. Kindell.

Research Interviewing by Elliot Mishler (1986)

A very challenging book. Mishler sets out to critique the contemporary view of interviews as controlled question-answer sessions. Instead, he argues that they are speech events and the respondents' personal contexts must be taken into account. He goes on to present an alternative and more sensitive approach to interviews.

3 Negotiated Language Choice

In this chapter we introduce you to language assessment at the Negotiated Level. We show how it differs from the Restricted Level covered in the previous chapter and the Free Level which we cover in the next chapter. In the first part of this chapter, we will discuss the social factors which influence language at the Negotiated Level. These include

- the multilingual outcomes when speech communities come into **contact**,
- the impact on language vitality when speech communities come into **contact**,
- different kinds of **social networks** that can develop,
- the importance of **economics** and **education** in contact situations, and
- the importance of **motivation** and **attitudes** to developing ability in languages.

The second part of the chapter will describe typical research questions that we consider when we work at the Negotiated Level. These include issues of multilingualism and language vitality, as well as the factors that influence these outcomes of language contact. We conclude the Negotiated Level with a look at a number of tools that we often use to answer these research questions.

3.1 Introduction

At the Negotiated Level we maintain our focus on understanding the sociolinguistic reality of the community we are working with, but we do so by looking at the influence of social factors that arise through interaction between the people in focus and neighboring communities that they consider to be "others." The key distinction between this and the Restricted Level is the inclusion of this element of negotiated interaction. This is because, unlike the Restricted Level, this interaction gives the people a measure of control over the social factors which influence their language choices. Interaction often takes the form of personal involvement, perhaps through meeting to buy goods in a market town or getting a job working alongside speakers of another language.

The interaction of any individual with another ethnolinguistic group is moderated by that person's attitudes towards the other group. Therefore, it is important for us to study attitudes to understand why people are making the choices they make.

Case Study 3A
Layers of Language
Chitral, Pakistan

Case Study 3A Source ▸ Ken Decker, International Language Assessment Coordinator, SIL.

In the Chitral District of the North-West Frontier Province (NWFP) of Pakistan there are several languages used for different purposes. Some of these languages can be used for more influential purposes. Some languages are used for their perceived beauty and others for religious purposes. When people prefer to use one of these languages rather than languages that are not considered as influential, beautiful, or religious there is impact on the less influential speech communities. English, Arabic, and Persian as world languages have some impact even on the smallest speech communities. English is available through media such as radio and television. People conduct religious ceremonies in Arabic, some people are able to recite Arabic verses from the Koran, and a few people may be able to read and understand the language. Persian is a highly valued language for poetry. Urdu is the national language of Pakistan and the prescribed language of education. However, in the Chitral District, most people can live their lives without knowing any of these languages.

Pashto, the language of the Pushtoons, is a lingua franca of the NWFP and much of neighboring Afghanistan. While Pushtoons are only a small minority in the Chitral District, they control as much as 85 percent of the economy (Decker 1992:21). It is hard to go to any market in the district and not need to use Pashto. Khowar is the language of the Kho, the largest language group in the district. Pashto and Khowar are both in the early stages of language development. The Pushtoons and Kho have pride in their languages and their cultural hegemony. There are several smaller less-influential languages and, at the language borders, where language homelands meet, people also feel the sociolinguistic effects of these smaller languages upon one another.

Typical parameters at the Negotiated Level will usually involve identifying the sociolinguistic features which enable us to differentiate speech communities like those in Case Study 3A. At this level, we define speech communities on the basis of criteria determined by the people. We may view two groups as linguistically similar, but if the people view each other as different, then we need to look at the relationships from their perspective as well. Likewise, there are groups who see themselves as one people, but we recognize enough language variation to consider that the people speak different languages. We need to study such a situation to determine how the speech communities are dealing with the differences. This is where the distinction between language and speech community becomes helpful. On a purely linguistic basis, we may arrive at very different conclusions about inter-group boundaries than the very people who provide the data. We need to understand how the people themselves define the various speech communities they may be part of through exploring the sociolinguistic factors which they use to define them.

When we consider the linguistic distance between two speech varieties, we need to allow for some ambiguity in our description of "different languages." It is easy to talk of distinct languages when the languages come from different language families or when the languages are only distantly related. However, it becomes less clear when the two languages are closely related and may be considered by some people as dialects. For each assessment project, we need to realize that the differences between the Negotiated and Free levels are often based on the people's view of who is in their social group. Often, the Free Level can be defined as interaction between people who consider themselves to be a social unit. The Negotiated Level involves interaction between speech communities that distinguish themselves as being different from one another.

CROSS-REFERENCE ▸ See the discussion about distinguishing dialects and languages in **Section 1.1.2** on page 5.

Assessment at the Negotiated Level will usually reveal the impact of forces that were studied at the Restricted Level. When a national government makes a policy that the national language will be taught in all schools, without involving a fully democratic dialogue, this is a Restricted-Level issue. The impact is seen in the community when children, who have never heard the national language, now listen to it for hours nearly every day.

Assessment at the Negotiated Level can often give us a good idea of the major factors that will inform language development because it gives us a broader perspective to interpret the data we get from Free-Level research. For example, research at the Free Level might tell us that 50 percent of the community's children go on to high school at the age of 15. This may sound good, but if the figure for neighboring speech communities is over 90 percent, this raises questions. We can only interpret data accurately when we understand its context.

There are two sociolinguistic questions that are at the core of all we will discuss in this chapter:

- Interaction and Contact: What happens when people from different speech communities meet?
- Attitudes and Motives: How do they feel about everything involved with meeting?

3.1.1   Interaction and Contact

CROSS-REFERENCE ‣ For more on language contact, see **Section 3.2.1** on page 53.

When two or more speech communities come into contact with each other there are two possible responses. They may try to avoid any intimate interaction and sometimes this is a violent response, or they may choose to interact to some degree, which usually results in a peaceful response. When discussing language choice, there isn't usually much of interest to say about the avoidance of interaction. Our interest is in learning about the interaction and negotiation involved in the language choices that are made. While contact can refer to both responses, in most cases, when sociolinguists talk about language contact they are referring to the latter response.

CROSS-REFERENCE ‣ See **Section 2.2** on page 25 for detailed discussion of these factors.

Contact between different speech communities comes about through any of the factors discussed earlier, as a response to economic, political, conflict, or disaster forces. It can also come about by local or regional growth of speech communities. As available land and resources become scarcer there will be competition and often domination. Contact also becomes an important means of expanding trade and influence.

Contact between speech communities at the Negotiated Level usually has the effect of forcing or offering language use choices. When people from two groups meet, which language (or languages) will they use? The choice is often not simply between A or B. In many cases, neither person has full control of the other language. Sometimes the choice can involve mixing of the two languages. There might be a third language, which neither control well, but is considered more neutral or appropriate for such a situation. Diglossia may be present and people are able to use the language appropriate for the situation. We need to assess the linguistic forms that are being expressed in response to the language contact situation.

CROSS-REFERENCE ‣ See the discussion about diglossia in **Section 3.3.1.4** on page 83.

When people make choices to use languages other than their heritage language or to begin mixing features of other languages into it, there can be a negative impact on the maintenance of the heritage language. We need to assess the impact of language contact on the vitality of each of the languages and discover how strongly the people are identifying with one speech community over another.

3.1.2   Psychological Variables

Language choices are the result of a complex inter-relationship of attitudes, desires, beliefs, motivations, and social norms. The interplay of these psychological variables is beyond the scope of this book. Simplistically, we can say that language choices are the result of desires motivated by attitudes and beliefs, moderated by social norms. The attitudes people hold towards anything can be based on past negative and positive experiences, beliefs, learned information, or conditioning.

CROSS-REFERENCE ‣ For more on attitudes and motivation see **Section 3.2.2** on page 68.

There can be a wide range of attitudes that affect language choices. People may like or dislike the sound of a language, they may like or dislike the people who speak a language as their heritage language, they may like the social or economic benefits that come from using a certain language, or they may dislike the cost of learning another language. These attitudes are the emotional feelings one has about something.

A motive is a reason for a certain choice of action. Motives can come from beliefs, attitudes, or desires. People can be motivated for many reasons, such as a desire for economic or social benefits, following traditional social norms and patterns, maintaining traditions, or religious convictions. A person may have a negative attitude about a certain language but may still be motivated to learn the language anyway due to their belief about the potential benefits and their desire to attain those benefits.

In this next section, many types of language choices will be described along with the role played by attitudes and motivations.

3.2   Social Factors and Language at the Negotiated Level

There are very few settlements around the world where people live in bubbles of linguistic isolation. For many people, interacting in languages other than their own is a daily norm and is so natural a situation that they hardly ever think about it. This is a natural result of two processes at work: contact and motivation. This section will focus on these two aspects of language learning.

Young children learn language from the input that is available to them without the need for any motivation other than the need to communicate. If they are growing up in a multilingual environment, they may learn parts of different languages. Or they may develop good proficiency in each of the available languages.

NOTE ‣ The CRITICAL PERIOD HYPOTHESIS proposes that there is an age at which language acquisition moves from being a subconscious to a conscious activity. Scientists still have very little insight into exactly when this occurs or why. For more about theories of how we acquire languages, see details of the book *How Languages Are Learned* in **Section 3.5** on page 112.

From around the age of puberty, people find they have to make more of a conscious effort to activate the ability to acquire languages (Brown 2000:54). They do this by proactively creating the right conditions, or they may be forced into language contact situations through factors such as population growth, migration, war, natural disasters, or slavery.

Language learning in adults is affected by many factors. Some of these factors are not very important considerations when studying multilingualism in a community. For example, an individual's language learning ability and success will be affected by their learning styles and strategies, as well as personality and mental ability. However, these individual differences between language learners in a community are not going to have any effect on the overall direction a speech community may take towards maintaining their heritage language or shifting to another language.

To be successful at language learning people need to be able to adjust the amount and complexity of language they receive and produce so that it matches their ability. If an adult wants to learn another language in a typical natural social environment, they can sometimes choose the people they associate with and the amount of time they spend in that learning environment. Their motivations for language learning will affect the depth of their language acquisition. Adults have the freedom to compensate for a lack of contact by increasing their motivation to make the most of the limited opportunities they do have, particularly if they have access to various media in the other language. This motivational freedom distinguishes adults from children in one very important way: they can also choose *not* to acquire languages even if there is plenty of contact with another speech community. Thus, for adults and in contrast to children, motivation becomes the factor which more clearly determines which languages they will acquire and to what degree.

3.2.1   Contact

For people to acquire additional languages, they must have an opportunity to do so. Such opportunities usually come about through some type of contact. This may be contact through listening to a radio program, through conversations with other passengers on a bus, meeting people at a shared well or market, working together with people from different speech communities, or it could be through enslavement.

In language assessment, we must consider how this contact has come about, what form it takes, and how much there is. Importantly, we must not assume that contact involves the interaction of two or more homogeneous and mutually exclusive speech communities. The danger of such a view is that we consider each community to be a monolingual group of people who use one language each for all purposes. Such communities are rare; some would even argue that they do not exist.

Contact with other languages does not affect everyone in a group to the same degree. More commonly we find ethnolinguistic groups whose individuals are members of any number of speech communities. Thus, the majority of groups we assess use a variety of languages for different purposes on a regular basis. People may use one language at home, another at school or work, yet another at the market, and still another when they attend their place of worship. But not everyone in the group will attend school or work in an area that requires another language. Not everyone will attend the same place of worship.

The factors that have contributed to such a multilingual situation have happened naturally, often over centuries or at least several decades. So, instead of assuming that contact involves the process of speech community A meeting speech community B, we need to appreciate the multilayered and complex nature of multilingual communities. The result of multilingualism is not like the careful and thorough mixing of red and blue to produce purple, it is more like an explosion in a paint factory.

Because such language contact situations have developed over time, we can often learn a lot about the complexities of the present situation during the secondary research stage. Historical records may show migration patterns that were the results of conflict or economic factors. Such data may tell us whether it was in-migration or out-migration, and census data may give an idea of the scale of this in relation to the speech community. Secondary research may indicate trends and may begin to explain the present situation, but there are some things it cannot tell us. Most importantly, it cannot tell us the reasons the people themselves have for establishing or maintaining contact, or their motivations and attitudes that drive this. It is hard to get an accurate idea of the current extent and forms of contact without collecting primary data.

3.2.1.1 Social networks

QUOTE ‣ *Understanding more about the social network structure and interaction of a particular individual can help the investigator understand more about the maintenance of vernacular norms.* (Marshall 2004:23)

CROSS-REFERENCE ‣ See Case Study 3D on page 65 for an example of how understanding contact through social networks enabled a more efficient approach to language assessment.

Societies, ethnolinguistic groups, speech communities—whatever type of social organization we want to talk about—these are formed by people who have social relationships with one another. We can describe webs of connections between people as social networks. The study of social networks can provide very useful information about the relationships that unite people or reveal distinctions between groups. In the study of social networks we identify

- who talks to whom,
- the frequency of contact,
- the topics of discussion within the networks,
- how information flows, and
- places where people from different groups meet.

From the data gathered in a study of social networks we can learn

- where there are centers of communication,
- where there are boundaries of communication,
- the presence of sub-groups,
- the groups people identify with, and
- who has influence.

This research also provides evidence of the attitudes people have towards the different languages—which ones they identify with and which ones they consider prestigious.

Social networks form through different processes and for different purposes. In some societies social networks form as a product of people creating their personal identities—people associating with other people they want to be like. In other groups, people may be more limited as to who they can associate with, for example, places where people can only associate with others in their caste.

Often there is a strong association between language and identity. For example, a national government might promote a policy that all citizens should speak the national language or members of a certain ethnic or religious group might believe that all members of their group should speak the same language. In some regions, such as South Asia, caste and religion may define a person's identity and allegiance to a national or religious group more than to a language or ethnicity. It is important in our studies of language vitality to understand the relationship of the people's identity and their languages and this is best done through a study of social networks.

CROSS-REFERENCE ‣ For more on the relationship of language and identity, see **Section 4.2.3** on page 123.

CASE STUDY 3B
DEPENDENCE AND LANGUAGE
CHITRAL, PAKISTAN

In the Chitral District of Pakistan there is a small language group called the Phalula. Some Phalula villages are in fertile side valleys off the main Chitral River valley. Other villages are located on the hillsides of the main valley, between the side valleys. The people in the side valleys are economically self-sufficient, but the people on the hillsides are dependent on their labor relationships with Khowar speakers, who are the largest group in the main valley. This dependence has only developed in recent decades. The people in the side valleys prefer to marry with other Phalula, but those on the hillside prefer marriage with Khowar speakers. People in the latter group said that they want the children of the next generation to grow up as Khowar speakers so that they will have better socio-economic opportunities.

CASE STUDY 3B SOURCE ‣ Ken Decker, International Language Assessment Coordinator, SIL.

When we understand the social factors involved in Case Study 3B, it is not surprising that the Phalula on the hillsides of the main valley are shifting to Khowar while those in the side valleys are continuing to maintain the use of their language. The case study illustrates how the desire to be a part of a social network may drive language choice decisions. Parents wanting their children to have better access to economic benefits may choose to encourage an L2 in the home. However, the parents may not have access to social networks that allow them to gain proficiency in the

CROSS-REFERENCE ‣ For more on economic forces driving language decisions, see **Section 2.2.1** on page 25.

other language, so they may not use the language well. This then influences the language production of the children and may influence their choices of social identification (Luycx 2003).

A person has an identity in each of the various groups they participate in whether it be their immediate family, a larger clan, a town, an organization, an ethnolinguistic group, or a nation (Coste and Simon 2009:171). Groups often use language to distinguish their own identity from that of others. In this way, membership in a group requires adopting a particular identity and conforming to the language associated with it (Wardhaugh 2009:127). Therefore, at the Negotiated Level we are trying to understand language choices like these because development activities that go against these patterns of pragmatic choice may have little chance of success.

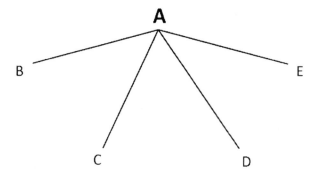

FIGURE 7 ▸ A *loose* social network.

Social networks are simple representations of the relationships people make with each other. Consider Figure 7. It shows A's relationships with four other people: B, C, D, and E. No one in A's social network has any contact with any other member, so we call this a loose network. A's heritage language is L1. If anyone in A's network only understands another

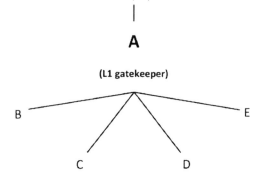

FIGURE 8 ▸ A loose social network with a gatekeeper.

language (L2), it is obvious that A must be bilingual to some degree to have established this network.

In many speech communities people are free to make association with whomever they choose. But in some speech communities people are limited in their ability to associate with others, and this will have an impact on the language environment. In some networks, such as described in Figure 8, one person may have a unique role within the network. Person A is designated as a gatekeeper who manages connections to the outside world for the rest of their community. The gatekeeper has enough contact with another speech community to maintain a high level of bilingual ability while the rest of the group does not. This person serves as an intermediary for the rest of the group. Since contact with the L2 is available only to the gatekeeper, ability in anything other than L1 is restricted for the rest of the community.

Exploring social networks may reveal attitudes about the L2 that are crucial to successful language development. Gatekeepers function in different social networks than the rest of their speech community, and may have different attitudes than the others in their speech community. Their unique role may influence how they filter sociolinguistic information to us about their community.

Figure 9 shows a dense network. In a dense network, people who interact with A also know and interact with others who know A. The members of a dense network may only interact with one another in one language. Or the network may have multilingual members from different speech communities who interact with one another in a variety of languages. It may be that their attitudes towards the various languages enabled them to make these connections, or it may be that the relationships have affected their attitudes towards the languages. These attitudes, however, may be positive or negative towards the languages and people since people are sometimes forced into relationships and gain multilingual

CROSS-REFERENCE ‣ For more about the influence of the position of our participants on our data, see the quote from Duranti at the end of **Section 2.4.2** on page 39 above.

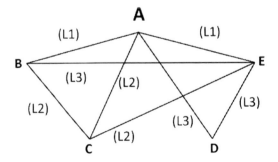

FIGURE 9 ‣ A *dense* social network. The L1, L2, L3 refer to the language used between two people.

proficiency pragmatically rather than by preference. When there are multiple languages used in a dense network, such as described in Figure 9, people may use different languages for different domains. These relationships, attitudes, and domains are all important aspects for the surveyor to explore.

Relationships in any social network may exist for more than one reason, and this is another important aspect to remember. For example, C is not only A's business partner but her husband, too. A and B may be relatives, members of the community governing body, and participate in the same religion. With each of these relationships there are more opportunities for interaction and more domains in which language is used. Each relationship will possibly strengthen identity and allegiance to the language used for the interaction. Communities like this, in which the members have multiple relationships with other members, are called multiplex social networks.

In dense social networks, ones in which everyone or nearly everyone uses the same language, the speech of the members will tend to accentuate unique language features. However, when there is a multiplex social network and a significant number of interactions occur in a language or languages, other than the heritage language, the opposite can happen in a process called **LINGUISTIC SWAMPING** (Wolfram and Schilling-Estes 2006:128; Landweer 2010:363). Linguistic swamping describes situations in which one speech community (A) is overwhelmed by a large number of immigrants from another speech community (B). The speakers of language A may have pride in their language and use it in most domains of their lives. Members of group B may be quite willing to learn language A. However, when people from group B learn language A, there may be some features of the language they don't adopt and due to the overwhelming numbers of group B a new altered form of language A becomes the norm. Furthermore, if group B does not want to learn language A, they may force group A to shift to language B.

DEFINITION ▸ LINGUISTIC SWAMPING is a process by which an immigrant population overwhelms a local speech community.

The networks that we have described in this section do not happen by chance. In most cases, social networks develop through individuals making choices as to who they want to associate with. There are a multitude of reasons why people will make these choices, but these pragmatic choices revolve around a number of real concerns that people have, and we will explore some of these in the following sections.

3.2.1.2 Economics

We saw at the Restricted Level that minority communities can be influenced by economic factors beyond their control. In contrast, at the Negotiated Level, people have some degree of control over economic factors that impact them. They can choose to adapt to changing economic circumstances in the regions where they live and they do so in different ways. At the Negotiated Level, labor and trade are the important economic concerns.

When people lose their ability to be self-sufficient, they become dependent on a larger network and economy. They need employment or some other resource to offer in exchange for what they want and need. Proficiency in another language will be required as they seek membership in additional speech communities that offer employment. Better jobs, better pay, and better benefits usually require better proficiency in the language of the workplace, and this enables access to more economic power and can also provide access to greater political power. Most jobs in civil service, education, government, and military service will require the use of an LWC or national language, and this can provide strong motivation to gain competency in that other language. In contrast, lower-paying, less-prestigious occupations tend to require less bilingual proficiency. Often, labor situations are arranged so that a more bilingual manager can oversee the work of numerous laborers who need very little, if any, bilingual proficiency. Even when working within one's own speech community bilingual proficiency can open doors to social networks outside in new speech communities. In Case Study 3B for example, we saw how Pashto-speaking sellers were functioning within Kho villages, which brought contact with Pashto into the Kho homeland.

Greater economic power can also be attained through trade in some form of goods. These goods might be manufactured products or crops grown for sale. As with labor, the locations for production and sales can have an influence on language use choices by bringing people of different languages together. In some situations, sellers will refuse to use anything other than their own language, forcing others to adapt to them, as in Case Study 3B. In other situations, sellers will use either an LWC or learn the languages of their patrons. In either situation, there is motivation for one party to learn the other language to improve trade. When the sellers maintain their L1, this establishes their language as the dominant language, and the buyer must learn it to get a better deal for purchases.

QUOTE ▸ *[P]ragmatic considerations – of power, social access, material advancement, etc. – are of the utmost importance in under-standing patterns of language use and shift; by extension, they are also the primary determinants of success for any language-planning exercise.* (Edwards 1985:94)

CROSS-REFERENCE ▸ For more about LWCs, see **Section 2.3.1** on page 33.

If sellers are willing to learn other languages, they gain a greater selling advantage by being able to better negotiate with the buyers.

When we are gathering information on individuals about the potential influence of economic factors on language use choices, it is important to consider past as well as present occupations because both will have an impact on multilingualism. Individuals may have spent time away from their home community for work. We will need to find out as much detail about this as possible including how they travelled to their employment and what languages they spoke when they were there. We also need to find out whether these individuals were exceptions in their ethnolinguistic group or whether migration for work purposes is a trend. In contrast to individuals moving away from the community, an employer may have come into the geographic area of a speech community to employ the local people in mining, logging, construction, or other industries. Again, we need to find out as much as we can about how this has affected language use.

3.2.1.3 Education

There are numerous ways that formal education may influence language use choices. These influences include languages used by teachers, parents, and children, proficiency in available languages, academic achievement, as well as the vitality of the heritage language. In this section, we are only considering the environment of formal education and not informal education, which includes apprenticeship and other passive ways children learn life skills outside organized schools.

CASE STUDY 3C
LANGUAGE AND EDUCATION
VANUATU

CASE STUDY 3C SOURCE ▸ Jim Stahl, international training consultant, SIL Vanuatu.

Epi Island lies in the center of the Vanuatu island chain. Just off the northwest coast of the island lies Lamen Island. Many years ago, there was an English medium District School on Lamen Island. Staff and students coming to the island to work and study did so in English and the use of any other language on the campus and particularly in the classroom was discouraged. Outside the school, however, the local islanders spoke Lamenu. It was common for staff and students to learn Lamenu and use this to interact outside the school. In time, a high school was built on Epi Island in a location where Lamenu was spoken. Despite Lamenu still being the local language in the area of the new school, staff and students at Epi High School stopped using Lamenu and instead started to use Bislama, the national language, to communicate with the local people.

In most places in the world, formal education is conducted in the national or official language. When a school is built in a community where a minority language is spoken and a different language is used in that school, we have a language contact situation. While this may be obvious, there are a number of factors for the surveyor to consider that are less apparent. These include the L1 of the teacher, the prescribed language of instruction, the proficiency of the teacher in the language of instruction, the proficiency of the teacher in the students' L1, and the teacher's attitudes and academic abilities to use the students' L1 for instruction. Table 1 describes these, and Case Study 3C above illustrates the choices that staff and students will face in this kind of situation.

EDUCATIONAL SCENARIO	ADVANTAGES	DISADVANTAGES
The teacher's heritage language is the prescribed language of instruction. This is not the students' L1, and the teacher does not know the students' L1.	The teacher is a good model of the L2 for the students to learn from.	The teacher will have difficulty communicating with students depending on how much they have been exposed to the teacher's language outside of school. Students may become frustrated and leave school before there is any significant benefit.
The teacher's heritage language is the prescribed language of instruction, which is not the students' L1, but the teacher has some useful proficiency in the students' L1.	The teacher is a good model of the L2 for students to learn from and is more capable of communicating in the students' L1.	The situation intrinsically reduces the value of the students' L1.
The teacher's heritage language is neither the prescribed language of instruction nor the students' L1, and the teacher doesn't know the students' L1.	None.	The teacher is neither a good model for learning the language of instruction nor able to use the students' L1 for clarification.

TABLE 1 ▸ Advantages and disadvantages of language contact through education.

The teacher's heritage language is not the prescribed language of instruction or the students' L1. The teacher has some proficiency in the students' L1.	The teacher has some ability to communicate with students.	There are still significant barriers to communication between the teacher and the students.
The teacher and students share an L1 that is different from the prescribed language of instruction.	Somewhat helpful to the students. The teacher can clearly and easily communicate with them.	The teacher may not be a good model of L2 use. Very little of the L2 may be taught.
The teacher and students share the same language which is also the language of instruction.	Language is not a barrier to any communication in the classroom between students and teacher.	There is no bilingual ability.

REFERENCE: Evidence of the high value of primary education in the heritage language is found in numerous studies from around the world. A good summary of recent research can be found in Kosonen (2005).

In Table 1, we have not included the provision for multilingual education. The teaching methods that are used can have a major impact on the effectiveness of the schools to educate. The use of multilingual education strategies may actually be even better than the scenario that was listed last in Table 1. Research has shown that children who have the opportunity to learn first in their heritage language before adding another language later have a greater potential for becoming highly bilingual. The converse has also been shown: children who are not taught in their heritage language may never gain significant bilingual proficiency. Furthermore, if teachers are unable to adapt their teaching approaches for different learning styles, some students will have less of an opportunity to learn effectively. All of these factors affect the potential for acquisition of the various languages that are available to the students. That is why it is important for a complete assessment of a speech community to include a description of language use in education.

The first factor for a survey team to identify is the availability of formal education. It is obvious that the language of education in a formal educational program will have little impact on language choices, if there are no schools or no teachers for the school. However, parents have choices that may make formal education more available for their children. If schools are not geographically close, parents may either choose to send the children away to a distant location where there are schools, or the whole family may relocate. The school may possibly still be within the territory where their own language is spoken, or it may be where another language is dominant. The student may thus have more or less contact with other languages in the proximity of the school. Access to formal education may also be limited to certain social or economic classes. This is a more difficult barrier to overcome and may impose other non-linguistically oriented choices, such as a farmer choosing to grow a more lucrative but illegal crop so as to be able to afford school expenses.

If children are unable to attend school, for whatever reason, there may be shame over this situation. Sometimes when people are interviewed about school attendance they may greatly inflate the numbers of children that attend school and the number of years they attend. It is also possible to overestimate the impact or value of reported time in school. In remote locations, sometimes teachers don't show up for school or the time spent in school is not spent well. Some teaching methods may be quite ineffective in teaching anything to the children.

Formal education, if it does not take place in the heritage language, may impact the local speech community and heritage language in several serious ways. Firstly, it not only involves years of sustained contact with the L2, but the early years of education are years when the ability to acquire languages is strongest. Secondly, formal education introduces the student to many new concepts and domains of knowledge. If the student's L1 is not part of the learning experience, the student will only learn vocabulary and structures for talking about these new topics in the L2. Depending on the policies that are influencing the education system, the educational experience can shape the student's attitudes towards themselves and the groups they are part of. Particularly if there are strong restrictions on the use of the student's heritage language, the impact of these factors causes the devaluation of the heritage language and culture. This can have a major effect on choices a person makes about language and identity in later life and can cause divisions in communities where older generations, who lacked educational opportunities, use languages that are different from those who are being or have been educated.

When the prescribed language of education is different from the heritage language of the student's speech community, there can also be influence on the heritage language and culture. Parents are often highly motivated to ensure their children gain access to education and may choose to encourage use of the language of instruction in the home rather than the heritage language. In such a situation the children have the double impact of predominantly hearing and using the L2 in the home and school and hearing less of their L1. As the students gain proficiency in the L2 and become more accustomed to using it in various contexts, the L2 may even have an influence on the linguistic structures of the heritage language. In extreme cases the children may even grow up with little competency in the heritage language of their parents and little sense of being connected to their parents' heritage identity.

The surveyor also needs to consider the possible impact of historical changes in the government and its policies. For example, students educated under a foreign colonial government may be highly motivated to learn the language of the colonial power. But with a shift to nationalistic sentiments, the students may become more loyal and motivated to learn and promote a local language. Government policy may then change to recognize the legitimacy of minority heritage languages for use in education. Students educated during each of these different periods will have different attitudes towards different languages.

The regional status of the language of instruction in the surrounding area may encourage or discourage its use outside school. It may be only one of many languages that students are exposed to in their geographic area. Therefore, it may be important to see how people rank their languages with regard to prestige and value. The absence of fluent speakers of the language of education in the region may lessen the importance of becoming bilingual in that language.

Formal education may also have an impact on the ability of people to participate in our research. Some of the types of questions that we ask, behavior we require, or the issues that we investigate can be quite different from anything the participant has ever experienced or considered. For example, to evaluate comprehension we ask questions that require them to repeat information after listening to a recording. Such questions can be confusing if the participant has no experience of them in formal education as this kind of behavior is not typical in their experience of normal conversation. They may be aware that we are listening to the recording and already know the answer to the question, so they don't understand why we are asking them. Likewise, questions about language use, or hypothetical situations, may be concepts that the participant has never considered. This is not to say that an uneducated person is not intelligent or unable to participate and provide valuable information, but we need to be aware of the possibility of this kind of a situation affecting the research.

We have been describing many ways that education can have an impact on the language use choices of a minority community. However, the presence of these factors does not tell us whether they contributed to any kind of bilingual proficiency. Further in-depth study of all these factors can be very expensive in terms of time and money. Therefore, it may be worthwhile for the research to focus on proving the absence of potential for bilingualism. Read Case Study 3D as an example.

CASE STUDY 3D
NO EDUCATION =
NO BILINGUALISM
NORTHERN PAKISTAN

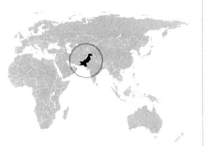

CASE STUDY 3D SOURCE ▸ Ken Decker, International Language Assessment Coordinator, SIL.

In northern Pakistan, we found that most people could not have significant proficiency in Urdu, the national language, unless they had at least five years of education. Schools were about the only place in the region where Urdu was used. So, we would find out how long there had been a school in the village. If there was no school available or it had been there less than five years, we knew it wasn't possible that more than a few people could have any significant proficiency in Urdu. If a school had been there longer than five years, we asked if girls attended the school. If not, then at least approximately 50 percent of the population could not have significant proficiency. Then, we would ask about the numbers of the different age groups of the boys who attended school. This helped us gain a profile of the potential for bilingualism. In most cases there was very little potential.

In Case Study 3D, the surveyors only needed to ask some simple questions to establish whether bilingualism was relevant to the survey. If so, they would have had to assess bilingualism in Urdu, but if not, they then saved precious resources for other kinds of assessment.

3.2.1.4 Other factors

There are a few other factors that may influence language use choices that the surveyor should consider. In the following paragraphs we will briefly discuss potential influence from politics, religion, travel, media, and gender.

In most cases, people in minority speech communities will need to learn the national or official language in order to participate in national and possibly regional politics. Typically, politicians do not use minority languages with their audience unless they share the same heritage language with them. Any speech community who does so will probably gain some prestige from association with that politician. Furthermore, multilingual ability may be a prerequisite to hold a position of leadership within some ethnolinguistic groups. Thinking back to our social network models earlier, we can see why this might be so: the gatekeeper is the person who moderates interaction with the outside world. This gives them influence within their own speech community. The more people one knows, the more likely they are to be an influential leader, although not necessarily a politician. Greater power and influence may well require or provide opportunity for membership in speech communities other than one's own. Also, being part of a larger network within these other speech communities will provide more opportunities to develop the language skills necessary to strengthen these relationships and establish more.

CROSS-REFERENCE ▸ See **Section 3.2.1.1** on page 54 for more on social networks and gatekeepers.

In some ethnolinguistic groups, the only contact with another language is through activities they carry out as part of their religion, such as the use of Arabic among Muslims, Hebrew for Jews outside of Israel, literary Sanskrit for some Hindus, literary Tibetan for some Buddhists, or European languages in some Christian churches. People following these religions are highly motivated to learn these languages so that they can participate fully in their religious speech communities. However, use of the L2 only in the religious domain limits the individual's proficiency in that language.

CROSS-REFERENCE ▸ See **Section 2.2.3** on page 30 for a description of the impact of geographic disasters on language use.

We have considered how geographic disasters are a factor at the Restricted Level in that people have little ability to control them. However, geographic features such as mountains, deserts, rivers, and other bodies of water are a Negotiated-Level issue because people learn to deal with their presence. Mountains and deserts tend to be barriers to contact, but they may also guide contact. In Case Study 3B we described how the location of Phalula villages on mountainsides or in valleys influenced the amount and kind of contact with the regionally dominant Kho. The locations of oases in the Sahara have historically controlled where people could travel and who they had contact with. Rivers and other bodies of water may restrict or enable contact. Some raging rivers, which are virtually impossible to cross by boat, limit people to where they can cross on bridges. People have known how to use boats to travel on rivers and other bodies of water for a long time. Therefore, rivers and lakes may actually enable contact rather than restrict it. Similarly, people have been able to deal with geographic distance for so long it is not necessarily a barrier to contact. When towns or villages are closer to roads, there is more potential for multilingualism. Modern transportation has made it much easier for more people to travel long distances and have contact with other speech communities. When members of a speech community have opportunity to travel, they can bring other languages back with them. Nomadic communities may or may not be multilingual depending on whether they are self-sufficient or dependent on people in the areas they travel through. Furthermore, variations in contact over time may result in only particular age groups being members of particular speech communities, and the economic and political factors we mentioned above may influence only particular socially-mobile sets of the community, such as young adults.

Increasingly though, proximity is becoming less of an issue; contact through media such as radio, television, mobile phone, and the Internet is increasingly able to sustain social networks of various kinds. The main issue with regard to language in the media is prestige. Languages used for widespread broadcasting are chosen because they have prestige and widespread currency, or the government wants them to have more influence. This initial prestige is further reinforced by being used in the media. This combination can provide strong motivation for people to learn the languages used in mass media. In addition, media has enabled something which has never been possible before: virtual mobility. Without leaving their homes, people are able to become sociolinguistically mobile in completely new ways. For example, video capabilities with phones make it possible for the Deaf to communicate electronically.

QUOTE › *[P]articularly for young people, exposure to the media constitutes one of the major vectors of socialization and individual development. It involves coming into contact with circulating stereotypical conceptions on one hand, and role models with which youngsters can identify on the other. Furthermore, it is a means of access to the outside world and to others.* (Coste and Simon 2009:171)

Finally, gender can play a part in language contact, as we saw in Case Study 3D where gender distinctions meant that girls in some villages were unlikely to be proficient in Urdu. Gender also influences occupation, leadership, and care-giving roles, and these in turn will influence language use choices. Marriage customs may mean that men and women marry spouses from other speech communities. Cultural choices based on gender will affect the socialization of children and the eventual vitality of languages. In speech communities where gender distinctions are not marked though, it follows that there is unlikely to be a distinction in the amount of contact that either sex will have with other speech communities.

CROSS-REFERENCE › See **Section 4.2.5** on page 129 for more about socialization.

3.2.2   Motivations and Attitudes

CROSS-REFERENCE ‣ For more on attitudes and motivation see **Section 3.1.2** on page 51. See the introduction to **Section 3.2** on page 52 for an explanation of the relationship between motivation and learning.

REFERENCE ‣ Karan and Stalder (2000) describe a useful approach to studying motivation.

QUOTE ‣ *[A]n attitude is a disposition to react favourably or unfavourably to a class of objects...an evaluative orientation to a social object of some sort.* (Garett, Coupland, and Williams 2003:3)

DEFINITIONS ‣ INSTRUMENTAL MOTIVATION happens when someone wants to learn new skills for some other aim such as finding employment, while INTEGRATIVE MOTIVATION focuses instead on the social benefits of learning; the learner wants membership in a new speech community, for example.

Up to this point in the chapter, the discussion of how contact affects language use has included a number of references to motivation. Motivation is particularly important when people learn languages as adults. Although factors like colonization may force people into contact with users of other languages, no one can force people to be motivated to learn another language. Motivation is fundamental to language learning because without it individuals in an ethnolinguistic group will simply refuse to learn. To inform language development planning, we want to understand why people would go to the effort to learn a language other than their heritage language. We need to be aware of their motivations.

There has been much research on the relationship of motivation to second language learning. There are several different models that have been proposed to describe the different kinds of motivations or factors that affect motivations. While Gardiner's Socio-Educational Model (Gardiner 2001) may be considered out-dated by some, it is appropriate for describing situations in which whole ethnolinguistic groups may be involved rather than only in a classroom. A simplified form of the model describes motivation along the lines of **INSTRUMENTAL** and **INTEGRATIVE MOTIVATIONS.** People are said to have instrumental motivation when they want to learn new skills for some other aim than the attainment of that skill, for example, learning another language to improve the chance of finding employment. Integrative motivation focuses instead on the social benefits of learning; the learner wants membership in a new speech community, for example. Some features of these motivations can be found in Table 2.

Motivation and attitude are very closely related (Schmidt 2006). It is the presence of motivational factors such as economics, educational policies, demography, etc., which determines the attitudes that a speech community might have towards an L2 and the people who use it. Clearly, from Table 2, if we want to be able to estimate the linguistic future of a speech community, it is important for us to be able to assess accurately what motivations people have for any learned multilingualism.

	INSTRUMENTAL MOTIVATION	INTEGRATIVE MOTIVATION
Social reasons for learning L2	economics (trade, employment), education, language planning policies, invasion/colonization.	prestige, social mobility, international status, psycho-linguistic (e.g. ethnic identity, trends, idealism).
Given reasons for learning L2	"The L2 opens doors of opportunity for the gain of our L1 speech community."	"The L2 speech community can be our speech community."
Feelings towards L2 community	Positive or negative. Desire for gain from L2 is greater than any negative attitudes. No interest in other social aspects of L2 group e.g. culture, customs, dress, etc.	Usually very positive. Tries to blend in as many ways as possible by adopting culture, customs, dress, and possibly even religion.
Feelings towards L1 community	Usually very positive, at least to insiders. Pride in L1 speech community is an important part of identity.	May be positive, neutral, or negative. May try to distance themselves from socio-cultural aspects of their L1 speech community.
L2 ability	Only as necessary. Usually in a limited number of domains.	As much as possible in as many domains as possible.
Bilingualism type (Myers-Scotton 2002:48)	Often additive: L1 continues to develop, and L1 investment is made in L1 culture.	Often subtractive: L1 may be replaced, and L1 culture suffers from effort to acquire L2 culture
Awareness (Myers-Scotton 2002:1)	Often very aware of impact of L2 on L1 including culture and may be protective of L1.	May not be aware of any impact of L2 on L1 and may be neutral or even positive about this.
Community policy	Leaders/caregivers may have a policy to limit membership of the L2 speech community to certain individuals in the speech community or certain domains.	Leaders and caregivers may have a policy to limit membership of the L1 speech community to certain individuals in the speech community or certain domains.
Impact on language vitality	L1 not influenced by L2 to any significant degree. If future needs change, speech community may no longer be members of L2 speech community in future.	People may not use L1 at home. Children may start learning L2 as L1. Language shift may occur, and speech community may lose membership of L1 speech community.

TABLE 2 ▸ Characteristics of learners who have either instrumental or integrative motivation.

Most studies of language attitude are carried out according to the mentalist view which states that the more we know about someone's attitude, the more accurately we can predict their behavior (Baker 1992; Babajide 2001; Ihemere 2006). But attitudes are particularly difficult to assess. They are often subconscious, and we need to bear this in mind when we design questionnaires and other tools to measure attitudes. For all sorts of reasons (honesty, fear, hospitality, self-protection, etc.), a person may feel that they should give a particular answer in an interview about attitudes towards another language. While this in itself shows an attitude to the assessment process, it may not give us the information we are looking for. It is therefore important to triangulate this data with observations of behavior that may reveal hidden attitudes.

CROSS-REFERENCE ‣ See **Section 3.4.2** on page 98 for more about questionnaires and **Case Study 2D** on page 39 for an example of providing particular data.

CROSS-REFERENCE ‣ See **Section 1.2.2** on page 13 and **Section 5.2.6** on page 187 for more about triangulation.

CASE STUDY 3E
ATTITUDES TOWARDS SUCCESS
CHILE AND USA

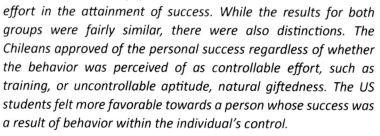

CASE STUDY 3E SOURCE ‣ Hector Betancourt and Bernard Weiner (1982).

Chilean students and students from the United States were studied for their attitudes towards the value of personal effort in the attainment of success. While the results for both groups were fairly similar, there were also distinctions. The Chileans approved of the personal success regardless of whether the behavior was perceived of as controllable effort, such as training, or uncontrollable aptitude, natural giftedness. The US students felt more favorable towards a person whose success was a result of behavior within the individual's control.

QUOTE ‣ *There is obviously a need for a combination of approaches to language attitude assessment; in particular, given the decontextualised nature of much social psychological work, both direct and indirect methods should be supplemented with real-life observation.* (Edward 1985:150)

It is important also to differentiate between attitudes and beliefs. Because attitudes are often subconscious, people may state their beliefs instead of their attitude, particularly if we don't design questionnaires with this distinction in mind. In a study in Nigeria (Igboanusi and Ohia 2001), data showed that Hausa was the most widely used indigenous lingua franca among respondents. In a seeming contradiction though, data from the same respondents indicated it was the most "hated" lingua franca, too. If these respondents were given a question such as "Is it important for you to be able to speak Hausa?" they would have responded positively. But this would only reveal their belief that Hausa is necessary in some way. If this same question was employed to gauge attitude, it would be badly designed.

Just as there are two kinds of motivation, there are also two kinds of attitudes: instrumental and sentimental. **INSTRUMENTAL ATTITUDE** refers to viewing language as a means to an end. This is the kind of attitude revealed in the Hausa example we just saw. In language development, this is important to distinguish from **SENTIMENTAL ATTITUDE** which is about a symbolic value of language. In the Republic of Ireland, relatively few people use Irish Gaelic on a daily basis. However, a study focused on sentimental attitudes towards Gaelic would have markedly different results from one on instrumental attitude. Links between ethnic identity and Irish Gaelic remain very strong in Ireland despite only 3 percent of the population using it on a daily basis. These two kinds of attitudes are related though, and the Irish government's twenty-year plan to make the country bilingual is founded on the belief that sentimental attitudes are simply latent instrumental attitudes waiting to be directed (ÓLaoire 2008; Baker 1988:125).

Case Study 3E shows us how a belief in the value of personal effort resulted in a positive attitude towards someone for US students, but was not a deciding factor for Chilean students. In this Case Study, success was attributed to the valued effort. Likewise, if people in speech community A admire something about community B, and people in A consider the language of B as a part of what they admire, then people in A will behave more positively towards people in B and their language. For example, numerous studies have established that there are certain English accents that are more trusted in certain contexts, and that the speaker's gender may make a difference for certain purposes. Such positive attitudes can be evoked simply by hearing someone's voice, as Case Study 3F illustrates.

DEFINITIONS ▸ INSTRUMENTAL ATTITUDE considers language as a tool which enables people to achieve their aims. **SENTIMENTAL ATTITUDE** views language as a symbol of the identity of a people.

CASE STUDY 3F
PASSENGERS AND PILOTS
UK

Four out of five airline passengers feel more at ease if their pilot speaks with a "posh" voice, according to new research. And while air travelers are also reassured by Scottish and Newcastle accents, 76 percent said that they would take no comfort from hearing a Birmingham voice over the tannoy [loudspeaker]. Female pilots are also less trusted than their male colleagues, the survey suggests, with 83 percent of people preferring to have

CASE STUDY 3F SOURCE ▸ Matthew Moore reporting for *The Daily Telegraph* newspaper (2010).

their flight briefings delivered by a man. While the stereotypes revealed by the research may be outdated, it appears that pilots are more than happy to play along. More than half of 53 pilots surveyed admitted talking to passengers in more formal phrasing.

DEFINITION ▸ ATTRIBUTION THEORY was first proposed by Fritz Heider in 1958. It is based on the idea that we do not want to see behavior as random but as the result of what we believe about behavior. These beliefs are so strong that we even have them in situations where they can be proved to be invalid.

REFERENCE ▸ Dörnyei (2005) gives a good overview of the development of different theories concerning motivation and second language learning.

Attitudes about languages are usually linked to attitudes about the users of those languages (Fishman 1999:154). According to **ATTRIBUTION THEORY,** in order to make sense of the world around us, we interpret what we observe and use it to draw conclusions about the relationship between certain causes and effects. People want to be able to explain the world around them. The conclusions we draw and explanations we form, combined with our beliefs about the way things should be, determine our attitudes. A sports team may attribute their loss to their poor training, for example.

These attributions fashion our attitudes and influence the way we act towards people when we hear their language (Padilla 1999:112). People form these attributions when either they admire or fear something about another group. For example, consider a situation in which large numbers of a large ethnolinguistic group are moving into the lands of a smaller group. The people of the smaller group may fear being overwhelmed and the destruction of their culture. The people of the smaller group may begin to attribute their negative feelings toward the larger group to such things as the larger group's perceived poor morals, rudeness, or the ugliness of their language. They may say something like, "We don't like these people moving into our town because their poor morals will corrupt our children." Thus, if someone from the smaller group learns and uses some of the language of the larger group, members of the smaller group might associate the language with the behavior and react negatively towards that person. Therefore, attributions and their resulting attitudes may be quite strong.

These negative or positive attitudes become associated with languages particularly at the Negotiated Level where inter-group communication is our focus. It is only when confronted with other ethnic groups that issues of our own ethnic identity become relevant (Padilla 1999:118). If these attitudes are associated with negative attributions towards another group and there are motivations for the preservation of ethnic identity, those people may be sensitive towards any questioning of their attitudes and motivations. Therefore, our questions may be uncomfortable or downright unacceptable to some participants.

3.2.3   Maintenance and Shift

There is a time in the life of a language when the people who speak that language find identity and affinity with that language. They are most proficient in it, and they feel the most commitment to communication in that language resulting in behavior that seeks to maintain and perpetuate its use. This is called **LANGUAGE MAINTENANCE.**

DEFINITION ▸ LANGUAGE MAINTENANCE refers to behaviors in a speech community that tend to preserve the use of a language.

As often happens, they then begin to believe that another language offers greater benefits. Sometimes, people are forced to change their speech habits by a change in circumstances such as enslavement. To make these changes requires a time of learning the other language and a change in the level of commitment and identification with this new language. This process is called language shift. In the process of shifting to the L2 from heritage language maintenance, there is a tipping point. It does not occur at the same point in time for everyone in the speech community; it is an individual and, probably, imperceptible change in attitudes and identification.

This tipping point is a major phenomenon that we look for in our research. In most cases, outsiders such as ourselves will see that some parents are no longer teaching their children in the heritage language, but some may be. It is hard for outsiders to really know what is going on in the intimacy of the home. Many people will be exhibiting proficiency in the L2, but since we cannot test everyone, we don't really know how widespread this might be. Except in forced situations, people will be expressing positive attitudes towards the L2, but we cannot be sure if their attitudes are sufficient motivation to signify their true allegiance or commitment. Therefore, it is often very difficult for us to really know if the community as a whole is leaning more toward maintenance or to shift.

3.3   Typical Research Questions at the Negotiated Level

Due to the fact that the Negotiated Level is concerned with interaction between different speech communities, questions about multilingualism and language vitality are of primary importance in our research. Since it is so difficult to identify the tipping point between language maintenance and shift referred to in the previous section, we have to look for evidence in multilingual proficiencies, reports of language attitudes, and observed language use behavior. Multilingualism may have a negative impact on the use of heritage languages that become perceived as less valued as a means of communication. Therefore, questions regarding language vitality are also quite relevant when determining the potential for

CROSS-REFERENCE ▸ See **Section 3.3.3** on page 88 and **Section 4.2.4** on page 128 for more on the impact of multilingualism on language vitality.

language development. In this section, we will also discuss partnerships with others who are interested in language development and studying multilingualism. Some of the larger questions to be considered at the Negotiated Level are

- What are the languages used by members of the ethnolinguistic group?
- How do they gain proficiency in each of these languages?
- How proficient are they in each of the languages?
- For what purposes do they use each of their languages?
- Does everyone have multilingual proficiency or how does it pattern through the group?
- If we are working with a speech community that is transitioning from the dominant use of their heritage language to the dominant use of another language, what are the factors that have motivated this shift?
- If children are no longer learning the heritage language, how endangered is the future use of the language?
- What are the relationships of various potential partners who are stakeholders in the decisions that affect the different communities?

3.3.1   Multilingualism

Multilingualism is of particular interest to us in language assessment. For any successful language development, it is vital to understand the roles of the different languages used by people we work with. We need to understand the distribution of multilingual abilities in the speech community. But more than simply understanding the present situation, we also must understand the historical factors that have led to the current multilingual state. Understanding these historical factors may help us to predict, to some degree, the linguistic futures of the various languages. With all of this information we hope to ensure that their desired future for their languages and development align.

While this section is titled *Multilingualism,* and it is a fact that people frequently speak more than two languages, it will be easier to talk about issues concerned with bilingualism. When multilingualism is present, the features of bilingualism are simply more complex.

According to Clyne (1997:301), "there are probably more bilinguals in the world than monolinguals." If we mistakenly assume monolingualism is the norm, this will prevent us from being able to visualize the sociolinguistic reality of the communities we work with. In fact, bilingualism will increasingly be the norm because without it contemporary global society could not function (Aronin and Singleton 2008:2; Coste and Simon 2009:169).

When languages come into contact with one another, people either learn some of the other language, expect that the others will learn their language, or they may both learn a third language that is not the heritage language of either. In some cases, after a time of contact, people are able to intentionally switch between languages. However, in other cases, the languages may merge to a degree that people are not aware which parts of their language come from another language.

In his book *Multilingualism*, Edwards (1994:34) makes two important points:

- no one speaks multiple languages just for the sake of it but rather because of self-determined necessity and
- those abilities in different languages will not be equal but only extend as far as that necessity determines.

We therefore need to be aware not only that multilingualism is the norm for most ethnolinguistic groups, but also that both its purposes and its extent are variables which we will need to determine as best we can for each assessment situation.

CROSS-REFERENCE ‣ See **Section 5.2.4** on page 183 for more about data variables.

One of the first considerations to discuss in this section is that there are several kinds of bilingualism. There are different issues involved when bilingualism involves closely-related languages compared to bilingualism in unrelated languages. The processes by which a person becomes bilingual can result in different abilities. There are also differences between interactive and passive bilingualism, and spoken bilingualism can be different from literary bilingualism. There can even be individual differences in bilingual proficiency resulting from variation in intelligence or physical deficiencies with the mouth or ears.

While everyone will have differences in their individual bilingual proficiencies, there is something we call **COMMUNITY BILINGUALISM**. This describes a situation in which a community is comprised of portions of the population with similar bilingual abilities, but each individual has reached his or her own level of proficiency by similar yet separate paths. To gain an understanding of the overall impact of bilingualism in a particular community, we will need to gain a deeper understanding of its overall distribution. In the following section, we will briefly describe some variables that are involved in gaining bilingual proficiency.

DEFINITION ‣ COMMUNITY BILINGUALISM refers to the distribution of differing bilingual proficiencies throughout a community.

3.3.1.1 Types of bilingualism

Cross-Reference ▸ See Section 1.1.2 on page 5 for more about the difficulties of defining *language* and *dialect*.

As we saw earlier, there is a considerable amount of disagreement between linguists as to the definitions of the terms *language* and *dialect*. To discuss different types of bilingualism we need to consider a multilayered continuum of factors. At one end we have the identical language of two people. They need not spend any time learning the speech, or signs, of the other in order to make intelligible communication or to have complete comprehension of the other. Furthermore, they consider that they use the same language. At the other end of the continuum are two people who use languages that are linguistically very different so that they consider them different languages. These two people would need to spend considerable time and effort to learn the other's language for there to be significant communication. Somewhere in between, we can identify cases in which there is some amount of linguistic difference and which would require some amount of learning for clear communication. But the people who use these speech varieties consider that it is all one language. The learned ability to use both varieties is called **BIDIALECTALISM**. Bidialectalism can be considered a type of bilingualism because it requires learning to develop communicative ability.

Definition ▸ **Bidialectism** is the learned ability to use two different dialects.

Nearby on the same continuum, we can identify cases in which there is some amount of linguistic difference, possibly even less difference than the previous case. Clear communication would require some amount of learning. But the people who use these speech varieties consider that they use different languages. The learned ability to use both languages is called bilingualism. Case Study 3G describes two different situations on this bilingual continuum.

CASE STUDY 3G
JAPANESE AND TOK PISIN
JAPAN AND PAPUA NEW GUINEA

Case Study 3G Source ▸ John Grummitt, Language Surveyor, SIL Papua New Guinea.

In 1998, I moved from my native UK to Japan. I spent six years working very hard at learning Japanese. Although I achieved a fairly high degree of fluency, nearing the end of my time there, I would still sit through church services grasping for meaning from the fast-flowing sermons. Often, I'd be completely mistaken about even the sermon topic, let alone the details. It was very frustrating.

In 2009, I visited Papua New Guinea for the first time and, the second Sunday, visited a local church where the sermon was in Tok Pisin, the local trade language. To my utter amazement, I could follow almost the entire discourse. Afterwards, a local mistook me for a seasoned worker there and engaged me in conversation telling me about the history of the church. He didn't realize I spoke almost no Tok Pisin, but it didn't matter. Later I checked the details of the sermon and the church history with a veteran expatriate who'd attended. With few exceptions, my interpretations were completely right!

In Case Study 3G, we can see that John had some bilingual ability in Japanese. Furthermore, we know that no one considers Japanese and English to be related languages. John required six years of studying Japanese to reach a significant communicative ability. However, it took much less time to gain some comprehension in Tok Pisin because it shares some of its vocabulary, phonology, and syntax with English. While English and Tok Pisin share some similarities, no one would say that they are dialects of the same language, yet, the similarities will aid an English-speaker to learn Tok Pisin. While there is no commonly used term for this phenomenon, Kloss and McConnell (1974:36) proposed calling it **INHERENT BILINGUALISM.** The concept of inherent bilingualism is only discussed here to describe why some languages may be more easily learned than others.

We can contrast inherent bilingualism with **LEARNED BILINGUALISM**. With learned bilingualism, learning the L2 is intentional. It happens because people choose to do it, and they must make an effort to do so, overcoming all the differences between their heritage language and the language they choose to learn. In Case Study 3G, John became bilingual in Japanese, but because we know that Japanese and English are extremely different linguistically, we know that the majority of his bilingual ability must have been learned and that this took time and effort. Inherent bilingualism differs from this. If another language is very similar to yours, you will understand some of it simply because it contains similar linguistic features. When John visited Papua New Guinea, from the very moment he arrived and with very little effort, he was able to understand some Tok Pisin phrases. While a certain level of bilingual proficiency is possible depending on the linguistic similarity of the L1 and L2, intentional learning is still necessary to improve one's proficiency in the L2. Of course, we know that social factors will influence proficiency independent of any linguistic relatedness. If, for example, there has been a long-held and

DEFINITION ‣ **INHERENT BILINGUALISM** is the ability to use another language that is due to similarity between the speaker's heritage language and the L2. This is not a commonly used term. It differs from Learned Bilingualism which results from a learner choosing and making an effort to learn.

CROSS-REFERENCE ‣ See **Section 4.3.1** on page 133 for more on inherent intelligibility.

abiding hatred between two linguistically related speech communities, it might well be pointless to go to the effort of assessing how much linguistic affinity there might be because there is no social affinity.

In addition to showing how linguistic relatedness influences potential bilingual proficiency, Case Study 3G also reveals a crucial social difference between these two types of bilingualism: learned bilingualism *often* requires some measure of interaction with the L2 speech community whereas inherent bilingualism does not. At the Negotiated Level we will only consider bilingual proficiency that results from the interactive contact between speech communities.

NOTE ‣ We accept that people can also learn another language through books, language learning courses, or through some audio-visual media. However, to gain significant fluency, there needs to be contact with fluent speakers of the language.

DEFINITIONS ‣ **INFORMAL LEARNING** refers to a typical natural way of gaining a more native-like proficiency in another language through social contact with users of that language. **FORMAL LEARNING** refers to learning a language through a structured program of learning.

The process by which people gain their bilingual proficiency can create differences in the expression of their bilingual ability. These differences can be described on a continuum from **INFORMAL LEARNING** to **FORMAL LEARNING**. Of course, the way a second language is learned, or acquired, is not the only factor influencing the outcome. As discussed above, motivation and personal differences are important also. In many situations around the world, people gain bilingual proficiency in another language through social contact with users of that language. There can be different results to this kind of informal learning depending on a number of variables. The amount of contact is important as is the context of the contact. If the contact is only in one domain, such as purchasing food in a market, the amount and types of vocabulary and sentence structures will be limited. However, if a woman from one speech community marries into another and spends much of her day in various social situations with her mother-in-law, she may have the opportunity to gain extensive proficiency in the L2. The proficiency of the people providing the language model may be another variable. For example, the marketplace may be filled with people from several speech communities and they all use an LWC which is a second language to all of them. None of them speak the language with great proficiency and do not provide a good source from which to gain greater proficiency.

DEFINITION ‣ A **MIXED LANGUAGE** is a language that forms from the combination of features from two or more input languages.

If a child grows up in a very bilingual environment, for example a neighborhood where speakers of two different languages live side by side, the child may hear similar quantities of both languages. In such an environment, the two languages might become quite mixed and inseparable in the child's mind. The child may not even be aware that he or she is mixing two languages and would have difficulty communicating with someone who only understands one of them. Such a situation may even evolve into the creation of a **MIXED LANGUAGE**. This can create quite a difficulty for surveyors if we are trying to identify a person's heritage language. In a typical scenario the children will eventually learn to sort out the different languages and use them with the appropriate people.

At the formal learning end of the continuum is a situation in which a person learns another language in a formal classroom situation with no contact with native speakers. The L2 is presented using teaching methods which provide a standardized form of the language. The child learns to use proper grammatical structures and, despite becoming quite proficient, may still have difficulty understanding the typically idiomatic speech of a native speaker of the language. This could describe many situations in which children learn the national language in school but have little or no interaction with native speakers. Such people may appear to be fluent bilinguals to outsiders, but this kind of bilingualism has much less of an impact on the speech community than other forms.

At a mid-point on this continuum would be a typical situation in which the child hears idiomatic use of the L2 in environments that are distinct from those of the child's L1. Furthermore, the child may also receive a formal introduction to the L2 in the classroom. The child's bilingual proficiency will depend on the frequency of such contact, domains in which there is interaction, the child's age, the child's motivation to learn and use the L2, and the ability to differentiate between the languages. Potentially, a person growing up in such a situation could attain native-like use of the L2.

Through this section there have been references to people having various levels of proficiency in another language, and this will be discussed more fully in the next section. These differences usually refer to **LINGUISTIC COMPETENCE;** this can be contrasted with **COMMUNICATIVE COMPETENCE** which does not necessarily require a high level of proficiency. It does, however, require a good understanding of the culture. This latter competence is a skill which is learned through frequent opportunity to interact. This kind of bilingualism can open many social and economic opportunities for the individual as they use the language in appropriate ways. Generally, when people learn another language in a more artificial environment such as a classroom or from mass media, they develop linguistic competence but not communicative competence. They don't have the opportunity to interact with people who use the L2 as their heritage language. While linguistic competence gives the individual some access to the L2 culture, it is not as significant as developing communicative competence.

> **DEFINITIONS ‣ LINGUISTIC COMPETENCE** is the ability to control the formal linguistic patterns of a language. **COMMUNICATIVE COMPETENCE** is the awareness of the appropriate situational use of the language.

It is also important to recognize that bilingual speaking proficiency does not necessarily include reading or writing proficiency. It is possible for someone to gain better proficiency in reading and writing the L2 than in speaking it. This may happen in the religious domain when people study the written scriptures in an L2 but have little contact with speakers. It can also happen when someone learns the L2 in a formal educational environment. Since there is so much illiteracy in the world, it is probably more common for people to have bilingual speaking proficiency in the L2 rather than being literate in the L2. In some cases, an L2 is a regionally prestigious LWC that has little or no literature. Language developers need to make the distinction between speaking, listening, writing, and reading proficiencies because different strategies will be needed for the further development of each form.

3.3.1.2 Levels of bilingualism

Bilingual proficiency is not simply a matter of being bilingual or not, there are varying levels of proficiency in multiple abilities. For example, if we know the Arabic greeting *as-salaamu 'alaykum*, we have a very limited bilingual ability in dozens and dozens of languages. When on a survey, we may frequently meet people who identify themselves as being bilingual in another language; yet they have no more ability than this example. There are numerous scales that describe varying levels of bilingualism. Obviously, a person would need much greater bilingual proficiency to adequately communicate in another language. We will briefly describe the **INTERAGENCY LANGUAGE ROUNDTABLE (ILR) SCALE** as an example for reference.

NOTE ▸ The **ILR SCALE** is used to measure oral language proficiency. Formerly known as the FSI (Foreign Service Institute) scale, it is used here because it is the most discriminating index at higher levels. There are many other similar scales, such as Council of Europe, and the Diplôme d'Études en Langue Française (DELF).

TABLE 3 ▸ Descriptions of the five levels of the ILR Scale.

WWW.SURVEYWIKI.INFO ▸ For more detail of the levels of the ILR scale, including links to audio samples of each in English, visit the ILR page on Survey-Wiki.

CROSS-REFERENCE ▸ See **Section 3.4.5.2** on page 107 for an example of the use of the ILR scale in assessment.

The ILR scale for speaking and listening is numbered from 0 to 5 with + levels in between (0, 0+, 1, 1+, 2, 2+, etc.). The whole-numbered levels are labeled as in Table 3 below.

LEVEL	DESCRIPTION
0	No proficiency
1	Elementary proficiency
2	Limited working proficiency
3	General professional proficiency
4	Advanced professional proficiency
5	Functionally native proficiency

The ILR provides full descriptions of each of the levels. Oral (not including reading and writing) bilingual proficiency can also be described as having five different components:

- **Comprehension:** how well the subject understands what is said in the L2,
- **Discourse** competence: speech above the sentence level, including how well the subject organizes information and handles face-to-face interaction,
- **Structural precision:** the ability to use the standard grammatical, morphological, and phonological systems of the L2,
- **Lexicalization:** the breadth and appropriateness of the lexicon available to the speaker, and
- **Fluency:** the continuity, quantity, and accessibility of the speech produced by the speaker.

When using this scale to evaluate the bilingual proficiency of an individual, each of these competencies is rated on a further scale of performance (B. F. Grimes 1987). The levels from lowest to highest are:

- **Blocking:** misunderstandings of very simple language; unable to produce continuous discourse; lexicalization inaccurate and very narrow; subject speaks with difficulty;
- **Dysfunctional:** subject recognizes non-understandings, which are quite frequent; minimally elaborate use of discourse features; lexicalization range is narrow and inaccurate, highly unnatural for the language; fluency is irregular;
- **Intrusive:** difficulties in comprehension slow down the interaction; limited range of discourse devices shows lack of cohesion; lexicalization is unusual and/or imprecise; subject speaks readily but not fluently;
- **Acceptable:** exhibits understanding quickly when clarification, repetition, or paraphrase is given; discourse is cohesive; lexicalization is clear and relatively natural; subject speaks readily, suitably filling pauses;
- **Successful:** understanding is limited only by cultural background; discourse is well organized; very infrequent imprecision of lexicalization; performance is fluent; and
- **Superior:** understanding is essentially complete; broad, flexible control of functional rhetorical speech devices; lexicalization is precise; the flow of speech is effortless and smooth in every respect.

The point of providing this scale is to help the reader understand the components of oral bilingual proficiency and the progressive levels of competency in each one. The combination of evaluations of each of the component parts results in a general overall description of an individual's proficiency in the L2.

3.3.1.3 Distribution of bilingual proficiency

CROSS-REFERENCE ▸ See **Section 3.3.1** on page 74 for an introduction to how bilingual proficiency is distributed through a community.

As introduced earlier, oral bilingual proficiency is distributed in patterned ways through a speech community. The patterns depend on how people have gained their proficiency in other languages and the purposes they have for using the languages. For example, if older women gain their bilingual proficiency through contact in the marketplace, they will have a different level and expression of their bilingualism than young women who have recently begun to learn the L2 in a school in the village. Older men who are primarily occupied with shepherding may have very little bilingual proficiency compared to young men who travel outside the speech community for extended periods of work. In this example, bilingual proficiency is distributed through the community based on gender, age, education, and occupation. Case Study 3D, concerning education in Urdu in Pakistan, described a different pattern. Every speech community will present different patterns.

At the Negotiated Level, therefore, we have a number of questions to answer in relation to bilingualism. We need to know

- which languages the people in a community have any proficiency in,
- who is proficient in which languages,
- how proficient they are, and
- what this proficiency is dependent on or limited by.

As we do this, it is important to realize that community bilingualism differs from individual bilingualism. Not only do individuals have different needs, abilities, and motivations to use other languages, but whole demographic sub-groups often show marked differences in bilingual proficiency because of these factors. The final assessment of a speech community's multilingual ability does not simply equal the total number of languages that people in the community can use, it also includes a profile of the individual language repertoire and the relative proficiencies in each language.

Bilingual proficiency varies throughout the speech community, but it is not random; it is influenced by social, economic, and other variables. If we can identify the variables, we will find that it follows somewhat predictable patterns of distribution. Therefore, before we assess the ability that is there, we have to take time to find out what it depends on. It is important to consider reasons behind bilingualism and the relationships between languages, the people who speak them, and the different roles people play in the social networks and speech communities they are part of. This involves looking at the factors that drive motivation and contact that we mentioned earlier. Once we have done this, we are usually able to identify sub-groups we can study who possess some kind of bilingual ability. For example, in Case Study 3D, the survey team was aware of the fact that schooling influenced bilingual ability. Once they had established the amount of schooling there was, they were able to decide on who was likely to have some bilingual ability in Urdu. This is a very necessary step in bilingual assessment because we do not have the resources necessary to test everyone in the speech community. Instead, we estimate the bilingual ability of the entire speech community by testing a small but representative sample. However, even if we select the right strata of the population to test, we should always be aware that within this, individual proficiency can vary for all sorts of personal reasons (Myers-Scotton 2002).

CROSS-REFERENCE ‣ See **Section 5.4.2** on page 195 for more about sampling methods.

3.3.1.4 Diglossia

There is another way that multiple languages are used in some speech communities called diglossia. As it was defined earlier, diglossia is a social situation in which two or more languages, or language varieties, co-occur in a speech community, each with a distinct social function, maintained as socially normative behavior.

CROSS-REFERENCE ‣ See **Section 2.3.1** on page 32 for an introduction to diglossia.

The term, as it was first proposed by Charles Ferguson (1959), only referred to a speech community that used two varieties of the same language in distinct domains. The two varieties were distinguished as one variety having a high (H), or prestigious, function and the other variety a low (L) function. An example of this is Haiti, where French (H) is used in formal domains and Haitian Creole (L) is used in informal domains.

Other linguists, notably Fishman (1967) and Fasold (1984), have adapted and expanded the definition of diglossia and described different types of diglossia. These distinctions are not very relevant to us. We will understand that there are bilingual speech communities in which the heritage language is not necessarily threatened if we simply remember some basic points of the definition:

- diglossia is socially defined,
- it is normative behavior,
- it involves high and low varieties, and
- it can apply to languages as well as language varieties.

It is important to distinguish diglossia from bilingualism. The term bilingualism can be used to describe the language use of an individual or of a speech community. There can be one bilingual person in a community. If a community is described as bilingual, each bilingual person in the group will have a different level of proficiency in the L2. Diglossia develops from the establishment of societal norms; we would not have an individual in a group who is diglossic. In a speech community with diglossia, virtually everyone has about the same level of proficiency in the L2. Individuals in diglossic speech communities are more constrained by the societal norms of language use than people in bilingual speech communities. The motivation to become bilingual usually comes about through some kind of contact with other speech communities whereas in a diglossic speech community it comes from compliance with social norms. Bilingual individuals may personally choose to use more than one language for many or only some social situations. With diglossia there are established patterns for language use. Bilingualism may actually alter the linguistic features of the languages over time. The linguistic features of the languages in a diglossic situation tend to maintain their distinct linguistic forms and structures.

3.3.2   Language Use

Every language has some variation in the way it is used in a speech community according to the domains where people use it. Thus, in our heritage language, we may speak one way when talking to a farmer and another way when talking to a politician. Linguistically, this is because different vocabulary, pronunciation, and even syntax may be required for different domains. As a feature of heritage language use within the speech community, this is an issue at the Free Level and will be discussed in more depth in Chapter 4.

When a community's social networks involve more than one language, and there is variation in the way people speak to one another, there are different effects. In both a more monolingual environment and a bilingual environment people will accommodate their speech to the expectations of people in their networks (Wardhaugh 2009:112). However, in the bilingual

CROSS-REFERENCE ‣ See **Section 4.2.3** on page 125 for more information about language accommodation theory.

environment, the variation can range from alternate pronunciations of certain words to a choice between different languages.

> *The individual's plurilingual repertoire is therefore made up of various languages he or she has absorbed in various ways (childhood learning, teaching, independent acquisition, etc.) and in which he/she has acquired different skills (conversation, reading, listening, etc.) to different levels. The languages in the repertoire may be assigned different, perhaps specialised functions, such as communicating with the family, socialising with neighbours, working or learning, and...provide building blocks for affiliation to groups which see themselves as having shared cultural features and their own identifying languages. Signalling group affiliation by these means also has the social function of providing a basis for hetero-identifications that give the group added solidity. (Beacco 2005:19)*

QUOTE ▸ *The bilingual uses the two languages separately or together for different purposes, in different domains of life, with different people. Because the needs and uses of the two languages are usually quite different, the bilingual is rarely equally or completely fluent in the two languages. (Grosjean 2008:23)*

One example comes from certain parts of Nigeria where accommodation occurs to reinforce group identity (Ogunsiji 2001:84). When a customer who uses Yoruba enters a shop, the owner switches to that language. If another customer enters, whose ethnicity the owner does not know, he switches to English. As English is common to all speakers in that area, the switch in effect acts as a welcome to the newcomer. Conversely, the inability to accommodate may limit a person. For example, lower proficiency in an L2 may limit what the person can do at a market. It may keep the person from getting a good price.

Social network domains where different language use choices tend to be made as users accommodate themselves to expectations from the network members	• the market place • public transport • law enforcement • traditional instruction	• the home • school • work • sport

FIGURE 10 ▸ Domains of language use relevant to bilingualism.

Social situations in which people tend to use a specific variety to perform specific speech acts	• religious teaching • addressing a gathering • with someone of higher status • ritual ceremonies

People often use different languages for pragmatic reasons just to meet some need. People who use an L2 only in a certain domain will probably have limited proficiency in the L2. This will affect how we approach assessing bilingualism. For example, if a person only uses their L2 at a market in a neighboring speech community, they may perform very well when tested on vocabulary from that context. But, if they listen to a story about a car accident, they may not understand much of it. Thus, we need to determine the domains in which they use each of their languages. We call this the study of the *domains of language use*. Figure 10 shows some of the more common domains we usually investigate on surveys where we are assessing learned multilingualism.

Understanding the variations in language use across domains is important for the assessment of bilingualism. But obviously, we cannot assess every domain of language use. We can sample a selection of domains, but if our assessment tools are too narrow, we risk missing domains where bilingualism exists. This would result in a false idea of the sociolinguistic reality of the speech community. Some people choose to use an L2 in certain domains and with certain people in an attempt to raise their social status. Therefore, it is particularly important to investigate any domains associated with status, such as those which provide economic or social benefits.

DEFINITION ▸ LANGUAGE DEATH is the result of language shift when people stop using a language for social communication. This may be because the people who use the language have themselves become extinct, or it may be because they have decided to use other languages to replace it.

When a person chooses to use an L2 in a given domain, these choices have consequences that may be positive or negative. The choice may give the speaker some social or economic benefit. Choosing to use the L2 in more and more domains may lead to language shift and **LANGUAGE DEATH**. Furthermore, a negative effect of language choice may produce a positive impact on the user. For example, a person may have feelings of anger against the need to use the L2, but this may also increase motivation to improve their proficiency. The cumulative impact of such negative effects on individual users may influence the language use practices throughout a speech community, such as the development of a pervasive belief that children should use the L2. Sometimes, these choices bring slow changes that may not be apparent even to the speech community itself. However, the changing needs can occur quickly and the community may be quite aware of what is happening.

The attitudes of the members of the L2 speech community towards L2-learners are almost as important as the attitude/motivation of the L1 speaker trying to use the L2. If they are hostile and closed to others learning their language, they may inhibit the acquisition of the L2 by L1 speakers (essentially slowing or preventing accommodation). If they are welcoming and helpful, accepting even poorly spoken L2, shift might be accelerated. French (in France) might be an example of the former, English (generally) an example of the latter.

The development of patterned behavior is usually not a conscious or intentional process. Often there is only subliminal negotiation between people as to what becomes normative behavior for language choice in these domains. Through domain analysis we can find patterns of language use that indicate the speech communities' decisions. While we may find that there is increasing use of the L2, sometimes there is only minimal impact from such contact. In Gambia, for example, English is used for numbers in communication that is entirely Wolof otherwise. One explanation is that as schools use English to teach numeracy skills, these Wolof users have no remaining vocabulary for numeracy in their heritage language (Peter and Wolf 2001:98). A situation like this may appear to the surveyor as an example of bilingualism, but it might be of only minimal impact on the heritage language.

When the local speech communities' social networks involve more than one language, the resultant language use may look like one of the groups is shifting to the other language. Although a community that uses more than one language across domains has obviously undergone some amount of language shift, the shift may not result in the L1 being replaced by the L2. As was described in the last section, there can be diglossia in which there is a balance between the languages. In this case, societal norms promote the maintenance of the heritage language in certain domains.

CROSS-REFERENCE ‣ See **Section 2.3.1** on page 32 and Section 3.3.1.4 on page 83 for more on diglossia.

In our discussion of bilingualism, we have seen how it occurs when individuals choose to use more than one language. Diglossia exists when there is a social norm for the patterned use of different languages. In a stable diglossic situation, the individual has to step outside of social norms to make a personal language choice. Formation of this kind of stability can often take decades of contact and may last for hundreds of years. It may not be obvious that a community is in transition from a situation with multilingualism with no diglossia, where no social norms have been established, to a situation of diglossia, when the social norms have been established. What appears to be an increasing amount of multilingualism may not be evidence of language shift.

CASE STUDY 3H
CHOOSING TO SHIFT
PAKISTAN

In   northern   Pakistan,   we
visited   a   village   where   the
people   said   there   was   a

CASE STUDY 3H SOURCE ‣ Ken Decker, International Language Assessment Coordinator, SIL.

*certain day in about 1960 when they decided to stop using their L1
and shift to using only the L2. As far as we could determine, they
were able to accomplish this successfully. However, it could only have
been possible if everyone had already become significantly bilingual.
They did this for religious reasons since their heritage language
was considered a corrupt language. Other villages still use the L1 in
order to maintain their unique identity, even though there are many
pressures on them to shift.*

_____

3.3.3   Language Vitality

CROSS-REFERENCE ▸ See Section 3.2.3
on page 73 for more on language shift
and Section 4.2.4 on page 128 for
more on language vitality.

Case Study 3H clearly shows us where issues of language vitality start:
pressure to change or greater opportunity through change. As we have
already seen in this chapter, changes to social networks may place speech
communities in contact with others whose influence may motivate them to
choose languages other than their L1. This pressure is particularly strong if
people use the L2 in social or economic status-raising domains. It can also
be reinforced if the L1 speech community doesn't have a strongly positive
value of its own ethnic identity. Infrastructure networks, such as new roads,
telecommunications, radios, or television, may bring previously distant
speech communities into contact with each other. A cultural pattern of
EXOGAMY not only introduces new languages to a speech community but
usually also means that these languages are involved in the socialization of
children through primary caregivers.

DEFINITION ▸ **EXOGAMY** is the practice
of marrying outside the community.
Traditionally, for example, the Jewish
community does not allow exogamy.
In contrast, in the Vaupés in Colombia,
exogamy is required (B. F. Grimes 1985).

Once the social pressure is in place, language shift may begin, and language
shift can lead to language death. Although the pace of change can seem
rapid when compared with the history of the ethnolinguistic group,
language death does not happen overnight. For example, Nancy Dorian
(Dorian 1981) documented over 1000 years of decline of Scottish Gaelic,
and there are still speakers. There are significant thresholds in the process
of language shift. If we recognize these thresholds we are not only able to
assess how much shift has taken place but also assess the appropriateness
of language development proposals. We will investigate these thresholds
and the issue of vitality further at the Free Level in the Chapter 4.

Earlier, we stressed the special relationship between language and
identity. Schmidt (2006:37) reminds us that "language is not only one
among many, but a very central element of identity." When a speech
community feels positive about its own identity, it often feels the same
about its language variety. Even when under the extreme social pressures

that usually accompany language shift, positive attitudes can provide the support to sustain a language and culture. As David Crystal puts it in his book *Language Death,*

> [W]hen it comes to endangered languages, attitude is what counts – how people look at their language, and what they feel about it when they do. If speakers take pride in their language, enjoy listening to others using it well, use it themselves whenever they can and as creatively as they can, and provide occasions where the language can be heard, the conditions are favourable for maintenance. (2002:81)

However, when a minority language is in contact with another language that offers access to desired benefits, positive attitudes toward the heritage language may not be enough to prevent language shift. Minority languages do not often fare well in competition with more dominant languages. Sometimes, minority groups do not always feel positive about their own identities and can see their heritage language as a form of social stigma or as a hindrance to pursuing social goals.

Once they make this attitude shift, they may seek a language that provides alternative access to their desired goals. As people stop using and transmitting their heritage language, language death may result. While this does not necessarily also mean the death of the people or the culture, it is often associated with the loss of the people's unique identity.

Language Shift

0	International
1	National
2	Regional
3	Trade
4	Educational
5	Written
6a	Vigorous
6b	Threatened
7	Shifting
8a	Moribund
8b	Nearly Extinct
9	Dormant
10	Extinct

Language Development

TABLE 4 ▸ The 13 levels of the Expanded Graded Intergenerational Scale (taken from Lewis and Simons (2010)).

WWW.SURVEYWIKI.INFO ▸ See the **EGIDS** page on SurveyWiki for much more detail about this scale.

The death of a language can mean the loss of unique knowledge that was only expressed in that language. The effect on the speech community itself can be more damaging still; loss of identity can lead to psychological trauma and social dysfunction.

At the Negotiated Level, we saw that language shift does not happen overnight. As language shift occurs, there are significant thresholds in the process that we can learn to recognize to help us evaluate the extent of shift in the speech community. Lewis and Simons (2010) have developed a scale to help us recognize these thresholds.

Based on original work by Fishman (1991) and UNESCO (2003), Table 4 shows the Expanded Graded Intergenerational Disruption Scale (EGIDS). The scale contains thirteen different levels of language vitality and use from 0, which represents a language as having international functions, to 10, where we regard it as extinct. The criteria for each level include both domains of use and profiles of who uses the language. The design of the scale means that, using only a few questions, we can potentially assess the status of a language.

The most important indicator of language maintenance or shift for us to identify is what language, or languages, caregivers are using with children in the home domain. As a threshold for determining endangerment, Stephen Wurm (2001:14) considers that any heritage language that is not learned by at least 30 percent of the children in a speech community is endangered. The home domain is key and, as well as being the most likely arena for the vital process of socialization, is also the most intimate domain. The more private the domains in which people use their language, the more impervious the language will be to outside forces of endangerment (Edwards 1985:97). If people do not use the heritage language with children in the home domain, we then need to assess the extent of language shift by looking at how old the youngest users of the language are. We can identify this because "the youngest generation of proficient speakers in an unbroken chain of intergenerational transmission provides an index to the progress of language shift" (Lewis and Simons 2010).

While it is important to understand the level of vitality, it is equally crucial to learn as much as we can about why the speech community is at that level of vitality. The reasons for a speech community having a negative view of their own identity and language are complex and usually have their roots in the socio-historical, socio-political, or economic environment of the area. Determining the level of vitality will help us to determine not only what development strategies might be appropriate but also how potentially successful they might be. If we do not fully understand vitality though, programs may only address the symptoms of issues that language development hopes to tackle and not the original causes.

The EGIDS scale is also helpful for gaining a projection of the potential viability of the variety we are surveying. According to Lewis and Simons (ibid.) there are only four levels that are stable:

- Level 4 – sustainable literacy,
- Level 6a – sustainable orality,
- Level 9 – sustainable identity, and
- Level 10 – sustainable history.

If the language vitality of a speech community is at any of the other levels, and there isn't effort to maintain and develop the functions of the language, it will shift to the next level down the scale. It takes great intentional effort to move the speech community to a higher level. Therefore, the EGIDS scale is not only useful for identifying a level of vitality but also provides a way to discuss the possibilities for the future functions of the language.

WWW.SURVEYWIKI.INFO ‣ The INDICA-TORS OF ETHNOLINGUISTIC VITALITY can also be used for studying vitality in small speech communities. See the Language Vitality page on SurveyWiki for details.

3.3.4   Extensibility of L2 Literature

Sometimes, we begin to study multilingualism in a community only to find that the people are no longer multilingual, they have shifted completely to another language. If there are strongly negative attitudes against the development of the heritage language or the heritage language is no longer spoken, then it is obvious that there is probably no point to attempting language development. However, there have been rare cases of languages that have come back into use after many years of disuse, for example Hebrew and Cornish.

Throughout this book there is an assumption that the heritage language is the preferred language of choice for development. Often, if a language is still used vigorously in a speech community, they will desire development. Numerous studies in recent years have shown that children learn better when they are able to begin their education in their heritage language (Kosonen, Young, and Malone 2007). If there is vitality and interest, development of the heritage language has many potential benefits.

However, there can be situations for which promotion of L2 literacy is a preferred strategy over the literary development of a vigorously used heritage language, but there are several criteria that must be met at a very high standard. Let's briefly consider why the high standards are required and the meaning of lower standards.

1. Literacy in the L2 should already be widespread and highly valued. If widespread literacy has not already been established through a few generations, then the potential for it would be hypothetical and the established fact is that people tend to gain literacy better in their L1 first. Thus, the recommendation would be for development of the heritage language.

2. Both languages must be used in all domains. If it was not so, the domains limited to the heritage language would almost probably be the intimate domains, such as in the home. This limitation would indicate a closer identification with the heritage language. As such, there could be topics that, in literature, would not speak so profoundly in the L2.

3. The level of bilingual proficiency needs to be very high, such as ILR 4. If people had a lower proficiency (ILR 3), it is questionable as to how deeply literature might meet their deepest needs. People with lower proficiency have limited vocabulary, control of rhetorical structures, and discourse structures.

4. Virtually everyone needs to be highly bilingual. If this bilingualism was lower for some segment of the population, those people would have limited access to some knowledge. If they relied on spontaneous translation from the highly bilingual, this would require someone highly bilingual to be skilled at translation principles so that they could produce accurate, natural, and coherent translation. It is unlikely that this kind of scenario would exist.

5. People must have positive attitudes towards any use of either language. If there are negative attitudes towards the heritage language, we would have to ask why they maintain it. If the negative attitudes are towards the L2, then the people are probably not receptive to having literacy only in this other language.

Such a situation is probably rare, and we should be on the alert for evidence of language shift, which would be expected if most of these criteria are being met. When two languages are accessible to a speech community, one of them will virtually always have more prestige. It may be the heritage language for sentimental reasons or the L2 for economic advantage, but the people will be either maintaining the heritage language or shifting to the L2. If the heritage language is being maintained, then literature in that language will communicate most clearly and deeply to the people.

Furthermore, if both languages are used equally well in the home, and this situation has existed for two or more generations, the relevance of one of the languages being a heritage language is lost. The people are not identifying with one language over the other, and the language with literature is as much their L1 as the language without literature.

3.3.5   Partnership

One final consideration at the Negotiated Level is the role of partnership. We have been discussing the interaction of a speech community with its neighbors and the potential this interaction has for partnership will need to be assessed. It may be that language development programs are already taking place in speech communities that the people we are working with are already members of. The sociolinguistic factors that could enhance or impede such partnership will need to be assessed. Also, it could be that contact with other speech communities will have an impact on the partnership opportunities with external agencies or other stakeholders, particularly if there are issues of ethnic identity or conflict.

There are several tools that can be used to identify stakeholders, such as the stakeholder analysis tool. This involves brainstorming with members of the speech community about people who may have interest in the development activities and outcomes. This part of the process would not normally be carried out by surveyors. However, if we are familiar with the area and people, we may be able to make a valuable contribution to the discussion.

NOTE ▸ To properly understand SECTION 3.3.5, you should first be familiar with the definitions and rationale presented earlier in SECTION 2.3.3 on page 35.

CROSS-REFERENCE ▸ See Section 4.4.5 on page 161 for a description of participatory methods that can be used for partnership discussions.

CASE STUDY 3J
A LASTING IMPRESSION
TANZANIA

When we started the survey among the Malila speech community, we expected to be the first SIL International people ever to have arrived at the Division Office of that area. We had never surveyed Malila before.

CASE STUDY 3J SOURCE ▸ Susanne Krüger, Language Assessment Coordinator, SIL Uganda-Tanzania Branch.

When we arrived in our Land Cruiser, the Divisional Secretary came out to meet us and told us that he was glad to see us again. Again? We explained that we had never been in the area before, but he insisted that he remembered the car and that a team had visited him some years back. We scratched our heads and tried to think of who that might have been. He kept telling us about "Tanna" and two other ladies who had come to talk about Malila. We really couldn't make it out.

In the end he brought out all his old visitor's books (every office in Tanzania has one and it is customary that you sign the book even if you only come for a few minutes) and looked for the entry. And sure enough he found it. Some years back the survey team under K. Turner had come all the way up the mountain when surveying the neighboring Safwa language as there were some people who insisted that Malila was really part of Safwa. They only stayed a few hours as they quickly found out that Malila was different enough and far enough away to warrant individual research to be done later. But they made a lasting impression on this Divisional Secretary.

It reminded me again of how important it is how we relate to people. I have met so many people in close to nine years of survey that I can only remember a small part of them. But we are special when we come to visit and people remember. What a privilege and what a responsibility!

DEFINITION ▸ The term **PARTNER AGENCIES** is used to refer to the organizations, institutions, or agencies who are working together with an ethnolinguistic group for language and community development. If the surveyor has a supervisor, this person is the representative of the partner agencies.

Survey teams are not autonomous; we work either at the request of our administrators, in coordination with advisors, or at the request of partners or **PARTNER AGENCIES**. If the assessment is conducted at the request of an organizational administrator, the research should be part of a larger plan that anticipates a response to possible findings of the research. This larger plan will coordinate the assessment with the work of other people. If the research is part of an academic study plan, the research should fit into a larger picture of theoretical development. This requires partnership also. We may need to work with a university advisor or a local-level liaison who functions as an advisor; we may cooperate with local academics; and we will definitely need to work cooperatively with the local people.

We may be asked to do survey with a community that has already begun discussions relevant to partnerships. It is from these partnership discussions that questions may arise. For example, local education providers may want to know whether a particular community is bilingual enough to receive general education in a regional language. It is at this point that they may request that a survey team investigate levels of bilingualism.

While survey teams are not usually partners with speech communities throughout the life of a language development program, it is important for us as surveyors to understand our particular role in any public relationships for a number of reasons.

- Survey teams may be the first development representatives that a speech community engages with. As such, we may have the privilege of being the first to have the involvement needed to establish a relationship. If so, first impressions can mean a great deal, as Case Study 3J shows, and we must take care to represent our development partners accurately.
- We must ensure that discussions use terms that stakeholders understand and consider relevant to issues that they face.
- Once assessment is completed, we have a responsibility of advocacy to accurately represent the speech community to the partners.
- Partnership is essential for successful primary data collection. It is impossible to carry out a recorded text test, for example, without the often time-consuming cooperation of a number of people from a number of speech communities.

We cannot underestimate the value of our ability to initiate and sustain working partnerships. If the development efforts do not meet the perceived goals of the stakeholders, they will have no commitment to the sustainability of the efforts.

3.4   Typical Negotiated Level Research Tools

At the Negotiated Level we want to gather information on attitudes, domains of language use, multilingualism, and language vitality. In this section we will look at some of the typical research tools we use to gather information on these topics. Good secondary research at the Restricted Level and Negotiated Level will enable good planning for primary research. The most common ways of exploring attitudes, domains of language use, and language vitality at the Negotiated Level include observation, ethnographic interviews, and questionnaires. For assessment of multilingualism in an L2, L3, etc. at the Negotiated Level there are several types of proficiency evaluation tools we can use. A good understanding of the sociolinguistic dynamics at the Negotiated Level is vital for successful planning of a survey trip as it provides knowledge about climate, infrastructure, festivals etc.

It is important to remember to seek answers to research questions through multiple tools. Different tools gather different kinds of data in different kinds of ways. This is important because there is a very significant dichotomy between

- *language usage,* what people do with language;
- *language image,* what people think they do with language; and
- *language posture,* what people claim they do with language.

There are things that we can observe and measure that are different from what people will tell us. This is not to say that they have any intentions to deceive; sometimes people don't know about something so intimate as their own language, or they have different perceptions about what they do and how they feel about things like someone else's language. There are a number of **QUANTITATIVE** and **QUALITATIVE** ways to measure bilingualism, as well as other phenomena.

3.4.1 Observation

As discussed throughout this chapter, there are a number of social and linguistic aspects related to multilingualism that may need to be studied in an assessment of a speech community. The most basic way to investigate multilingualism is by observation. Basically, observation is watching what people do and noting the context in which they do those things.

3.4.1.1 Rationale

Behavior is motivated by attitudes, values, and beliefs. While it is important to understand these attitudes, values, and beliefs, they are not easy to investigate. People probably have not consciously thought about these things and they may not feel like being open about them. Therefore, it is important to investigate attitudes, values, and beliefs through other means. Through observation the surveyor can notice what languages people use with one another and who they associate with.

Many of the tools we describe in this book involve the participation of the local people or others. When people participate with researchers in

DEFINITIONS ▸ QUALITATIVE DATA is information that describes a subjective quality such as someone's attitude. **QUANTITATIVE DATA** is information that describes an amount or quantity of something such as someone's age.

WWW.SURVEYWIKI.INFO ▸ See SurveyWiki for detailed guidance on observation. We strongly recommend you read these details and, as you develop experience in assessment, contribute to SurveyWiki.

CROSS-REFERENCE ▸ See **Section 4.4** on page 140 for more on other multilingualism testing methods.

providing data, we have to acknowledge that their involvement with us will influence the data we collect to some extent that is often difficult to measure. Observation is the closest we can get to gathering data that is least affected by the artificial nature of participation. But even observation isn't completely unaffected by the assessment process. The moment a surveyor makes a deliberate attempt to observe, we impact (and skew) the possible observations we can make simply by inserting ourselves into the situation. People may behave differently just because we, as outsiders, are there. This phenomenon is called the observer's paradox. Even though observation has this potential flaw, it is still vital to the assessment process (Wardhaugh 2009).

QUOTE ▸ *[G]iven the decontextualised nature of much social psychological work, both direct and indirect methods should be supplemented with real-life observation. (Edwards 1985:150)*

Skilled surveyors use observation to

- confirm information that has been provided,
- deny information that has been provided, and
- identify information that people have not provided.

Observation thus provides a very valuable form of data we can use to triangulate our findings from other tools.

3.4.1.2 Methodology

In order to guide the observation so that we collect information which is in line with survey goals, the first step is to draw up an observation schedule. This is a list of specific categories of behaviors, linguistic or otherwise, which we want to observe. Having a schedule helps us to be intentional and focused and have a way of recording what we observe. It is important to observe behavior in a variety of locations to see if people behave differently in different places and with different people.

With each observation we document as many potential variables as possible, and within reason, so that we can identify by correlation which factors are relevant. Potential variables include who talks to whom, where they meet, when they meet, how long they meet, what they talk about, and any observable impact of the meeting – such as if one party leaves angry.

We carry out observation as unobtrusively as possible. This might mean not carrying a notebook or observation schedule with us but recording important details as soon after the observation as possible. Once we have completed the observation, we need to summarize the notes we have taken by typing them up according to the categories in our schedule.

NOTE ▸ It may be possible to find ways to be unobtrusive or to distract people from our presence. For example, we may stay alert when closing our eyes to prepare for an afternoon nap, or get adults talking amongst themselves about an engaging topic, or give children a toy to play with. We must be careful that we aren't unethical though.

3.4.1.3 Evaluation

Observation is, by nature, subjective. It is probably the least reliable of the tools we employ because no two observers are going to note the same behaviors even if they watch the same event. However, subjective variation in observations can be reduced if the observers are "socialized" to a set of standards and consciously work at following those standards. Someone who knows the culture and traditions of the speech communities being researched can assist the observers in understanding better what they are seeing. Typical situations being researched can be analyzed together (role played, video recorded vignettes, etc.) and the behaviors identified. All of this is done ahead of time so that when behaviors are observed "in the field" they can be reliably and consistently categorized by all observers. This process is helpful to the individual doing observation also. This can minimize the effect of learning on the observation process, which typically leads the observer(s) to throw out their early data because "we didn't know what we were looking at."

As long as we do not rely on observation data alone as our primary data source, the weakness of the method isn't restrictive. The strength of observation as a tool is that it enables us to paint a larger picture of the sociolinguistic situation we are assessing. Against this backdrop, any inconsistencies in data from other tools will stand out. This is where observation is valuable because investigating those points of conflict often reveals key features of the sociolinguistic reality that we might otherwise have missed.

One area where observation is particularly useful is in assessing attitude. Because attitude is revealed by behavior, observation can suggest what people's attitudes actually are. Often though, when explicitly questioned about their attitudes, people may well give answers that reflect just their beliefs or what they feel we want to hear. Sometimes people are unaware of their attitudes. Observation and reflection on what we observe can often provide valuable insight into the accuracy of other tools such as questionnaire data.

3.4.2   Sociolinguistic Questionnaires

WWW.SURVEYWIKI.INFO ▸ See Survey-Wiki for detailed guidance on administering questionnaires. We strongly recommend you read these details and, as you develop experience in assessment, contribute to SurveyWiki.

Oral questionnaires can be one of the easiest and most direct ways of collecting information. These are questionnaires that are administered orally; we don't ask the people to fill out a form themselves. They must be very carefully constructed to gather the information we want and cultural sensitivities need to be considered.

3.4.2.1 Rationale

Although we can observe what people do, and carry out tests to measure ability and other linguistic factors, we must remember that while we do these kinds of things, it can be difficult not to treat people as subjects of study instead of human beings. Questionnaires allow us to interact with people more than most other assessment tools and, for that reason, they are uniquely valuable.

CASE STUDY 3K
BELIEVE THE BIRD!
PAPUA NEW GUINEA

In Papua New Guinea it is common for people to respond with what they believe the surveyor wants to hear. Thus, it is helpful to confirm local reports of language use with actual observation. Sometimes observational confirmation comes in unusual forms.

CASE STUDY 3K SOURCE ‣ Lynn Landweer, Sociolinguistics Consultant, SIL Papua New Guinea.

In the mid-Watut survey in Morobe Province, the adult population told my partner and me that they spoke only the traditional vernacular to their preschool children. Unfortunately, on this particular survey, observation of language use by preschool children was made impossible by the apparent terror the children felt of the surveyors. At the end of the survey, returning to our starting point, we were resting and chatting with the local adults when a cockatoo flew up and promptly produced a phrase in the local trade language (not the vernacular), which translated would have been calling the youngest child of that hamlet to dinner. Waka, yu kam kaikai (Waka, you come eat) is a perfectly formed Tok Pisin phrase. Obviously, Waka's parents didn't speak only the traditional language to 3-year-old Waka. In this case, I had to believe the bird.

CROSS-REFERENCE ‣ An **SRT** is a Sentence Repetition Test. You can find out more about SRTs in **Section 3.4.5** on page 106.

Cross-Reference ▸ See also **Case Study 2D** on page 39 for another example of participants providing information that might differ from what we expect.

Questionnaires are also unique in that they give the speech community some control over the data they provide. Often, tools like SRTs are an enigma to the speech communities we work with. Although people may cooperate and may understand what we want, it may still be hard for them to understand exactly why we want them to repeat sentences back to us. But as we engage people in answering a questionnaire, we allow them to elaborate, change their answers, invite comment from their peers, provide an alternative to reality, or even refuse to answer the question. This can be empowering for a speech community.

In addition, questionnaires serve as a valuable source of qualitative and quantitative data to triangulate with other forms of data collection (Edwards 1985:150). It can be revealing when questionnaire answers flatly contradict observed or measured data such as in Case Study 3K. We do not want to imply that the people have any bad motives, but they may have reasons for the information they give us, or withhold. They have a right to their own motivations in the ways that they respond, and it is our job to sort through the responses and identify the important patterns.

Cross-Reference ▸ See **Section 3.2** on page 52 for more information about these social factors.

Questionnaires are particularly valuable for assessing attitudes. These attitudes may include feelings about such wide-ranging topics as other speech communities, economic factors, and how the people feel about government programs. Studying attitudes is important but they can be quite difficult to assess directly. If we have a good grasp of the social factors

FIGURE 11 ▸ An approach to useful question construction.

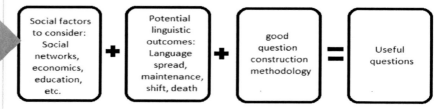

Cross-Reference ▸ See **Section 5.2.2** on page 179 for information on the construction of individual questions on a questionnaire.

and understand the link between them and their linguistic outcomes, this can help create useful questionnaires as shown in Figure 11.

Questionnaires are also valuable for helping to identify variables that influence language use choices. For example, we may find that all young people answer a certain question the same way, and differently from others. This tells us that age is a significant variable for the issue addressed in the question.

3.4.2.2 *Methodology*

Questionnaires are designed and pilot-tested to ensure **RELIABILITY** and **VALIDITY**. Questionnaires need to be limited to exploring areas relevant to the survey goals. On a survey assessing bilingualism, for example, this might include domains of use, social networks, education, demography, literacy, or attitudes. Usually the focus is on the participants as individuals, the speech community they are part of, or wider social networks and speech communities they may be members of.

It is possible to bias the responses from a questionnaire simply by the types of questions we use. Two types of questions we use are **OPEN** and **CLOSED** questions. We need to consider whether the possible answers given in closed questions include answers that the people may actually give and make sure our questions don't force them into answering in a way we want. There is another important distinction between two types of information that we may be seeking: objective and subjective. Objective information is factual; regardless of who we ask, we should get the same response. For example, although a question like "How many schools are in this city?" does depend on the responder's knowledge, there is a real, countable number of schools. Subjective information depends on an individual's attitudes, preferences, or perspectives. A question such as "Where do people speak your language the best?" is asking for subjective information; the answer is dependent on the individual's perceptions, judgments, and feelings. This has implications for how we analyze this data.

Questionnaires vary in the way that they require respondents to give their answers. Some questions, particularly subjective, open ones, invite the respondent to give a lengthy, personal answer. Others require numerical data or the respondent to choose one option on a scale such as a five-point **GRADUATED SCALE**. Scales and multiple-choice options can make data analysis and comparison much easier, but they also mean that we limit the responses we will get to only what we offer. However, if we do good pilot testing we can offer the options that are most useful. In this way, the types of questions we design determine the form of data that we collect and this affects how we then organize and analyze it. Because of this, it is very important to decide how we will analyze data before determining the type of questions to use.

We can also choose who we will administer questionnaires to. The most common use of questionnaires is a set list of questions administered to a sample of individuals. These types of questions tend to be designed

DEFINITIONS ▸ A test has **RELIABILITY** if it produces consistent results no matter who administers it and **VALIDITY** if it produces the data it was designed to produce and not something else.

DEFINITIONS ▸ OPEN QUESTIONS allow the participant to answer freely in whatever way they want. **CLOSED QUESTIONS** require the participant to choose from a number of options when they answer.

DEFINITIONS ▸ When a question asks the participant to rate their feelings about something, e.g., on a scale of one to five, this is a **GRADUATED SCALE**.

to gather a mass of quantifiable data. The questionnaires need to be relatively short with questions that are easy to ask and which produce answers that are easy to record. To help us verify data later and to remove pressure to note down every word, we might audio record questionnaire administration. We might also give questionnaires to groups so that the data reflects consensus within the speech community. In this way, we note down the range of opinion represented. This is not a preferable situation to giving individual questionnaires, but it is a useful way of carrying out a questionnaire when it is not culturally appropriate to question individuals. Usually, we focus on recording responses from one individual whom the group seems to agree with. Open questions can also be useful with a smaller group of people to stimulate discussion, revealing differences of opinion and points of consensus. We can also use a specialized questionnaire with key figures such as leaders or educators. These questionnaires explore more specific topics and special knowledge.

3.4.2.3 Evaluation

Questionnaires can look deceptively simple to design, but the old proverb is true: you get what you ask for. They are very sensitive tools; poor wording and even the order we place the questions in might influence participants. Badly designed questions not only provide information that does not match the goals of our surveys, they also deceive us into thinking that we have what we need.

CASE STUDY 3L
POTS
SOUTHEAST ASIA

CASE STUDY 3L SOURCE ▸ SIL's Mainland Southeast Asia Group survey team.

In the early days of training local surveyors, none of the trainers knew the national language so we couldn't oversee the translation of the questionnaires. This was a big problem, since the local surveyors didn't always understand the purpose of the questions or have enough sociolinguistic experience to make sense of the questions. Thus, a question like "What makes your ethnolinguistic group different from neighboring groups?" got translated as "What does your group make that is different from neighboring groups?" Answers like "pots" were not the answers we were looking for.

Questions can be difficult to word so that participants can answer appropriately as Case Study 3L demonstrates. It is all too easy to create an item like "Do your children like their school and teachers?" which in effect asks two questions at once: do they like their school and do they like their teachers. Another common error is to ask about information unknown to the participant, such as, "Do you feel education meets the standards you require for your children?" This may be beyond the experience of the participants as they may never have had an education themselves. Members of a survey team should discuss the questions so that they all understand what they are asking. They should also discuss possible answers and how they will record the answers so that there is consistency no matter who conducts the interview.

When working with minority speech communities there are a number of issues that may create problems for the administration of questionnaires. There are issues that are of deep concern to the surveyor, such as language attitudes, which the participant may have never considered. The educational level of the participants may influence their ability in other ways, too, particularly to understand and answer hypothetical questions. Participants may not feel it is appropriate to talk to us without permission from a leader. In some cultures, people may feel it is inappropriate to talk about others whereas in other cultures, it may be more useful to ask what other people do, rather than ask people to talk about themselves.

Attitudes towards us and attitudes toward the topics in our questionnaires will determine whether or not the people want to work with the surveyor and how much cooperation they will give. They may be suspicious of our motivations for doing the research. How the participant is feeling on the day may also affect their answers. They may feel pressure to give the "right" answer rather than their true opinion. We need to be aware of as many of these factors as possible so we can understand the influence of the environment where we collect our data. We need to ask a number of questions from different perspectives to take into account these factors.

Summarizing data from a questionnaire and working it into a presentable form can be difficult when writing a survey report. Taking care to complete the questionnaire in a clear and concise way while administering it can help with this. While questionnaires can seem like a relaxed tool for gathering our data, there is still a certain formality in administering them. This is more marked for a speech community that has no similar speech event in their culture. Particularly for these, there is a limit to the number

REFERENCE ▸ See Briggs (1986) for a classic example of this lack of a speech event causing conflict.

of questions a participant will endure before becoming bored or tired and giving less thoughtful or complete answers. Therefore, it is always a good idea to remember that questionnaires may still only give us limited insight into a speech community. In some cases, a surveyor can gather more valuable data during informal discussions with the people than by using questionnaires to probe for information.

3.4.3 Interviews

CROSS-REFERENCE ▸ For details about conducting interviews with knowledgeable outsiders, see SECTION 2.4.2 on page 39.

We have already introduced interviews in chapter 2. We also use them at the Negotiated Level, particularly to talk to knowledgeable insiders, such as people in leadership positions and others who are responsible for the welfare of the people in some way. Remember that interviews are different from the administration of questionnaires. Interviews allow the person being interviewed to talk as little or as much as they want on a topic. They can also change topics. The interviewer is able to explore other issues that arise during the conversation.

3.4.4 Matched-Guise

WWW.SURVEYWIKI.INFO ▸ See Survey Wiki for more details of Matched-Guise. We strongly recommend you read these details and, as you develop experience in assessment, contribute to SurveyWiki.

Matched-Guise is a way of assessing attitudes that one group of speakers has towards speakers of other languages. The term guise in this context means the appearance of a certain behavior. In this kind of test, people listen to recordings, thinking that the different utterances are different people.

3.4.4.1 Rationale

CROSS-REFERENCE ▸ For more on attitudes see Section 3.2.2 on page 68.

When there are multiple languages available for L2, L3, etc. it may not be clear why the L1 speech community chooses one language over another. As we have discussed previously, often, people who are learning an L2 have attitudes towards the kind of people who use the L2 as their heritage language. They may think that speakers of L2 are smarter or more successful.

At the Negotiated Level, we may want to understand the stereotypical attitudes L2 users might have towards members of the L1 who learn it. We may be interested in assessing L2 speakers' attitudes towards an L1 group we are working with. For example, we may need to know if the two groups have the positive attitudes towards each other, if they are required to work together on a language development program.

The Matched-Guise test is a method that can reveal these kinds of attitudes without letting the test participant know that they are giving opinions about the language.

3.4.4.2 Methodology

There are a number of ways a Matched-Guise test can be constructed, but the basic idea in devising the test is that we have a speaker do two different things. For example, they might read the same text in two different speech varieties. When respondents are later asked about the "different people," they have really been listening to the same person. The only real difference is the one thing that was changed in the test construction. Case Study 3E used a Matched-Guise test to investigate values.

Suppose we want to understand the attitudes people in the L1 community have towards the L2. We could first select a number of L1 speakers who have high levels of proficiency in their L2. We make recordings of each of them reading the same passage in both L1 and L2. The recordings are mixed so that it isn't easy to identify voices. We then play these back to other L1 speakers who are not aware that it is the same people reading both languages. We ask the listeners to judge the speakers on a number of personality, intelligence, or sophistication characteristics. For example, does the speaker seem more intelligent? Which speaker would seem to make a good friend? Which speaker would they not trust? Listeners typically reveal stereotypes as they assign positive qualities to one language and negative qualities to the other. Therefore, they may rate a person reading the L2 text as intelligent, and then rate the same person reading the L1 text as unintelligent. The only thing that has changed is the language, and the results thereby reveal attitudes towards the language, not actual intelligence.

CROSS-REFERENCE ▸ See **Section 5.4.2** on page 195 for more about sampling methodology.

3.4.4.3 Evaluation

Since the only variable in this test is the language and not the speaker, it can isolate the attitudes to the language itself. This provides a high degree of validity. However, it is very important to select speakers who have high levels of proficiency in both languages so that differing levels of language ability do not compromise the recordings. We also need good sampling to select listeners who are representative of their community so that we can generalize results to the whole population.

Using a Matched-Guise test may be difficult in some developing nations and some cultures. It may be difficult to find L1 speakers who are highly proficient in the L2. The test relies heavily on the particular language skills of reading and speaking. It may not be possible to find people who can read either or both languages. Recordings of the two passages are based on identical written texts. If either L1 or L2 are non-literate languages, it may be very complicated, or not possible to get two comparable texts. In smaller speech communities the test subjects may recognize the speaker's voice. The audio-based methodology of the Matched-Guise makes it unsuitable for assessing attitudes of sign language users.

The test may also suffer from cultural bias in that it relies on listeners' willingness to make public value judgments of strangers. Some cultures have high standards about not speaking badly of others, and, therefore, listeners may refuse to attribute negative qualities to anyone openly. If this is the case, alternative forms of assessment other than Matched-Guise will be necessary.

CROSS-REFERENCE ▸ For more on ethical considerations see **Section 5.1** on page 168.

Finally, some people have ethical concerns about this method since it does involve misleading the test subjects. This may be a problem for the test subjects, also, if they have felt misled and they may spread the word to other potential test subjects either skewing the results or making it difficult to find more test subjects. University ethics committees, who approve research proposals, may not approve the use of this method.

3.4.5   Sentence Repetition Tests

WWW.SURVEYWIKI.INFO ▸ See Survey Wiki for detailed guidance on carrying out SRTs. We strongly recommend you read these details and, as you develop experience in assessment, contribute to SurveyWiki.

Bilingualism testing may be an important part of research at the Negotiated Level. This is because bilingual proficiency will be evidence of the depth and successfulness of the contact between ethnolinguistic communities. There are many aspects of bilingualism that could be tested, such as comprehension, production, reading, and writing proficiencies. With so many aspects to test, it can be very costly in terms of time and effort. The Sentence Repetition Test is one method that has been developed to give a quick, but superficial, indication of possible bilingual proficiency.

3.4.5.1 *Rationale*

Fluency in any language depends on memory and that in turn depends on a phenomenon known as **CHUNKING**. An adult can remember seven units of information, plus or minus two (Norman 1976). The more we know something, the more information we are able to chunk together as a unit. As we learn languages, we begin to link together certain elements of vocabulary, phonology, and syntax in our memory. At the initial stages of language learning, we put our memory under pressure to forge these links and this slows down our comprehension and production. But as we reinforce long-term memory through practice, we develop fluency and are able to understand and reproduce elements of vocabulary, phonology, and syntax simultaneously in prefabricated chunks of language.

DEFINITION ▸ CHUNKING is the process whereby the human mind pre-assembles strings of languages together based on common patterns of vocabulary and grammar.

The rationale of an SRT is that the better someone knows a language, the more automatically they can reproduce utterances that they have recently heard. With very simple utterances, anyone can create approximate reproductions of any language they hear. But as the complexity of utterances increases, mimicry is not enough, and actual ability in the language becomes necessary.

NOTE ▸ We can adapt SRTs for use in sign language assessment. Instead of playing participants a pre-recorded sentence, we show them a video of a sequence of signs which they then reproduce. Scoring criteria are the same as for spoken tests.

3.4.5.2 *Methodology*

An SRT begins with three simple sentences in the second language to orient the subject. They are followed by a list of fifteen sentences, also in the second language. These sentences increase in linguistic complexity and length. We play the participant each recorded sentence and they simply repeat it immediately afterwards. We score the repetition according to whether it is perfect, has one or two errors, or contains a number of errors. If there are three or more errors, the subject scores zero for that sentence.

The construction of an SRT takes some time, but once it is created it doesn't take much time to test many people. The construction requires the selection of lots of sentences. The proper development of an SRT requires calibration, or comparison, with another method of measurement. For example, test a group of people using some other method, such as the Reported Proficiency Evaluation (RPE) or the oral interview method, and identify a group of people at each proficiency level. Then they are tested with the initial long list of SRT sentences. Through this calibration process, the long list is reduced to the most useful sentences which discriminate

CROSS-REFERENCE ▸ See **Section 5.4.1.2** on page 194 for more on calibration.

CROSS-REFERENCE ▸ See **Section 3.3.1.2** on page 80 for more about the ILR scale.

between different ILR levels. The prepared test is then administered to a representative sample of people.

3.4.5.3 Evaluation

Unlike most other evaluative tools we use to assess bilingualism in survey, the SRT provides a measure of productive bilingualism. Even as an uncalibrated test the SRT can be used to demonstrate differential ability within a population. For example, it could show that men score higher than women, or men under 30 score higher than everyone else, or those with at least six more years of schooling than everyone else.

With calibration, the SRT has been used to accurately discriminate between ILR proficiency levels up to 3 or 3+. We limit our confidence to no more than ILR 3+ because after twenty years of experience, we have never found an SRT that could accurately discriminate ILR levels above that. Of course, poorly constructed tests may not discriminate as high as level 3. Therefore, if a participant completes a well-constructed SRT, we cannot be certain of their proficiency over level 3+. We can only use SRTs to screen for a lack of bilingual ability.

Development of an SRT can be a lengthy process and this should be a major consideration when deciding whether or not to make one. However, once created, the application of an SRT is relatively rapid, meaning we can gather a large amount of data within a relatively short period. This is important because we need to test a relatively large sample to give a generalized measure of ability within the speech community. This stands in contrast to other, more rigorous tests (such as some oral interview methods), which give a more thorough and diagnostic assessment of an individual's bilingual proficiency, but require an unacceptable amount of time and skill to administer. Furthermore, if we have created an SRT in an LWC, we can use it with many different speech communities.

To provide a valid understanding of bilingualism in a speech community, we should combine data from an SRT with other sociolinguistic information, for example, information about how long schools have been available, attitudes toward the L2, reasons why people learn the L2. These and other factors help us interpret SRT data.

3.4.6   Other Bilingualism Testing Methods

There are many kinds of bilingualism tests. There are also several different types of proficiencies that get grouped together as aspects of bilingualism. Some tests focus more on production, others on comprehension, and still others on literacy skills. There are no tests that measure all aspects.

WWW.SURVEYWIKI.INFO ‣ See Survey-Wiki for more details of other bilingualism testing methods. We strongly recommend you read these details and, as you develop experience in assessment, contribute to SurveyWiki.

3.4.6.1   *Oral interviews*

The oral interview is a detailed method involving trained L2 testers and a rigorous evaluation process. Many government departments that need to evaluate civil servants for bilingualism use an oral interview type technique. Oral interviews generally involve an extensive interview in the L2 between the subject and at least one trained L2 tester. The L2 here is the tester's L1. The conversation ranges over a number of topics in different domains. The subject is instructed to lead the discussion for part of the test, and there may be other requirements for the subject. During the test, the tester tries to assess the subject's abilities and then tries to increase the difficulty of the discussion, requiring the subject to respond with increasingly more advanced vocabulary, more complex sentence structure, etc. until the subject's limitations are identified.

NOTE ‣ A version of the Oral Interview method that has been used in some SIL International bilingualism surveys is called SLOPE (Second Language Oral Proficiency Evaluation).

The use of well-trained testers, a standardized test procedure, and a thorough scoring process enables the subject's abilities to be diagnostically evaluated. It is possible to discriminate at all levels of the ILR scale. However, it is very costly in terms of time and money. It may take as much as an hour for each subject. When a survey needs to assess a statistical sampling of a speech community, it could take months to do all the required testing using this method. It may be most worthwhile to use an oral interview evaluation to calibrate an SRT during its construction phase.

3.4.6.2   *Recorded Text Tests*

The Recorded Text Test (RTT) method of testing bilingualism uses an audio recording of a text in the L2, approximately three to five minutes in length. The test subject listens to the text and answers questions based on its content. The RTT methodology was developed for comprehension testing which will be covered later. The construction of an RTT using the

CROSS-REFERENCE ‣ See **Section 4.4.3** on page 149 for more on Recorded Text Test construction.

traditional questioning method as a bilingualism test is not significantly different from making one for comprehension testing.

There are a number of difficulties concerning the use of RTT methodology for bilingualism testing. First, we must identify the proper form of the L2 to use for the text. This isn't particularly unique to RTT testing methodology, but since an RTT is usually used for measuring comprehension, the variety used for those tests is more obvious. Furthermore, it is fairly easy to pass an RTT without a high level of proficiency in the L2. Therefore, it should only be used when we are fairly certain that there is no bilingualism. It can be used if quantitative numbers are required to convince someone of the absence of adequate bilingualism.

3.4.6.3 Self-evaluation

A self-evaluation questionnaire involves questions that ask the participant to describe something about themselves, usually their own abilities in an L2. This is sometimes called the "Can you do this?" method. Typical examples include asking if the person can use the L2 to purchase a train ticket, give directions somewhere, describe how to make something, etc. This does not result in a quantifiable number or a defined level of proficiency. When given on a large scale to a wide sample of people, the results can present a useful picture of a range of abilities and which sectors of the speech community have those abilities. The problem with this method is that it relies on the ability of the participant to make a self-evaluation of their own proficiency. Participants tend to over- or underestimate their abilities based on cultural norms or social pressures.

Rather than simply asking a series of yes-no questions, one adaptation asks people to give autobiographical descriptions. These descriptions cover experiences of how they have used the L2 in a series of circumstances which would have involved increasingly complex language. Rather than a five minute yes-no question interview, this adaptation results in a much more useful thirty minute conversation that is less hypothetical.

Once again, along with RTTs, this is a method that may be used to identify the absence of widespread bilingualism at the Negotiated Level. Surveyors should avoid the temptation to assign an ILR level to the information gathered through this method. It is not really possible to assign an ILR level to a specific activity.

3.4.6.4 *Reported proficiency evaluation*

In this method, we seek out L2 speakers who have friends who use L1. We guide these participants through a process of evaluating and ranking their L1 friend's abilities in the L2. We ask them to consider past experiences of conversations and consider "can-do" type questions. This differs from the self-evaluation method in that another person is being asked to give a non-technical evaluation. Another important difference is that each person is ranked in comparison to other people and in comparison to the ILR scale. This method is calibrated to the ILR scale and evaluations up to mid-ILR levels have shown to be reliable. The method can also be used in more extensive surveys for identifying people who will be more useful for further testing or in-depth interviews.

3.4.6.5 *Conversation in L2*

If we know our own ILR level of proficiency in the L2 and are familiar with the ILR scale and level descriptions, it is possible to get an impression of the abilities of the speech community we are working with. We simply have L2 conversations with L1 speakers and evaluate whether each person has as good, worse, or better proficiency in the L2 than our own level. If this method is used with a wide sample of people, and the conversations extend into a wide coverage of domains, it is possible to gather valuable quantitative data that is conclusive.

In the past, this method was sometimes used with less scientific rigor. If the survey team expected that there was little bilingualism in the speech community, they would talk to some of the people who were assumed to be the mostly likely to be bilingual. If those people had little bilingual proficiency, then it was assumed that the rest of the speech community had even less proficiency. With the increase of multilingualism it is probably no longer safe to have those expectations and to make those assumptions.

3.5   Further Reading

Studying Bilinguals **by François Grosjean (2008)**

This is very good overview from a leading scholar in the field of bilingualism and includes both a rare chapter on bilingualism of the Deaf and an important chapter on biculturalism.

How Languages are Learned **by Patsy M. Lightbown and Nina Spada, (1999)**

Although written for English language teachers rather than linguists, chapters 1-4 and 7 of this book are excellent introductions to the issues involving both child and adult learners of languages.

Sentence Repetition Method for Studies in Community Bilingualism **by Carla Radloff (1991)**

This is the definitive guide to sentence repetition testing.

Getting What You Asked For: A Study of Sociolinguistic Survey Questionnaires **by Catherine J. Showalter (1991)**

Showalter challenges surveyors' tendencies to re-use questionnaire items repeatedly without evaluating their effectiveness and improving them. The paper's appendix is a long annotated list of survey questions. You might want to find this and then evaluate her suggestions for suitability to a context you are familiar with. This article can be found on pages 302-325 in *Proceedings of the Summer Institute of Linguistics International Language Assessment Conference* edited by Gloria E. Kindell.

Who Speaks What Language to Whom and When **by Joshua Fishman (2001)**

This article is the classic reference on domain analysis of language use. This can be found in *The Bilingualism Reader* edited by Li Wei which also contains many other essential readings.

Principles of Linguistic Change **by William Labov (2001)**

The entire volume provides discussion of classic social variables that accompany linguistic variation.

Designing Sensible Surveys **by Donald Orlich (1978)**

Practical discussion of data collection techniques: advantages and disadvantages of interviews and questionnaires as well as a focus on the construction of questions including various forms of questions.

Notes on Oral Proficiency Testing (SLOPE) by Barbara Grimes (1992)

Brief description of a standard bilingualism interview technique and provides very good descriptions of the ILR levels. This can be found in *Windows on Bilingualism* edited by Eugene Casad.

Observing and Analysing Natural Language by Lesley Milroy (1987)

The seminal text for understanding social networks was first published in 1980 and had a great impact on the development of sociolinguistics. This second edition contains a review of the theory since it was introduced.

 **FREE LANGUAGE CHOICE**

In this chapter you will be introduced to language assessment at the Free Level. The first section of the chapter will cover the interactions between social factors and language. At the Free Level, social factors of particular importance to language include

- understanding the demographic subgroups within the speech community,
- self-identity and how people use language to reinforce this,
- attitudes about self and how this affects the vitality of languages, and
- socialization and how it determines language.

The second part of the chapter will describe typical research questions that we consider when we work at the Free Level. These questions are primarily associated with intelligibility between dialects and extensibility of literacy materials between dialects of a language. In the last part of the chapter we will look at a number of tools that can be used to assess language at this level.

4.1   Introduction

The previous chapter on the Negotiated Level focused on issues arising from interaction between the community we are working with and groups they identify as others. This chapter now considers influences on language choices that originate within the speech community, with people who are self-identified as same or similar. These are the people they identify with most strongly. It is the introspective nature of the Free Level which makes it different from the Negotiated Level. In contrast to the Restricted Level, the Free Level is where the community holds the most unrestricted control over their language use choices. The influences at the Free Level come from within, and control of them rests with the people themselves.

Study at the Free Level can reveal the motivations people have for maintaining their own variety of a language. This information is crucial for making it possible for language development materials to be accessible to the largest number of members of the speech community. The success of any language development depends not only on the products of development but also the processes used to create them. Thus, it is important to work with the community in a way that is most motivating for them. Studying the Free Level is vital considering that, ultimately, it will be the same community who carries out the processes that create these products in whatever form they take. All sorts of factors can affect a group's ownership and involvement in language development and whereas at the Negotiated Level we focus on the community's attitudes to others, it is the attitudes of the people towards themselves that we investigate at the Free Level.

4.1.1   Language Variation

Cross-Reference ▸ For a discussion of the differences between the terms language and dialect see **Section 1.1.2** on page 5.

Definition ▸ **Idiolect** is the unique speech variety of an individual.

At the heart of research at the Free Level is the fact that speech varies from person to person. Earlier, we introduced a discussion about the difference between languages and dialects. We can make a further distinction by speaking of **IDIOLECTS**. Between any two individuals it is possible to find some variation in their speech. However, we are more interested in the way people will unite to form a group that has an identity based on a set of similar speech features. A dialect tends to have a set of similar linguistic features, and the people have a somewhat shared identity. At another level they will have a shared identity with speakers of other dialects, and this larger shared identity helps to identify a language.

In this chapter we will consider the identities and attitudes that people attach to their language and their dialect and other dialects. We are also interested in the linguistic realities of the shared features that identify dialects and languages and the linguistic features that differ between related speech varieties.

4.1.2   Centers, Boundaries, and Chains

Some large speech communities, such as the English speech community, include members spread over several countries with many different language varieties. There can also be a surprising amount of linguistic variation in much smaller, and seemingly homogenous, speech communities. In fact, it would be unrealistic to expect any speech community to be completely homogeneous. Case Study 4A shows that even in a small, nearly homogeneous group in a confined geographic area, some variation in language is often found.

CASE STUDY 4A
A SIMPLE SPEECH COMMUNITY
CHITRAL, PAKISTAN

CASE STUDY 4A SOURCE ► Ken Decker, International Language Assessment Coordinator, SIL.

Dameli is a language spoken in the Chitral District of northern Pakistan. It has a population of about 5000 located in eleven villages in an isolated mountain valley. It is classified as an Indo-European, Dardic language, but it is not very similar to any other Dardic language. It is easy to draw a line on a map to indicate geographically where Dameli is spoken. Even though this is a relatively small and homogeneous speech community, slight linguistic variations were noted between speech of the higher eastern villages and the lower western villages. Some nouns end with [o] and [ɪ] in the western villages, which have [u] and [e] in the eastern villages.

Case Study 4A represents a type of language group that is easy to identify as a speech community. The variation in the speech presents little evidence of anything that would divide the group identities, and all of the people identify themselves as Dameli speakers. With this much uniformity, the people still identified the speech of one village as more "pure." In many language situations it is typical for there to be a variety that is considered the central variety. The centrality of this variety is primarily based on its being the speech of people with the most socioeconomic power and/ or prestige. It may also be the most widely understood variety. People will usually identify this central variety as being pure, beautiful, sweet sounding, proper sounding or intelligent sounding.

For the purposes of language development it is most efficient to find the variety that is most widely understood, as well as considered prestigious. Therefore, many surveys will focus on identification of a variety that is most widely understood. When such a linguistic center is identified there will be increasing variation as one moves away from that center. In most situations, there is a boundary at which the speech forms change more

DEFINITION ▶ REFERENCE DIALECTS are language varieties which are standardized for formal purposes, such as literature and education. They tend to be identified as the best understood and most prestigious variety.

CROSS-REFERENCE ▶ See **Section 4.3.1** on page 133 for more on intelligibility and **Section 4.4.2** on page 141 for details of wordlists.

dramatically and beyond that boundary the people identify with a different central variety. When we identify a central variety that is both widely accepted and understood, and will be used for development, we call it a **REFERENCE DIALECT**.

The idea of a central variety with concentric varieties of decreasing comprehension differs from a **LANGUAGE CHAIN**, like that described in Case Study 4B. With a language chain it is often more difficult to identify a central variety.

CASE STUDY 4B
A SIMPLE LANGUAGE CHAIN
IRAN

The Taleshi language is spoken in Gilan Province, Iran, and the south of Azerbaijan. Within Iran, the area in which Taleshi is spoken extends about 120 km (75 miles) from north to south, and less than 40 km (25 miles) from west to east at its widest point. Wordlist collection and intelligibility testing in towns and villages along the length of the area revealed high similarity and high intelligibility between neighboring population settlements but lower similarity and intelligibility between settlements only 60 km apart. Intelligibility testing results also revealed that people living at either end of the area could not understand each other at all. Yet, the people all consider that they speak Taleshi.

DEFINITION ▶ A **LANGUAGE CHAIN** is a sequence of dialects that gradually change from one to another.

In Case Study 4B, there is no point at which one could clearly identify a division in identity or language between the ends of the chain. A language chain is not necessarily in a geographically linear orientation. Case Study 4C describes a situation in which multiple language chains run in multiple directions.

CASE STUDY 4C
A COMPLEX LANGUAGE CHAIN
INDIA

CASE STUDY 4C SOURCE ▶ Ken Decker, International Language Assessment Coordinator, SIL.

Across the Indian sub-continent there is a language chain that extends for thousands of kilometers in every direction:

Punjabi merges into Rajasthani, which merges into Khandeshi, and then into Marathi, etc. However, these names cover a great deal of variation, and those names may not be the commonly used names. For example, Gujarati covers Aer, Jandavra, Koli, Saurashtra, Vaghri, and Vasavi, but again, these are only cover terms for smaller divisions. There is a Kachi Koli, Parkari Koli, and Wadiyara Koli. Kachi Koli includes Rahabari, Kachi Bhil, Katai Meghwar, and Zalavaria. Often the names are simply the name of the nearest city. In villages midway between cities, people from one household may identify their language by the different city names, but the speech is no more like one city than another. There is no place where a line could be accurately drawn to separate speech communities. Furthermore, away from the cities, people may only have a very weak identification with the language of the city people.

Case Study 4C describes a situation where there is no clear boundary between varieties that are considered central.

PIDGIN and **CREOLE** speech communities represent another kind of variation. Usually, the creation of a pidgin or creole has been influenced most by another, more prestigious language, referred to as the **SUPERSTRATE**. For example, 70 percent of the vocabulary of Fanagalo, a pidgin used in South Africa, is from Zulu; Nefamese, a possibly extinct pidgin in India, had a large percent of vocabulary from Assamese; Jamaican, a creole spoken in Jamaica, has a vocabulary that developed predominantly from English; and Haitian, a creole spoken in the nearby country of Haiti, has a vocabulary that is largely from French.

> **DEFINITION ▶ A PIDGIN** is a language that no one speaks as their heritage language. It has formed by a process of reducing grammatical structures and the number of lexical choices from the selection of languages available to the speakers of the pidgin.

> **DEFINITION ▶ CREOLE** is a language that was once a pidgin but now it is the heritage language of a people. It is typified by a process by which it has expanded the grammatical structures and lexical choices that are considered part of the new language.

When a creole language and its superstrate language are spoken in the same region, a continuum of lects forms. The form that is most different from the superstrate language is called the **BASILECT**. The form that is most similar to the superstrate is called the **ACROLECT**. The various forms that are produced between the basilect and acrolect are called **MESOLECTAL** varieties. Generally, no one controls the entire continuum from basilect to acrolect. A person will be able to speak in the basilect for less formal speech and then shift into a mesolect for their most formal speech. In this discussion of language variation, it is the mesolectal variations that are most interesting. There is no one standard or uniform variety of the mesolect. Everyone speaks it somewhat differently. Therefore, in a creole speech community, we can have people speaking a language with considerable variation within one home.

> **DEFINITION ▶** The **SUPERSTRATE** is a language that has had the most significant influence on the creation of a pidgin or creole.

> **DEFINITION ▶ BASILECT, MESOLECT,** and **ACROLECT** are terms used to describe various forms of a creole language between the form most different from the superstrate (basilect) and the form most similar to the superstrate (acrolect).

In reality, we see that it is difficult to identify the boundaries of speech communities as many people live in ones where there are a number of languages being used or varieties of one language being spoken. It is in situations like Case Study 4B and Case Study 4C, and the situations of creole continuums, that we encounter difficulty describing differences between dialects and languages or identifying specific varieties as reference dialects. In such situations, it is better to identify centers rather than boundaries. However, this may mean that there are people in areas between centers whose language needs are not well met.

4.2   Social Factors and Language at the Free Level

4.2.1   Impact of outside language contact

As has been pointed out numerous times in this book, we no longer expect to find speech communities in which everyone speaks the same or languages that do not show any similarities with neighboring languages. There are various factors which influence people who come into contact with another language. They may begin using a new sound from the other language or there may be a shift in word order as a result of contact. People may pick up words from another language; we call this **BORROWING** of loanwords.

DEFINITION ▶ BORROWING describes the practice of taking words from another language and incorporating them in the vocabulary of one's own language.

These shifts or borrowings may initially occur randomly in the speech of some people. If the use of the new feature becomes consistent throughout the speech community, we know that it has become a new part of the language. During the transitional phase between when the first people begin to use new features and when it becomes a standardized behavior, we call this **CODE-SWITCHING**. Code-switching may involve the use of a pronunciation typical in another language, a word or a phrase from the other language, or switching entirely between different languages when talking to someone who also uses the speaker's heritage language.

DEFINITION ▶ CODE-SWITCHING happens when people mix two or more languages for certain words, phrases, or sentences while communicating with another member of their own language group. When one language forms the basis for syntax and another language is used to vary vocabulary or other non-structural features, you have the makings of pidginization and, eventually, possible creolization.

4.2.2   Demographic and Ethnographic Information

As we have discussed previously, we can understand data only when we compare it to other data. This means we can better understand linguistic data when we compare it to other ethnographic and demographic information. At the Negotiated Level, we saw how knowing about surrounding speech community norms enabled us to understand the people we work with in relation to their neighbors. In contrast, the Free

CROSS-REFERENCE ▶ See **Section 3.1** on page 47 for an example of the importance of context for interpreting data.

WWW.SURVEYWIKI.INFO ▶ For more about the link between demography and vitality, see the **Language Vitality** page on SurveyWiki.

Level provides us with a context which enables us to understand our data in relation to the speech community itself. We can document quantifiable facts (demographic) and observe cultural behaviors (ethnographic) in each group. These provide information to help us understand the context of other social and linguistic behavior. For example, when we investigate vitality at the Free Level, it is important to collect demographic information such as birth rates and ethnographic information about practices like exogamy. Vitality can be an issue for smaller speech communities in particular, if there is a birth rate that is below replacement levels or fewer women, all of whom will, by tradition, marry and move away to become members of other speech communities. Thus, regardless of the research question, we always collect certain types of demographic and ethnographic data about the speech community to help us understand the context.

We also realize that there can be variation between individuals in a speech community. There can be variation in attitudes, perceptions, and beliefs, as well as language use. So, when we test, interview, or collect social and linguistic information from individuals we also want to collect some factual information about each person so that we can better understand any variation in data collected from each person. Table 5 summarizes typical key information we need to do our best to collect.

NOTE ▸ See **Section 5.7.2** on page 209 for information about recording of metadata for data sources.

SPEECH COMMUNITY DATA	• population estimates (distinguish between the number of people who identify themselves as part of the ethnic group and the number of people who claim to speak the language) • in and out migration patterns • proximity and type of any communication infrastructure (media, telecommunications, transport) • utilities (power, water) • places where they may come in contact with other speech communities: market town, roads, collections of expatriates including: mission stations, mining operations, plantations, oil explorations, etc. • education (including attendance information (by age and gender) and language/s used) • social and political structure of speech community (including economic activities, marriage patterns and ethnic homogeneity) • reported expectations for language use within the speech community
ETHNOGRAPHIC INFORMATION	• social and political structure of speech community • economic activities • marriage patterns and ethnic homogeneity

TABLE 5 ▸ Typical essential data to collect at the Free Level.

INDIVIDUAL LANGUAGE HELPER DATA	<ul><li>name (or data source reference)</li><li>gender</li><li>education (including location of studies, language used and level attained)</li><li>languages and self-evaluation of proficiency</li><li>where born, when (approximation if unknown) and language/s used with parents at home as a child</li><li>current residence and, if for a significant time, where else and language/s used there</li><li>current and, if any, long term contact outside of the speech community for the purposes of employment or experience</li><li>first language of spouse and language use patterns of that spouse with language helper and their children</li></ul>

NOTE ▶ See **Section 5.1** on page 168 for ethical considerations. Some people may not want to give personal information and/or we may need to gather informed consent from language helpers.

We may add to this data depending on the specific research questions we have on a particular survey. For example, religious affiliation may be important to know if this is likely to mean a preference for a particular language variety. Because of this, consider Table 5 only as an indication of essential data and not as containing everything you will need in every case.

The *ethnography of communication* is a field of study related to language assessment, which focuses on the speech events within a speech community. Hymes (1968) identified fifteen main components of the speech event that are important to study to understand the ethnography of communication. These are presented here as a reminder to us of the details of language use at its most essential level.

1. **Message form**: how something is said
2. **Message content**: the topic of what is being said
3. **Setting**: when and where something is said
4. **Scene**: the cultural descriptive context of the speech event
5. **Speaker**: an interactive member of a speech event
6. **Addressor:** a deliverer of a speech event
7. **Hearer:** the one who receives a message and may interact with the speaker
8. **Addressee:** the one who passively receives a message
9. **Purpose – outcomes**: a specific intentional reason for what is said
10. **Purpose – goals**: a more general, less intentional reason for what is said
11. **Key**: the tone, manner, attitude of what is said

12. **Channel**: method of transmission: oral, written, semaphore, recitation, etc.
13. **Form**: REGISTER, code, dialect that is chosen for what is said
14. **Norms of interaction**: the cultural rules governing normative behavior
15. **Norms of interpretation**: normative understanding of behavioral meaning

DEFINITION ▶ REGISTER is a particular style of language such as formal or informal, technical or simple.

From this list we see that there are many components of each communicative interaction between people. It's helpful for us to be growing in our understanding of these things, but to study it in any depth would provide greater detail than we need for most surveys.

4.2.3 Identity

Within any speech community there can be a range of amounts of linguistic variation. In some communities there may be very little linguistic variation. As was described earlier, there can be so much variation that we are not sure if the two varieties should be considered different languages. When there is very little variation, the people will tend to be unaware of it. At some vague point in this continuum, language varies enough that the members of a particular speech community are able to distinguish between their own variety and those of others. Some people will consider a slight amount of variation to be a strong indication that there are different identities. Sometimes there will be a large amount of linguistic difference between varieties, and yet the people still consider that they are all one people, one identity.

CROSS-REFERENCE ▶ See **Section 1.1.2** on page 5, **Section 3.3.2** on page 84, and **Section 4.1.1** on page 116 for more about variation.

QUOTE ▶ *[P]ossession of a given language is well-nigh essential to the maintenance of group identity.* (Edwards 1985:3)

QUOTE ▶ *Languages... supply the terms and other linguistic means with which identities are constructed and negotiated. On the other hand, ideologies of language and identity guide ways in which individuals use linguistic resources to index their identities and to evaluate the use of linguistic resources by others.* (Pavelenko and Blackledge 2004:14)

At the Free Level, we need to be able to understand the sociolinguistic reasons that groups within a particular speech community consider themselves as having different identities and those who relate to each other as having the same identity. They may do this linguistically, by focusing on how other groups pronounce words differently, or they may do this culturally in some way. However, as Case Study 4C and Case Study 4D show, there may be ambiguity about self-identity and the relationship to others which can arise because the people may never have had to elaborate concepts such as these before. Language development activities can be very illuminating for an ethnolinguistic group.

CASE STUDY 4D
WHO IS WHAT?
SOUTHEAST ASIA

CASE STUDY 4D SOURCE ▶ SIL's Mainland Southeast Asia Group

In one remote survey, the question "What is the name for your ethnolinguistic group?" prompted a panic and the village leaders quickly called a village meeting to resolve the question. Each person involved had a different idea of what they should call their group and they could not reach a consensus before the survey team had to leave the village. In another survey, the question "What is the meaning for your ethnolinguistic group's name?" created a local controversy. The local leaders gave an answer and the survey team moved on to the next village. After reflecting on their answer, however, the local leaders became very distressed when they realized it was wrong. They went in pursuit of the survey team (over days of hiking) to give them the corrected answer for the meaning of their group name!

We need to be able to isolate the different factors that mark the different identities, whether they are linguistic, cultural, or some other factor. The factors are called **VARIABLES.** Sociolinguists classify variables into two types: **INDICATORS** and **MARKERS** (Wardhaugh 2009:143).

DEFINITIONS ▶ VARIABLE are parts of language which vary depending on the social context. An **INDICATOR** has no social value attached to it. Linguistically, it has other forms but these do not have any social significance. Contrast this with a **MARKER** which does have social significance.

An indicator is a linguistic variable that has no social value attached to it. In other words, linguistically, there is a difference but socially there is none. Perhaps it is just a difference in aspiration on a consonant. The speakers may or may not even realize that there is any difference in their varieties. If the only variation that occurs is at the level of an indicator, the two speakers will most likely identify themselves as being from the same speech community and accept that they both use the same dialect. In fact, even when presented with linguistic evidence for differences, people may deny this and insist that they communicate in exactly the same way. This reaction to linguistic evidence alone shows that if we study speech communities at the level of the indicator, we are liable to produce linguistic evidence for differences between speech communities that the people themselves do not accept.

In contrast to an indicator, a *marker* is a linguistic variable that has a social significance of some kind. For example, pronouncing /h/ in the word *hotel* is still a feature of middle-class English in England, unlike some other social classes. Most people in Britain would predict someone's social group from whether or not they pronounced the /h/ in *hotel*. People are very much aware of markers because they use them to distinguish social groups and, in particular, membership of their own social group and others.

These markers are distinctive linguistic features that can be very influential in shaping our attitudes towards people and their languages. Markers, along with other social factors, help us form attributions that we use to define identity. Even before we interact with someone, we subconsciously identify these attributions through factors like roles, ethnic identity, clothing and even the setting where we might meet the person (Foley 1997:343). Because of this, we have developed tools such as Matched-Guise to help us screen out attributions based on visual information so that we can focus on language alone. Because these attitudes are important in identifying language varieties, we need to investigate the social reasons for these attitudes as well as linguistic reasons as to why people distinguish language varieties.

CROSS-REFERENCES ▶ See **Section 3.2.2 on page** 68 for more about attribution theory and see **Section 3.4.4 on page** 104 for more about Matched-Guise.

CROSS-REFERENCES ▶ See **Section 3.2.1 on page** 53 for more about contact and its effect on language.

Language variation can often reflect boundaries between social groups. When individuals from different social groups meet, they often vary their language to reflect roles they take in different kinds of interaction. For example, when meeting those of higher status, people use a more formal way of communicating than normal. When speaking to someone from another variety area, particularly if they want to appear friendly, people will often take on qualities of that other person's dialect. We call this **ACCOMMODATION**, and here is how it works:

DEFINITION ▶ ACCOMMODATION THEORY attempts to explain why it is that people change their language to become more or less like that of the person they are with.

> Attitudes brought to interactions are based on socio-historical backgrounds, as well as individual histories comprised of the previous experiences of similar interaction and perceived social norms. Initial orientation is also based on the larger social context, particularly the intergroup and interpersonal history. This orientation may be modified...by interactants in conversation...in this view, attitudes are both brought into the interaction and negotiated within it. This dynamic in turn influences the ways in which behaviour is labelled and how it is attributed...and thence to overall evaluation of other interactants. Finally evaluations determine the initial orientation in future interactions with the other person or the person's group. (Gallois, Watson, and Brabant 2009:610)

CROSS-REFERENCE ▶ See **Case Study 3F** on page 71 for an example of accommodation.

In other words, there is a circular process by which we enter new interactions based on evaluations of past experiences. Then, as we adapt our conversation in a new interaction we evaluate the success of our adaptations. Thus, we create a new perspective from which to enter the next interaction.

CROSS-REFERENCE ▶ See **Section 3.3.2** on page 84 for a discussion of domains of language use.

In larger, more socioeconomically diverse speech communities there are sub-communities within the larger speech community. These sub-communities may be associated with certain domains of language use. For example, the speech in the religious domain usually makes use of words that people rarely hear elsewhere. Other professions or trades will have their own vocabulary and manners of speech. There can be other variation in speech in domains of language use, such as pronunciation when addressing a gathering of people is usually clearer than in one-to-one conversation. Depending on an individual's social mobility, they may have more or less ability to shift their speech to meet the expectations of others in that domain.

If people choose not to change their speech by accommodating their language in any way, there may be a social cost, and this will increase as the differences between the varieties increase. The same thing is happening when people shift dialects or languages when they change domain or location. This is because a shift in dialect reflects underlying attitudes towards what the dialects represent, such as group solidarity or social mobility. Understanding why people find particular dialects more appealing than others will help identify appropriate reference dialects.

CASE STUDY 4E
RELATED, BUT ONLY ON PAPER
REPUBLIC OF THE CONGO

CASE STUDY 4E SOURCE ▶ Annette Harrison, SIL Central Africa Group.

In 2006–2007, our team worked in northern Republic of the Congo to study the linguistic ecology of the main town of the area. We studied speech repertoires via questionnaires and observation, studied patterns of intermarriage, and collected texts and wordlists from several of the language groups. I worked principally with men from the Ngundi, Imassa, and Jasua groups in an attempt to gain enough confidence of the speakers that they would let me record natural interactions between family members and friends. Imagine my surprise one day while working on a kinship chart of the Imassa man to find that he was the son-in-law of the Jasua man. And then imagine my further surprise to discover that the Ngundi man and the Imassa man were related through their mothers!

Though these three men firmly insisted that they belonged to different ethnolinguistic groups, they were all related to each other.

Traditionally, linguists have shown languages on maps drawn with distinct boundaries between languages. However, due to the complexities involved in language variation, this does not reflect the reality of many speech communities as Case Study 4E shows. Instead, speakers themselves draw boundaries in a variety of ways as they choose language varieties at the Free Level depending on what they use language for and how they identify with the different communities.

The people we work with may, or may not, use terms of reference that we understand. For example, they may use geographical boundaries or features such as rivers and mountain ranges to define language varieties. The Pahari, Potwari, and Northern Hindko varieties of northern Pakistan are very similar, but they are considered by the local people to be separate, and they are named after their geographic locales. Pahari, meaning 'hill language', is located in the hills north of the capital Islamabad; Potwari is spoken on the Potwari Plateau in the area around Islamabad; the name Hindko is related to the name of the Indus River along which Hindko is spoken. Political boundaries rarely take into account the ethnic makeup of the people on the ground. As a result, speech communities that share the same variety of language at the Free Level can find themselves divided by a political boundary and they may, or may not, use this as a basis to distinguish themselves from others.

The identity in creole language communities can be somewhat problematic for language development. The people will generally consider that they speak a poor form of the superstrate language, or they may not even be aware of the significant difference between their basilect and the national language. For example, in Jamaica there has been a small minority of people who advocated for the literary development of Jamaican Patwa for over 40 years—an effort that has been strongly opposed.

CROSS-REFERENCE ▶ Creole languages and concepts related to the creole continuum were introduced in **Section 4.1.2** on page 116.

While not exactly a creole situation, there is a continuum of forms between Indonesian and numerous mesolects. On the island of Papua, there is a continuum of varieties from those that are more similar to Indonesian to those that are quite different. Those varieties most different—those most basilectal—often resemble the local Papuan languages used in that particular area. People who speak these varieties may not be aware that they don't speak Indonesian and might be quite resistant to the idea of developing their local variety as something different from Indonesian. Despite this, they are unlikely to understand literature in standard Indonesian. Recently, many Papuans have begun to attribute a separate identity to a somewhat homogenous mesolect, calling it Papuan Malay. This may open the door to possible production of materials in a variety that is more intelligible to large numbers of Papuans.

This example of Indonesian clearly shows that issues of identity must be addressed or they may prevent language development. To understand the sociolinguistic reality of identity in speech communities, it is necessary to have an open mind and ask the people themselves to explain the differences between varieties from their point of view.

4.2.4   Attitudes and Vitality

CROSS-REFERENCE ► See **Section 3.2.2** on page 68 for more about attitudes.

At the Negotiated Level, we discussed the relationship of language attitudes and identities and the impact of these issues on minority languages when in contact with more dominant or prestigious languages. All of these issues are also true of more and less prestigious dialects of a language. Just as people can choose to shift to the use of another language, they can also choose to shift to another dialect.

At the Free Level, we are interested in attitudes the people have about themselves and their heritage language and culture, and their particular dialect. This is very closely related to issues of identity as discussed in the last section. The reason for our interest in this topic is that any language development plan needs to be in line with the prevailing attitudes of the speech community. Unless people have positive attitudes towards the language variety that provides the medium for development work, they may well resist such development. And if the people are given no choice but to cooperate against their will, such as when Russian was forced on all speech communities in the former Soviet Union, the situation will be even worse.

Often, within the collection of dialects that form a language, there will be a variety that is identified as the best or "sweetest." It may also be identified with access to better education and economic benefits. People often aspire to adapt their speech to this variety. This can also have impact on the less prestigious dialects which become stigmatized as less attractive or desirable. People within the speech community identify the features that are indicators of the less prestigious dialect and will attempt to avoid those features.

It is also possible to find a group of people who speak a dialect that is stigmatized by others, and the speakers of this stigmatized variety are aware of the other peoples' opinions. However, the people who speak this stigmatized variety may not be ashamed of their speech, and they may willingly acknowledge that another variety is prestigious. A negative stigma is not necessarily sufficient to cause people to shift to another dialect.

4.2.5   Socialization

Nowhere at the Free Level are the language identities and attitudes revealed more apparently than in the socialization of children. As Ochs (2002:106) tells us, "[l]anguage of children and language directed to children is grounded not only in the immediate discourse context but also in the context of historically and culturally grounded social beliefs, values and expectations." Long before any formalized education may take place in a child's life, a child receives a more fundamental education in the values of its culture as parents and other caregivers teach it how to speak and behave in ways that conform to their accepted norms. As we observe speech communities that we visit, it is important to realize that socialization may take place in ways which differ significantly from our own cultures. People may often define the role of caregiver much more widely, for example, with older children or members of the wider community caring for younger children for significant amounts of time. Multiple caregivers may also be involved at once such as in Samoan society where children learn that addressing a request to a high status caregiver will result in its being directed to a lower status caregiver who then responds to the child's request (Ochs and Schieffelin 2009).

The majority of this socialization takes place subconsciously as children acquire language and behavior through simple imitation of their caregivers. This is socialization through language. In this form of socialization, behavior is the focus, not language. Even though language is not the focus, the language that parents choose to use for socializing children can provide important information. In Luycx's study of the Aymara people in Bolivia (2003), she noticed that whenever parents spoke about the topic of school, they would use Spanish, the language of education, instead of their heritage language of Aymara. We need to be aware that the language that caregivers choose (or don't choose) as a

CROSS-REFERENCE ► See **Sections 2.2.2** on page 27 and **3.2.1.1** on page 54 for more on the links between language and identity.

QUOTE ► *The process of becoming a competent member of society is realized to a large extent through language, by acquiring knowledge of its functions, social distribution, and interpretations in and across socially defined situations, i.e. through exchanges of language in particular social situations.* (Ochs and Schieffeli 2009:297)

QUOTE ► *[T]he verbal environment contains important cultural keys, tropes, metaphors, and rules. It also provides the material for learning one of the most important cultural systems and how to use it: language itself.* (Scheiffelin 1990:249)

medium for socialization reveals important information about the roles languages play in their speech communities.

In contrast to socialization *through* language, there is also socialization *to* language (Duranti 1997:26). It is often necessary for caregivers to make certain language explicit, particularly when children do not conform to expectations consistently. We can all remember being told the "right" way to say things when we were children. The varieties of language that caregivers insist on provide important clues about attitudes towards language because they explicitly reveal the importance of one versus another. This is especially so when caregivers choose to use a language other than the heritage language. This sends a clear message to the child about the value of the heritage language which will be reflected in their adult attitudes towards it and thus affect their own choices about which languages to use to socialize their own children.

As recent studies have shown (Kulick 1992; Pease-Alvarez 2003; Luycx 2003), language socialization may change over time. As social forces change, so do choices about which variety is best to use for particular purposes. The language choices made explicit in socialization are therefore a reflection of current social influences on the speech community. In this way, perceived future language requirements may influence the initial socialization that children might receive at home. While we investigate the socialization process through observation and asking the people we work with about their attitudes and practices at the Free Level, we should therefore bear in mind Luycx's advice to consider the influence of Negotiated and Restricted Level factors within the domestic environment:

> It is...somewhat artificial to treat the home as an isolated sphere with regard to language socialization, given that wider social pressures penetrate the most intimate of domestic interactions. In the wake of modernization, parental norms and attitudes become less central to children's post-infancy language development. Defined by the dominant society as linguistically deficient, many indigenous parents place their hopes for their children's linguistic success in school. Family language policy is often shaped in
>
> anticipation of the school's requirements. When it is, it may have negative consequences for the mother tongue; when it isn't, children's entrance into school is often traumatic.... We must therefore pay attention not only to family language policy per se, but to its articulation with the language policies of other spheres

such as the school, the workplace, the neighborhood, and the media. (Luycx 2003:40)

Socialization in the home is an extremely important determiner of language and attitudes to language. However, the home is not the only arena where socialization takes place. Socialization is believed to take place wherever people encounter a situation where they need to develop language in order to establish a social network. In this view, socialization takes place in a very wide variety of contexts. The language learning between playmates outside of the home is also important. For example, in Belize many parents try to use only English at home with their children to prepare them for schooling in English. However, for social interaction with other students, the children must learn Kriol, the local English-lexifier creole, which is used in most contexts outside the classroom. Other traditional examples include learning a trade, joining a religious community, or initiation rituals. More modern practices include using a telephone or interaction in social networking websites on the Internet. As surveyors, therefore, it is important that, as well as the home domain, we're aware of other areas where the necessity of socialization will have an impact on the language of the speech communities we study.

4.2.6   Deaf Communities

CROSS-REFERENCE ▶ See **Section 3.2.1.1** on page 54 and in particular **Section 3.3.2** on page 84 for more about domains of use.

Deaf people form their own unique kind of communities. Many deaf people are born to hearing families. Therefore, they are scattered through other language groups. The first way they learn to communicate may be through simple gestures called home sign. The development of home signs may be influenced by the syntax of each parent's spoken language. Sometimes when deaf people who use home signs come together, a new sign language may develop. When someone who has used home signs goes to a school for the Deaf, they will need to embrace a completely different sign language. The people going to a certain school may come from numerous different speech communities, but they now constitute another speech community in the middle of other languages but not necessarily influenced by the spoken languages used around them.

REFERENCE ▶ For more on the links between language and identity with a special focus on the Deaf, see Nash (1987).

While some sign languages are related to a spoken language, for example signed English, most have nothing to do with the spoken languages around them. American Sign Language and British Sign Language are nothing like spoken English and are mutually unintelligible.

4.3   Typical Research Questions at the Free Level

Having explored social factors arising within speech communities which directly impact their language, we now move on to consider typical research questions at the Free Level. Some of the major questions are:

- What is the linguistic variation between speech varieties?
- How intelligible are language varieties to users of other varieties?
- How extensible are materials from one language variety to another?
- How do people feel about their own speech varieties?
- Which dialects are more prestigious and which have less prestige?
- What are the possibilities for partnership?

Due to the fact that language varies in every speech community we work with, we need to find the variety in each that is best suited for development as a reference dialect.

It is rare to find a survey that does not explore differences between language varieties, and so we focus first on assessing dialect intelligibility. Questions about which dialects are intelligible to the community are usually of utmost importance at the start of language development. Also, questions about partnership are important at this point. By the time development has made some progress, there are sometimes questions about the potential for literature in one language variety to be extended for use in speech communities using other varieties. Although this chapter focuses on three areas—attitudes, vitality, and intelligibility—which are typically researched in language assessment, we cannot presume that these will be the only questions which need to be explored. We must remain open to the possibility that we will be involved in language assessment projects where our partners may have questions that we have never encountered before. Ultimately, any questions that need to be studied at the Free Level will be influenced not only by the project purpose but also by questions that have been raised at the Negotiated and Restricted Levels. Our data collection should provide a holistic view of the speech communities we work with.

4.3.1   Linguistic Variation

CROSS-REFERENCE ▶ See **Section 4.1.1** on page 116 for more about language variation.

There is linguistic variation between the speech of individuals and within the set of speech varieties that are identified as a dialect. This variation may be in the form of differing pronunciations, vocabulary, or grammatical structures. Sometimes these kinds of differences are noticeable markers of different dialects, but they can also be variation that people don't notice. Sometimes they can cause loss of comprehension, but in some cases they may not cause any loss of comprehension.

In Case Study 4A we saw how the Dameli people tended to end some nouns with [o] and [ɪ] in the western villages, which have [u] and [e] in the eastern villages. If we checked a larger sample of people in the western villages, we may actually find that some individuals actually pronounce their ending [o] as [ɵ], [ə], or [ʋ]. But these alternate pronunciations may not be considered to stray from the normative [o]. Case Study 4G presents another example of pronunciation variation between villages. There can also be variation in vocabulary. For example, in various parts of America a carbonated sweet drink is called a *soda, pop, soda pop, soft drink, coke,* or *cola.*

There tends to be less tolerance for variation in grammatical structure between varieties that would still be considered to be the same language. For example, where American English uses past simple tense, British English would use present perfect tense, thus

> American: Did you finish it yet?
> British: Have you finished it yet?

Speakers of English-lexifier creoles in the Caribbean tend to think that their creole speech is just "bad" English, but English nonetheless. But speakers of British or American English would tend to find it difficult to consider it as the same language because there are so many grammatical differences. For example:

> Plural marking:
> > Standard English: the boys
> > Jamaican: di boy dem
> Past tense:
> > Standard English: He chopped wood all day.
> > Jamaican: All day he bin chop wood.

When we study language variation, we need to consider the real measureable differences and balance this with the perceptions and attitudes that people have towards the differences. They may think that a little linguistic difference is sufficient to consider them different languages, or they may think that a great linguistic difference makes little difference. However, in the latter case it may be difficult to create a writing system or literature that really can be widely used.

4.3.2   Dialect Intelligibility

For language development, one of the most important questions we need to ask about language variation is how well people speaking these different varieties actually understand each other. We need to know what is meant when people say, "Those people speak a little differently." What criteria are they using to measure these differences? What kinds of difference are they talking about? How much do these differences affect comprehension and intercommunication?

In the introduction, we defined language, and part of that definition included references to dialects. Grimes (1995:17) defined a language as "a cluster of regional or social speech varieties ("dialects"), at least one of which can be understood adequately by everyone who speaks any of the varieties in the cluster natively." Sometimes, we call this **MUTUAL INTELLIGIBILITY**.

DEFINITION ▶ MUTUAL INTELLIGIBILITY is the ability of users of two different varieties to understand each other's language. Although the term *mutual* is used, we should not assume that they understand one another equally. Intelligibility is generally asymmetric or directional, which means that, for example, group A understands group B better than B understands A.

DEFINITION ▶ INHERENT INTELLIGIBILITY is the natural, unlearned comprehension of another language that is possible without any exposure to the other variety. This understanding is possible because of linguistic similarities. For example, American English speakers understand Australian English simply because it shares features of their speech. This is because both are descended from British English.

Grimes' definition of language reminds us of the important distinction between comprehension of another language and that of another dialect. When we study another language, we increase our comprehension as we learn. However, there are elements of comprehension that do not need to be learned; they are inherent at several levels. For example, due to similarities in human experience, it is possible for two people who do not share any language to communicate simple concepts. Through gestures alone, they can communicate a simple message, such as, "Sit down." When two people speak dialects of a language, there is comprehension due to the inherent features of similarity between the two speech varieties. There are shared grammatical structures, semantics, and vocabulary. We call this **INHERENT INTELLIGIBILITY**.

Comprehension is a complex concept. It includes the ability to hear and understand the phonetic and phonological properties of speech. It includes shared knowledge of the vocabulary and the semantics being used. It includes the ability to decipher the meaning that is communicated through the grammar and syntax of what is spoken. It includes understanding the social and cultural context of the speech event.

Inherent intelligibility is comprehension that is not learned and happens naturally, but the foundation of inherent intelligibility can be built on in other ways. Sometimes, learning one variety will increase the comprehension of a third variety even upon first contact. Of course, virtually any amount of contact increases comprehension. While there may be lower inherent intelligibility between two varieties, it may only require a small amount of contact for the comprehension to be increased. This may mean that, at the beginning of the research before there was any contact, tests seem to show that people do not understand the other variety enough for it to be useful for language development. However, if the people are given the opportunity to get more familiar with it, they might be able to quickly gain comprehension. So, we not only need to ask whether another variety is intelligible but also if it may be possible to plan for comprehension and, if so, under what circumstances. Sign languages in particular seem to be easily learned by signers of other languages.

CROSS-REFERENCE ▶ See **Section 3.3.1.1** on page 76 for an example and discussion of the difference between inherent and learned bilingualism.

We need to remember that communication is far more complex than simple linguistic relatedness. More often than not, attitudes play a larger part, overruling linguistic factors. Comprehension is a voluntary activity. We need to ask whether there are any attitudes that may prevent a willingness to understand people speaking another variety and so compromise apparent inherent intelligibility. For example, in some situations there is measurably low comprehension, but people will say that they understand one another because they use the same language. In other cases, although there is very little measurable difference in the varieties, people will claim not to understand one another. Often, social factors are behind attitudes like these which determine whether people regard another variety as a different dialect or a different language. Due to these facts, it is very difficult to actually measure inherent intelligibility artificially divorced from the social context. So we must infer it from measured comprehension, which we know can be increased by contact or decreased by negative attitudes.

This shows us that the difference between bidialectalism in another dialect and bilingualism in another language is not absolute but is very much related to the particular sociolinguistic situation we are studying.

CROSS-REFERENCE ▶ See **Section 3.3.1.1** on page 76 for discussion of bidialectalism and bilingualism.

4.3.3   Extensibility

We are interested in measuring inherent intelligibility as one indication of how widely materials produced in one variety may be useable in other linguistically close varieties, in other words, how extensible they are. These materials are not only written materials but may also be audio and video materials.

Simplistically, if there are materials in one variety of a language, and there is enough inherent intelligibility with another variety, then the two groups could be expected to be able to share the same literature. Any materials produced by or for the first speech community could simply be introduced to the second on the basis of inherent intelligibility. However, there are many other relevant factors that determine the acceptability and feasibility of sharing materials.

Linguistic factors alone cannot determine whether one language variety is acceptable to users of another, as described above; we need to consider attitudes. For example:

- Do people like or dislike the people who use the other variety?
- Do the people identify with the topics, values, and ideas of the materials?
- If the materials are translated from another language, is the style appropriate?
- Do the people consider that the orthography is linguistically representative of their language variety?
- Do the people consider that the orthography is visually representative of their language variety?

These questions are not about intelligibility. They are about suitability. Because suitability depends on extra-linguistic factors, it is not correct to say that just because people understand it, the materials will meet their needs. There are strategic considerations also. In a sense, any literature, audio recording, or video is extensible if the people are willing to give the effort to learn. The feasibility of sharing literature requires consideration of the costs and benefits to overcome any differences.

CASE STUDY 4F
ENGLISH ORTHOGRAPHY
WORLDWIDE

Written English is not particularly representative of anyone's speech; a Bostonian would have difficulty understanding the speech of a Singaporean English speaker, but they can both read the same literature. They both feel that it is worthwhile to overlook features that are unrepresentative of their speech to gain the benefit of the vast amounts of literature available in English, as well as the economic benefits of the large population that use English for written communication.

While English orthography receives a lot of criticism for its many inconsistencies there are some benefits from its design that help make it more widely useable. For example, representing the final phoneme in "electric" with a "c" rather than the more "phonetic" "k" allows for consistency in spelling derived forms like "electricity." While inconsistent, it is pedagogically helpful as learners can "sight" read both forms. The cost of this is that a lot of time has to be invested in learning how to spell these somewhat less phonetic representations that violate the one sound-one symbol maxim.

Central to the idea of extensibility is the premise that we can find a reference dialect that has a potential for greater impact than other varieties. There are several factors that can be considered as criteria for a good reference dialect (Sadembouo 1989; Sanders 1977). We list them below, not ordered by importance, but grouped into those criteria that are of primary importance and those that are secondary.

A: Primary Criteria

The variety

- has been measured as having the greatest linguistic similarity with the widest range of variation in the language.
- attracts a high level of positive attitudes.
- is considered to be the most prestigious dialect.

- is commonly identified as being more "pure." This may mean that it has the least evidence of borrowing from other languages, or it may be considered more melodic or expressive.
- has the largest number of speakers who identify with it as their language.
- is used in a central location, or has easy access by major transportation routes, where many people have contact with it.
- has a high potential for people to learn it, due to its geographic centrality and the amount of contact people have with it, even if there is not a high degree of inherent intelligibility.
- is recognized and learned by people who don't speak it as their heritage language.

B: Secondary Criteria

The variety

- is considered by the people to be "easy" to adapt to, understand, and learn.
- attracts government policy or preference.
- is used for the provision of government services.
- already has a history of being written.
- has more socioeconomic importance or influence.
- is considered historically central or original.
- has religious importance or connotations.
- has speakers whose social status is acceptable.
- has institutions, such as schools or mission stations, which may help with the establishment of teaching a standardized variety.
- or
    ◊ it was spoken by a socially, politically, or financially powerful person or group.
    ◊ it belonged to individuals who were interested in language development.
    ◊ it was spoken in a location where outside agents were able to have access.
    ◊ it was spoken by individuals who outside agents had access to.

There are examples of cases in which a synthesized variety has been created and used for standardization, such as "Central Igbo" (Sadembouo 1989). This method is chosen to avoid favoritism and create unity.

However, this method has not met with much success. Basically, it requires a person to learn a new language.

A survey team can help investigate many different issues related to the extensibility of literature and other materials. Our research can also help the potential users of shared materials understand what the costs will be and thus help them evaluate if it is worth doing.

4.3.4   Partnership

Assessment is only one relatively brief and intermittent part of a language development program. However, it is significant because plans and strategy for language development need to be informed. There need to be baseline studies and studies to assess progress. Therefore, the time we spend with the people is important and can have impact on the partnership and the future of the program.

CROSS-REFERENCE ▶ See **Section 4.4.5** on page 161 for a description of participatory methods that can be used for partnership discussions.

Local people are the primary stakeholders in language development. It is their language, and their collaboration and participation is essential. Exploring what they want and what they have to offer towards their goals typically forms part of our research. Answering questions about partnership often starts by exploring how the program partners can work together with the people. There are usually questions about who is interested in partnership and how these relationships will operate.

The speech community may have resources which they can offer to promote partnership. For example, on the Rai coast of Papua New Guinea, the Sam people had specifically chosen one man from the village and sent him to get a theological degree. On the surface, the intellectual resources this man could offer particularly benefitted the partnership; it also revealed the strength of deeply held attitudes motivating a commitment to development. In many respects, this commitment is the more valuable resource. At the Free Level, research questions involving partnership focus on the existence, quality, and potential of this commitment to language development.

Our cooperation with other partner agencies, organizations, and institutions is also important. As in any relationship there can be conflicts between different partners. Each agency, organization, or institution has its own identity, methods of operation, and goals. When working with these partners, it is important to try to understand their goals and methods in order to attain the best cooperation.

4.4   Typical Free Level Research Tools

Just as there are typical research questions, there are typical research tools that we use at the Free Level within the speech community to try to provide data to answer these questions. In this final section of the Free Level chapter, we will look in detail at four different tools and remind ourselves of three others that have been useful at other levels. Just as we must remain open to the fact that we could encounter research questions that are not typical, we must be cautious in our use of these research tools. We want to continually improve the reliability and validity of our methodology. New research questions could well involve us in developing new research tools for situations that we have not yet encountered. But typical research questions also require that we look at developing new tools to answer questions we have encountered before in new ways which might improve the quality of our data. Doing this is not only a challenge, it is a necessity. Taking on this necessary challenge has led in particular to the development of **PARTICIPATORY METHODS**, a recent development in language assessment that holds great potential for improving the quality of language development.

4.4.1   Observation, Questionnaires, Interviews

We have already introduced observation, questionnaires, and interviews as research tools at the Negotiated Level. At the Free Level, these tools are used to gather information about behaviors within the speech community.

Observation is used to check information that has been given or identify information that has not been given by other means. Observation provides a valuable form of data with which to triangulate our findings from other tools. We can use observation to verify if any other languages are being used within the speech community, if there is diglossia, or if words are being borrowed.

Questionnaires can be used to focus on issues that are specific to the speech community such as socialization routines, attitudes towards their own culture and language variety, and demographic information. Questionnaires can be used with other testing methods. For example,

DEFINITION ▶ **PARTICIPATORY METHODS** are discussion methods that harness the power of a local community to solve their own problems and make their own decisions. They also serve to restrain the power of the researcher.

CROSS-REFERENCE ▶ See **Section 4.4.5** on page 161 for a description of participatory methods that can be used for partnership discussions.

WWW.SURVEYWIKI.INFO ▶ See SurveyWiki for more details about observations, interviews, questionnaires, and more. We strongly recommend you read these details and, as you develop experience in assessment, contribute to SurveyWiki.

when collecting wordlists we can ask about the people's perceptions of language similarities and differences.

At the Free Level, we carry out interviews with knowledgeable insiders such as leaders, teachers, etc. Sometimes there may be knowledgeable outsiders who have spent sufficient time within a speech community and they have become very knowledgeable about things within it. In contrast to questionnaires, interviews are not limited to a set list of questions. While informed by specific questions (such as found on the questionnaires), guided interviews are interactive, where the content of the interview is determined as much by the interviewee and the direction he or she takes in discussion as by the questions that originally sparked his or her comments. These involve preparing some open questions to guide the discussion towards relevant topics in the hope that the discussion will develop in unexpected, but fruitful ways.

4.4.2   Wordlists

The collection of wordlists is one of the easiest ways to collect linguistic data. The idea of a wordlist is that we have a set list of words, and we collect the local form and pronunciation for each of the words from different locations. The lists are digitally recorded and transcribed using a standardized phonetic system, such as the International Phonetic Alphabet (IPA).

An early use of wordlists was to try to establish a specific point in history when two languages diverged. Words were chosen for the lists that covered a number of semantic domains and word classes and were thought to be the most stable and resistant to change. Wordlists are no longer used to try to set dates, but people still try to use words that seem to be more resistant to change. Recent studies using computers and the Internet are providing empirical evidence of words that are resistant to change and borrowing. See, for example, Haspelmath and Tadmor's detailed study *Loanwords in the World's Languages* (2009).

Wordlists can be used for several purposes, including both synchronic and diachronic studies. They can be used to identify the phonetic inventory for a language and consistent phonological changes between varieties. Often they are used to get a quick, rough comparison for the potential for intelligibility. They are also used to establish genetic

WWW.SURVEYWIKI.INFO ▶ See Survey-Wiki for detailed guidance on carrying out wordlists. We strongly recommend you read these details and, as you develop experience in assessment, contribute to SurveyWiki.

relatedness between varieties. Wordlists can also be used as part of the documentation of a language.

There are various computational methods referred to as **LEXICOSTATISTICS** or **PHONOSTATISTICS** which are used for the quantitative comparison of speech varieties. Lexicostatistical methods look at the relationships between words. They have historically been used to determine historical linguistic relationships. This requires using a wordlist that samples basic vocabulary, including semantic categories, for which the words tend to change least over time. Phonostatistical methods are used to calculate phonological similarity. These calculations can be made on any set of words that adequately sample the range of sounds used in a language.

CROSS-REFERENCE ▶ See **Section 4.4.3** on page 149 for more information about RTTs.

We can collect wordlists as a quick way to indicate where we need to do more in-depth intelligibility testing. For example, Recorded Text Tests (RTT), for studying comprehension, can be time-consuming and, at the start of a survey, it isn't always clear where the best locations for reference sites should be. Potentially, if travel isn't too difficult, we can collect wordlist data from a large number of locations in a relatively short space of time and use these to identify reference sites. Wordlists have frequently been used for the creation of linguistic atlases. In such cases, words are collected and related to geographic regions, thus showing the relationship of languages or language variation to geographic regions and features.

For the purpose of language documentation, one study attempted to identify the full phonetic inventory of a language. Surveyors expanded the standard wordlist to include words that revealed phones they expected to elicit. For example, in neighboring varieties there was a name for a bird that had the [ʒ] phoneme in it. The team put this bird name on the wordlist to see if [ʒ] occurred in the language variety they were studying. Another study attempted to identify the differences between two varieties rather than the similarities. The local people told surveyors about words they used that others did not use, and words they had heard but did not use. The study found that there were about 60 words that could be identified as unique to one or the other variety. However, the words did not seem to be a barrier to language development as they were mostly names for types of things like a particular kind of fish or grass. Surveyors were able to show that, although the different varieties did have different words, everyone knew both names so there was no intelligibility problem.

DEFINITIONS ▶ **LEXICOSTATISTICS** are computational methods used to determine the lexical relationship between comparative wordlists. **PHONOSTATISTICS** are computational methods to determine the linguistic distance between phonological elements of comparative wordlists.

4.4.2.1 Rationale

Languages are changing constantly. One of the most obvious ways that they change is in the words that are used and their pronunciation. When the changes become adopted as a norm for a segment of a society we have the development of dialects. Much has been written in the history of linguistics about the mechanisms for language change; this book simply focuses on recognizing the change.

Case Study 4G below presents a sample of word list information on the Balti language of Pakistan. From a quick look at the data, it would seem that the Balti language as spoken in Khapalu and Skardu is very similar with only some small variation between these towns. Without further research it is not possible to know which form is the older or if one has diverged from the other. When words can be proven to have come from the same earlier form, we say they are **COGNATES**. With this little evidence of Balti we can only say that they are apparent cognates.

DEFINITION ▶ COGNATES are words which are descended from the same root word. We can also say a word is *cognate with* another.

CASE STUDY 4G
LANGUAGE VARIATION IN
WORDLISTS
BALTISTAN, PAKISTAN

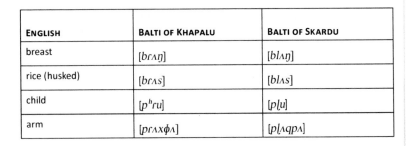

CASE STUDY 4G SOURCE ▶ Peter Backstrom (1992).

In the Balti language of northern Pakistan a survey team collected wordlists from two neighboring towns.

With just a quick glance, we see that when an [ɾ] follows a bilabial stop in the Khapalu, there is a lateral approximate [l] or [ɭ] in the speech of the residents of Skardu. Other than this, there is very little difference between the pronunciations of these words in either town.

ENGLISH	BALTI OF KHAPALU	BALTI OF SKARDU
breast	[bɾʌŋ]	[blʌŋ]
rice (husked)	[bɾʌs]	[blʌs]
child	[pʰɾu]	[pɭu]
arm	[pɾʌxɸʌ]	[pɭʌqpʌ]

In another set of words we find that some words begin with a [b] in Khapalu that begin with [β] in Skardu.

ENGLISH	BALTI OF KHAPALU	BALTI OF SKARDU
seven	[bdun]	[βdun]
eight	[bgyət]	[βgyt]
one hundred	[bgyə]	[βgyə]
(he) ran	[bgyuks]	[βgyuks]

Again, there is very little difference between the pronunciations of these words in either town.

We have to be careful about calling words cognate and making inferences about languages due to shared vocabulary. There are many words that appear to be cognates, and there are cognates that don't look very similar. Many languages share words that have been borrowed from somewhere. English and French, for example, have the following vocabulary in common: *weekend, cigarette,* and *television.* But we would be very unwise to think that English and French were closely related linguistically simply because they share these words. Although they are both Indo-European languages, they are from different branches of that linguistic family tree, the Germanic and Romance branches. And thousands of years ago, when Germanic and Romance branches diverged from some proto-Indo-European speech form, the people did not come from a culture where they spoke about smoking *cigarettes* at the *weekend* while watching *television.*

If two languages have a significant percentage of vocabulary items which are cognates, it means that they must be genetically related; they must, at some point in the past, have been united as one language. If we draw up a list of **LEXEMES** that are fundamental to all the cultures we are working with (and therefore represent words which users are unlikely to have to borrow), we can compare these between language varieties. Where we find similarities, we are also likely to find some degree of genetic relatedness. As that relatedness increases, we may also find more inherent intelligibility, though not always.

DEFINITION ► Lexemes are the minimal units of meaning that words can be reduced to. So, while English has *walked, walks,* and *walking,* the underlying lexeme is *walk.*

4.4.2.2 Methodology

As was said above, there are different reasons for collecting wordlists, and there are different procedures to follow for the different uses. Wordlists are versatile, and with a bit of creativity, we can adapt them for a wide range of linguistic purposes. However, many things can go wrong when collecting wordlists. They have been used to make unwarranted inferences about language relationships. Therefore, it is important to follow established procedures when available and carefully think through the meaning of the evidence.

The first step is to identify the list of words we will use. For most studies, there really isn't any reason to create new wordlists. In some locations and with some language groups there are established lists that have been used for years. If there is any desire to consider diachronic change, we should be careful to compile wordlists which share vocabulary with wordlists that previous surveys have used so that we can compare data. Most lists have 100 to 400 words on them and are based on the Swadesh list first created by Morris Swadesh in the 1950s (Hymes, Swadesh, and Sherzer 1971).

To create new lists we group words on the list according to **SEMANTIC FIELD**. Common fields include parts of the body, natural items, animals, foods, color terms, numbers, pronouns, and verbs. None of the words on a wordlist should be taboo, specialized, foreign to local culture, onomatopoeia (sound words), compound words, or vague in that they could refer to several things. It is generally considered that borrowed words should not be included. However, in some situations there may be reason to allow for borrowed words on a wordlist. If we are studying a speech community that uses a lot of borrowed words in their everyday speech, then the exclusion of borrowed words would present an unreal picture of language use. If our focus is on the comprehension of everyday speech, we base our understanding of extensibility on the actual speech performance of the speech community. If borrowed words are included, we need to be careful about our interpretation of the numbers computed for lexical similarity and the inferences drawn from those numbers.

A new list needs to be pilot tested to identify any potential problems with the words chosen or the elicitation procedures. Usually, we elicit words using a LWC, as long as the language helper is sufficiently proficient in the LWC. There should be locally established protocols for how words are elicited. For example, verbs should be elicited in a standardized sentence

DEFINITION ► SEMANTIC FIELD: a set of lexemes that are connected in meaning or type. In English, *head, arm,* and *tongue* are all part of the semantic field of body parts. In constructing a wordlist, we also want different word classes. For example *blue, broken,* and *big* are in the semantic field of adjectives.

for consistency. New surveyors need to practice eliciting wordlists to become aware of potential problems.

Once the wordlist has been pilot tested, and the surveyors are trained, we identify a selection of locations where we want to collect wordlist data. Sometimes a survey team may gather information from every place where the language is spoken, but often languages are spread over too large a region and the team needs to be selective. Members of the speech community should be involved in decisions as to where and how data is collected, as well as being involved in the data collection itself. There are a number of factors to consider when selecting elicitation locations, such as

- geographically central locations,
- population centers,
- alternate potential centers suggested by consultants
- locations at an extreme distance from the center, and
- isolated locations.

Participants are selected in each of these locations. Be sure that the language consultant has all of his or her teeth for clear articulation. They must speak the language as their heritage language, be knowledgeable about the language, and not prone to giving words from the LWC.

CASE STUDY 4H
SPITTING WORDLISTS
NIGER

CASE STUDY 4H SOURCE ▶ Annette Harrison, SIL Central Africa Group.

During my first survey in Niger, our fieldwork coincided with Ramadan, the time when devout Muslims fast from sunrise to sunset. The most pious do not even swallow their own saliva, and so there is quite a bit of spitting during that time. I was taking a wordlist in the south of the country. The gentleman who had been appointed by the group to pronounce the words for me was seated facing me. I noticed that as we went through the list, his speech began to sound "mushy," and he looked more and more uncomfortable. Finally, he turned to the side and spat—he had been holding his saliva in his mouth while giving me the wordlist. As a devout Muslim, he couldn't swallow his saliva, but I had not been pausing long enough in recording the elicitation to allow him time to spit. Once I realized this, we continued through the wordlist, pausing at intervals for him to empty his mouth.

The surveyor elicits the local equivalent of the terms on the list using an LWC or with the help of a trained language helper. The participant's words are recorded in two ways: firstly, by transcribing them using the International Phonetic Alphabet (IPA), or a similar established system, and secondly, by using a digital audio recorder. If at all possible, video recording is also considered to be a good practice in that it provides more information on the pronunciation, such as visual clues of lip-rounding, than an audio recording. It is also considered to be a good practice to collect and check the wordlist with a second person in each location. This adds to the time required but provides quality control and gives an opportunity for further discussion about words and language usage.

As with the construction, pilot testing and administration of wordlists, there are also standard protocols for analyzing the data they provide. Short wordlists, with 100 to 200 words, can be analyzed using lexicostatistical or phonostatistical methods of comparison. These calculations cover a wide range of methods including the very conjectural visual inspection method, the Blair lexical similarity comparison method (Blair 1990), and the more empirical Levenshtein Distance Method (Gooskens 2007). If it is important to determine that the words are true cognates, then the comparative method should be used to analyze the genetic relationships between languages. There are also computer programs to help us with comparative analysis.

WWW.SURVEYWIKI.INFO ▶ See the **Lexicostatistics**, **Phonostatistics**, **Levenshtein distance** and **Blair Method** pages on SurveyWiki.

Refer briefly to the Balti example above in Case Study 4G to help understand the comparative method. Each pair of words is lined up comparing like phone to like phone. We identify all of the times a phone is paired with an exact match and the number of times it is paired with a similar phone. An algorithm is used to determine the predictability of each pairing which is why the use of a computer program is helpful. This identifies the consistent differences between the two varieties. In this way, even though two words may look different, they can be proven to be cognates.

Sometimes, when interviewing people about language variation, they will say, "They sound different over there." Wordlists can also provide evidence of phonological variation between locations, which can explain such comments. As was shown in the Balti example above in Case Study 4G, we can identify consistent patterns showing the variation between varieties. When we compare the amount of lexical similarity with the types of phonological differences, we are able to gain an impression as to what the people may be referring to. If there are a lot of lexical differences and significant phonological differences between the varieties, then we know that it really must sound quite different to the interviewee. However, if there really wasn't much lexical difference and there were only minor phonological differences, then the person must only be referring to a slight, noticeable difference.

4.4.2.3 Evaluation

Wordlists are often relatively easy to compile and administer in the field and the data they provide is relatively easy to analyze and present. There are a number of computer programs that can help analyze wordlist data and, in the wider field of linguistics, wordlists are a very common form of data collection. This means our results have value not just to the speech communities we work with but with the wider scientific community also. Many wordlists we use around the world are standardized, and this means that we can easily and validly compare the data between languages and dialects, both synchronically and diachronically.

There are, however, some problems with collecting wordlist data. The first is in choosing the items that make up the list. Despite our best research, if any of the words are in fact borrowed from neighboring varieties, this may weaken any conclusions we make about genetic similarity. Numbering systems are sometimes borrowed. Sometimes there is really no way to know whether a term is borrowed from another variety or not. It is only recently that research has confirmed that certain concepts are in fact more resistant to borrowing than others (Haspelmath and Tadmor 2009).

Another common criticism of wordlists is that languages really do not have completely equivalent terms for concepts. *Sensei*, the Japanese term for the English word *teacher*, for example, also means *doctor* or *pastor*. Thus, it can be hard to know whether the term offered by the participant is actually equivalent to the term on the wordlist or not, unless we are careful in not just our selection of words but also our administration of wordlists. For this reason, a good word list will include a narrowly defined semantic range as an annotation on the item that may be problematic.

DEFINITION ▶ DOUBLETS are words which are distinct in meaning in one language but not in another. *Leg* and *foot* are distinct in English, for example, but in Japanese the word *ashi* is used for both.

Sometimes parts of numbers are repeated, such as in the items *forty-one*, *forty-two*, and *forty-three*. If these are included in the statistical analysis they introduce a bias. If we inadvertently elicit **DOUBLETS** in our wordlist data, what we initially thought were separate items become the same. These types of problems also mean we have less data to work with.

Therefore, if we suspect that items on the list may be doublets, we need to allow for this by increasing the overall amount of vocabulary we collect.

There are many other problems that can arise when some words are considered taboo in some languages or embarrassing to discuss. If the language helper is not sufficiently fluent in the language being used for elicitation, there can be further confusion and discomfort. Eliciting verbs can also be difficult if any of the inflectional information becomes confused.

Another problem involves working with the language helper. Sometimes they do not fully understand what we are after. If we do not know the language, as is usually the case, then we don't really know what we are getting. More than one surveyor has found out later that the language helper was playing word association. In other words, when the surveyor said *water*, the language helper said *river*.

Finally, there are a number of ways that the words can be compared and similarity percentages calculated. In the past, people used the visual inspection process, just deciding if they looked alike. This is very unreliable since words that look alike are not necessarily related. Furthermore, if someone else tries to repeat the counting process, they may not consider the same words as looking alike. A person who is very knowledgeable about a language family may be able to draw valuable information from such a visual inspection, but it is not a method to be used by someone with less familiarity. Even with familiarity, there are problems with wordlist analysis. Campbell and Poser (2008:200) warn us that if we compare enough data, we are likely to see correlation purely through chance. It is important for us to be able to demonstrate that whatever items of significance we find are not due to chance but due to relatedness.

4.4.3   Recorded Text Tests

A Recorded Text Test (RTT) is a short measurement of a person's comprehension of another language variety. The person listens to a short story from one place and demonstrates his or her level of comprehension.

Apart from the less-common use of RTTs for measuring bilingualism that we saw earlier at the Negotiated Level, there are two ways that RTTs are typically used at the Free Level. Both relate to assessing intelligibility of language varieties.

WWW.SURVEYWIKI.INFO ► See Survey-Wiki for detailed guidance on carrying out RTTs. We strongly recommend you read these details and, as you develop experience in assessment, contribute to SurveyWiki.

CROSS-REFERENCE ► See **Section 3.4.6.2** on page 109 for a description of the use of RTTs for assessing bilingualism.

CROSS-REFERENCE ► See **Section 4.1.2** on page 116 for a description of reference dialects.

CROSS-REFERENCE ► See **Section 4.3.1** on page 133 for more background on the Free Level research questions associated with dialect intelligibility.

As we saw earlier, in order to make the task of language development manageable, we need to identify varieties that can serve as reference dialects acting as common mediums of communication for speech communities that use related varieties. The identification of reference dialects is possible because in many speech communities, people who use secondary varieties understand the most common varieties adequately. On this basis, one of the ways we typically use RTTs is to identify a reference dialect as a precursor to producing a written, or oral, standard for language development.

4.4.3.1 Rationale

NOTE ► RTTs can potentially be adapted for use with sign languages. Instead of an audio text, test takers are shown a video of a signed story with signed questions on video which they then answer.

CROSS-REFERENCE ► See **Section 4.3.1** on page 133 for more background on the Free Level research questions associated with dialect intelligibility.

As explained earlier, it is difficult to separate intelligibility from other factors, such as attitude. Therefore, the best we can do is to test comprehension and try to eliminate other variables, such as attitudes, as much as possible. If we present a language helper with a sample of a language variety they have never heard before and they can demonstrate comprehension, then we can feel we are getting close to intelligibility.

4.4.3.2 Methodology

RTTs have been used for decades. In this time, as their strengths and weaknesses have become apparent, we have adapted the original test design as described by Casad (1974) to produce more appropriate variations to the original test. To distinguish it from other more recent methods, we now refer to Casad's original version as RTT-Q because it is a recorded text test RTT which measures comprehension by asking participants questions (Q) about the text they have heard. A variation to this methodology for use with groups for a rapid appraisal (RA) is called the RTT-RA method. Another variation requires the participant to retell (R) the story, so it is referred to as the RTT-R method.

RTT-Q development starts at our primary research stage where we identify locations of varieties which we think might work as reference dialects. We may use wordlist data to give us an idea of where these might be. Other sociolinguistic data may also help us such as population centers, locations with a dialect that is considered prestigious. We call these locations reference sites. Then we identify test sites, places where we want to find out whether the reference site varieties are understood.

At our first reference site, we elicit a story, in reference variety 1 (RV1). The story is someone's personal experience and not widely known in the speech community we are working with. From this story, we create 15–20 questions which we have translated into RV1. These questions are then pilot tested until we have ten that give reliable results. In other words, the questions are suitable when at least ten RV1 speakers score close to 100 percent. This is done to assure that the quality of the language sample and the test are such that someone can score 100 percent. When others score less than 100 percent we will know that it is due to something other than the quality of the recording or test, and that their unfamiliarity with the language variety is a probable explanation for the lower score. We repeat this procedure at each of the reference sites we have identified when we come to them on a survey so that we have stories and questions in RV1, RV2, etc.

At a test site, we carry out a number of tasks to prepare for the testing as Table 6 shows. First, if the speech variety of the test site is not one of the reference varieties for which we already have a test, we construct a **HOMETOWN TEST** in the local test variety (TV1) in the same way as we constructed the reference tests. The hometown test will serve as a screening device to verify that a person is competent in the local language variety and capable of passing the test. It also helps us become more familiar with the speech community we are testing and their language variety. Second, we translate the ten questions we created for each of the reference varieties we want to test (RV1, RV2, etc.) into TV1 and create the final test recordings. Third, we translate and record instructions and a short practice test in the TV1. The practice test serves as a warm-up to help train the people in the testing methodology.

DEFINITION ► A **HOMETOWN TEST** is a test in which people are tested on a language sample that is meant to represent their own language variety. This serves as a screening device to verify that a person is competent in this language variety and capable of passing the test.

PREPARATION PHASE	IN VILLAGE 1	IN VILLAGE 2	IN VILLAGE 3
RECORD A STORY IN	dialect 1	dialect 2	dialect 3
CREATE QUESTIONS IN	dialect 1	dialect 2	dialect 3
THIS CREATES TEST	story 1	story 2	story 3
RECORD INSTRUCTIONS IN	dialect 1	dialect 2	dialect 3
PILOT TEST	story 1	story 2	story 3
RECORD THE QUESTIONS FOR TEST STORY 1 IN		dialect 2	dialect 3
RECORD THE QUESTIONS FOR TEST STORY 2 IN	dialect 1		dialect 3
RECORD THE QUESTIONS FOR TEST STORY 3 IN	dialect 1	dialect 2	

TABLE 6 ► Procedures to follow in order to prepare an RTT.

To administer the test (see Table 7), we play the recording of the initial instructions, the practice test, and the hometown test in their local variety.

TEST PHASE	IN VILLAGE 1	IN VILLAGE 2	IN VILLAGE 3
PLAY INSTRUCTIONS IN	dialect 1	dialect 2	dialect 3
PLAY PRACTICE TEST IN	dialect 1	dialect 2	dialect 3
PLAY HOMETOWN TEST IN	dialect 1	dialect 2	dialect 3
WITH QUESTIONS IN	dialect 1	dialect 2	dialect 3
PLAY TEST OF	story 1	story 1	story 1
WITH QUESTIONS IN	dialect 1	dialect 2	dialect 3
ASK POST TEST QUESTIONS IN	dialect 1	dialect 2	dialect 3
PLAY TEST OF	story 2	story 2	story 2
WITH QUESTIONS IN	dialect 1	dialect 2	dialect 3
ASK POST TEST QUESTIONS IN	dialect 1	dialect 2	dialect 3

We use these initial tests to screen participants; it identifies people who are possibly not mentally capable or are too scared or emotionally confused by the situation, and they are excused from further testing. If they perform well enough on this, we assume they are capable of managing the test procedure. Next, they go on to do the actual test and hear the RV1 story interspersed with questions we translated into TV1. Participants thus hear a story in another dialect and questions in their own dialect. We record their answers to these questions and will later score them to see how well they understand the reference variety. We do not tell the participants where the stories come from.

We administer the test to at least ten participants in each test location. It is not necessary to use a sampling method for choosing participants because the principle is that everyone should have the same proficiency, if we are measuring inherent intelligibility. However, if at all possible, we want to be selective to try to avoid people who have had significant contact with the other varieties. If this is not possible because the people have had so much contact, then intelligibility may not be a relevant question.

For the RTT-RA (rapid appraisal) adaptation of the RTT-Q methodology, the testing is not done with individuals but with groups of people. RTT-RAs are a quick way to test a number of people, but we need to be careful to observe the group dynamics. One person will probably dominate the answering, but we do not know if that person's answers are really representative of the group. The tester needs to take good notes on the whole interaction as to who says what and how various people respond.

At the beginning of this section, an adaptation to the RTT-Q methodology called RTT-R (for retelling) was introduced. In the pilot testing of the RTT-R story the people are asked to retell the story. Then, the tester notes which elements of the story are considered critical for the retelling. When the story is subsequently replayed in another location, the participants are asked once again to retell the story, and the tester notes which elements of the story were included. These responses are compared with the responses gathered in the pilot test and a score of similarity is assigned.

FIGURE 7 ▶ Heidi Anderson, working with SIL International in Cameroon, carries out a recorded text test.

After each participant has taken the test, whichever adaptation is used, we recommend taking them through a post-test questionnaire. A post-test questionnaire asks for the persons impressions from the test:

- do they think they know where the language samples are from,
- do they feel like they understood the language samples,
- where do people use their language just like them,
- where do people use their language just a little different, but they can understand, and
- where do people use their language, but it is so different that it is hard to understand?

This can be an extremely valuable way of assessing the quality of the test we have designed as well as providing us with very important background information about how well the participant thinks they have done and why. We can also use this to gain more information on their perceptions of similarities and differences with other varieties.

It is important to remember that we are testing to find out how well other locations understand the reference variety rather than the other way around. RTT testing is complicated and requires that the procedure be well thought through. The process is further complicated by the fact that we cannot test the TV2 and TV3 stories when we first go to village 1 because we have not been to villages 2 or 3 yet. So, we may actually have to go to some villages more than once to do all the necessary testing. This is another factor to consider when planning a survey. We do not want to have to make multiple trips to the most difficult places to reach.

4.4.3.3 Evaluation

The RTT is a complex tool to develop and use. It takes a lot of resources to produce even one RTT. We need to find good language helpers, good texts, make clear recordings, develop good questions, and find good test takers. If the quality of our work in any of these areas falters, the reliability and validity of the test becomes questionable. Therefore, like all the tools we use, we should consider that the data we collect with RTTs are only one small view of a much bigger picture.

The collection of good texts is very difficult. Often people say they don't know any good stories, or they give a very short story. Another problem is when the story is about an experience that would be very foreign to most people in the culture, such as a story about flying in an airplane in a culture where few people have ever been in an airplane. Furthermore, a short story as is typically elicited for an RTT, only provides a small sample of the language. Intelligibility varies depending, on the topic, among other things. The use of specialized vocabulary by the story narrator may create a problem.

The reliability and validity of RTT data are also questionable. For one thing, unless we are very careful in how we set up and administer RTTs, we risk invalidating the data we collect. If one participant tells others about the story before they are tested, the data will be invalid. What is more problematic though is that because tests are constructed using stories and questions that vary from group to group by topic, quality, or some other factor, we cannot rely on comparisons of their data. In this respect, RTTs stand in contrast to wordlists whose data are much more comparable. Table 8 summarizes the pros and cons of RTT-Qs and RTT-Rs.

RTT-Q	RTT-R
In spite of the many potential problems with the method it has been used for many years in many surveys and has proven to provide useful data.	In spite of the potential improvements of this methodology it has not been validated in any way nor has it proven its usefulness over many years as the RTT-Q.
Content questions are unnatural and may be misunderstood by those who have not received formal education. In some cultures, questions are not asked for the sake of an answer but to promote learning by reflection. Thus, the purpose of questioning can be confusing.	The retelling of the story is very natural. Even with the RTT-Q method, people will often want to retell the story.
Translation of questions in each location can be time-consuming and a point of potential error.	Does not require any translation of questions. Does involve making sure that the key elements of the story are those that the local people perceive, not the surveyor.
Respondent answers can be analyzed fairly quickly but this assumes that the answers we have are the only possible answers. Therefore, it does not allow for alternative interpretation of questions which may be more natural to people in different cultures.	Recording and analysis of retelling is time-consuming and much more reliant on the participation of a language helper.
Score for an individual on each test is only based on ten points of information.	Score for an individual on each test is based on as many as 40 points of information.
Respondents may feel that they are limited to only answering the questions.	Respondents feel free to offer more information regarding their comprehension and attitudes about the language used in the story.

TABLE 8 ▶ The advantages and disadvantages of RTT-Qs and RTT-Rs.

We mentioned at the Negotiated Level how, if we are testing for learned intelligibility, we will need to test a variety of texts and not just one story. Testing only one narrative on a sample of only ten participants in a speech community assumes that inherent intelligibility is the only way that participants would be able to understand the text. However, many language situations are very complex and we cannot always assume that no one in the speech community has had any contact with users of the varieties we are testing and that there are not some levels of learned intelligibility. In some areas of the world, for example Papua New Guinea, speech communities are relatively small and contact with surrounding groups is therefore hard to avoid. Not only can it be difficult to find a story that not everyone has heard before, we cannot be sure that other people understand it because of learned intelligibility (Landweer 2009).

QUOTE ▶ *Separating inherent from acquired intelligibility in terms of their effects on RTT scores is most clearly impossible when testing involves communities speaking related varieties that are also in close geographic proximity.* (O'Leary 1994:5)

RTT construction and administration relies on a great deal of cooperation from the community. Firstly, in each reference or test location, we need to have a helper who knows the variety being spoken as well as a language we speak. They need to be willing to help create the test and record or interpret answers given by participants. Scoring is thus dependent on the ability of a local language helper. Taking the tests can also be tiring and the respondent's boredom or exhaustion can hinder their performance. In some speech communities, our test-taking procedures may conflict with local cultural practices; isolating someone for testing or wearing headphones may be a problem.

CASE STUDY 4J
TESTING WOMEN
PAKISTAN

CASE STUDY 4J SOURCE ▶ Ken Decker, International Language Assessment Coordinator, SIL International

Men of the SIL North Pakistan survey team were restricted from having any contact with women in most villages. So, on one survey we wanted to test both men and women to have a comparison of the differences between the genders on an RTT intelligibility test. First, the survey men had to build relationships with the men of the village before they could get permission to bring the survey women in to the village. During one point in the testing of the women, some became afraid that their voices were being recorded, which would have been forbidden. After they were reassured that there was no recording, the testing continued. But then one of the women recognized the voice of a male relative in one of the stories. She was concerned that this would be considered immoral for her to listen to his voice and both she, and some others, refused to participate any further.

4.4.4 Extensibility Testing

NOTE ▶ In this section, we are using the term "literature" in a very broad sense that is not just restricted to writing. In using this term, we therefore include other media such as audio for oral cultures and both video and printed versions of sign languages.

The methods that have been described up to this point have been considered as tools to be used at an early stage of investigation for understanding language variation. Wordlists and RTTs are usually conducted to predict the extensibility of materials. The following discussion of extensibility is primarily concerned with investigation where language development is underway or at least beginning. We want to test the extensibility of proposed or previously developed orthography, literature, or audio-visual materials. At the time of writing, there are no standardized testing procedures for extensibility. Since we are describing the testing of a number of different things, it may not be possible to develop one procedure.

4.4.4.1 Rationale

In situations where no literature exists, it is impossible to know how widely literature, once produced, could be used. Attempting to evaluate the extensibility of literature is of value, however, even if only its indicators—not extensibility itself—can be investigated. Once language development is underway, programs typically produce literature in a particular language variety. In order to maximize the value of these resources, we can carry out extensibility testing to find out whether users of any other language variety could also use this literature.

A number of situations may create a need for extensibility testing. For example, a program may have developed an orthography and materials written in one dialect, but we do not know if people in neighboring related dialects can also use these. Or maybe literature has been produced, but is not widely used. We may do extensibility testing as one way to assess the problem. Of course, it is better to do testing at each step in language development. Therefore, an orthography should be widely tested when it is being developed, as should beginning literature.

The extensibility of various components of language development should be considered as early as possible in the development of a written language. Furthermore, the consideration of extensibility needs to be an overt component of the language development strategy. For example, in the development of an orthography, the symbols chosen to represent the sounds or signs of the language should be tested to see how widely people identify with these decisions. When materials are translated into the language, these need to be tested to see if the word and idiom choices can be made in such a way as to reach a wider audience.

4.4.4.2 Methodology

Testing for extensibility is very difficult and time consuming. There are no widely agreed-upon tools or procedures for doing extensibility testing. Surveyors have tried several methods which are similar to checking

REFERENCE ▶ For more on extensibility, see from page vii in Mildred Larson's foreword *Meaning-Based Translation: A Guide to Cross-Language Equivalence* (1984).

procedures for translated materials. Enlisting the help of a literate, native user of the language of the test materials is essential. Bergman (2001:90) proposes that the best way to test extensibility is probably by teaching literacy classes and comparing performance between a hometown situation and a test site.

The first thing to consider when planning extensibility testing is to identify the "unit of work" for the study—how large of a social network should be considered so as to meet the needs of the entire social network. We want the materials to have the widest possible coverage. It may only be possible to create materials that reach a dialect of a larger language. This may be indicated by weak social network links with speakers of other dialects. Alternatively, it may be possible to design materials that reach people who call their language by a different name. This may be indicated by stronger than expected social connections across perceived language boundaries. Researching these possibilities will mainly be done through interviews with knowledgeable insiders of the speech community.

Before beginning a language development program, it is important to conduct research to identify the reference dialect, the best language variety center. This is identified as having prestige and a dialect with the best potential for extensibility. We may use observation, questionnaires, interviews, wordlists, and RTTs to help identify the best center. However, this research should be considered tentative until language development efforts begin.

Cross-Reference ▶ For more on the identification of reference dialects see Section 4.3.3 on page 136.

We have already proposed that extensibility testing should be a part of language development activities. Before efforts are begun on an orthography, there may be oral or video products that are developed. The testing of these materials may help to further identify the best reference dialect. If an orthography or literature has already been developed, we may need to determine if they are adequate for the original speech community they were intended for. In other words, we find out if the people whose language they are based on understand and use them. If the people they were intended for cannot understand them or do not accept them, there is little reason to expect that anyone else can either.

Next, someone, who is in another speech community, who is unfamiliar with the original text, reads it, or we read it to them. First, we ask if they can understand it and what they understand it to be saying. If there does seem to be some comprehension, we then ask them specific questions about each sentence to evaluate how well they understand the writer's original ideas. If we do this first as a hometown test and then with the people we are working with, we can compare results to see whether extensibility is viable.

If problems arise, a further procedure can be used to identify specific differences. If the test participant does not understand something, we can explain what the text was trying to communicate. Then the participant can try to propose a better local translation. This can be done well with a committee. If the written form of a word does not seem to represent the local pronunciation, they can propose something more acceptable. In this way, we get specific data illustrating differences within the speech community, if they exist.

In order to improve our ability to assess extensibility of written materials, it helps if we understand more about the decisions that were made in the language development process. For example, with the construction of an orthography, there may be reasons why extra symbols have been included that are not linguistically justified. If there were a people who spoke a variety of English, but had never seen written English, they may react to several different letters being used to represent the same sound (For example: <k>, <q>, <c>, <ch> = [*k*]).

NOTE ▸ <> are used to indicate that the symbol in between is a symbol in an orthography.

[ ] are used to indicate that the symbol in the center is a **phone**.

DEFINITION ▸ A **PHONE** is the smallest unit of sound in speech.

CASE STUDY 4L SOURCE ▸ Ken Decker, International Language Assessment Coordinator, SIL.

CASE STUDY 4K
BELIZE KRIOL
COLOMBIA

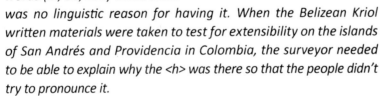

In the construction of an orthography for Belize Kriol, the people wanted to add <h> to the end of several short words (Ih, ah, deh) when there was no linguistic reason for having it. When the Belizean Kriol written materials were taken to test for extensibility on the islands of San Andrés and Providencia in Colombia, the surveyor needed to be able to explain why the <h> was there so that the people didn't try to pronounce it.

Readers from different dialects of a language can read the same written word and sound very different depending on their individual interpretations of the written symbols. Therefore, if the people being tested cannot read the material for themselves, a reader needs to be found that can read the materials for the people, using a locally natural pronunciation.

CASE STUDY 4L
GULLAH TESTING
THE BAHAMAS

A survey team wanted to take the Gullah New Testament from the United States to the Bahamas to test if people there could use and understand it. One aim was to see if anyone could read it using a Bahamian accent. Before leaving for the Bahamas, the team found a man that could read the Gullah materials in this way. Because of this, the survey team could assume extensibility for pronunciation and then narrow the research focus to the identification of other factors such as vocabulary and semantics.

CASE STUDY 4L SOURCE ▸ David Holbrook, former SIL Caribbean surveyor.

4.4.4.3 Evaluation

As stated above, extensibility testing can be difficult and time consuming. There are many variables involved and a number of problems that we might encounter when doing extensibility testing. The following incomplete list includes both technical and non-technical concerns.

- Literature can vary from easy to difficult based on content and style.
- Native-authored materials can be different from translated materials, and the quality of either can make a difference.
- The cultural content and perspectives may differ, whether they are within the reader's or writer's culture, or from an outsider's culture or perspective.
- The degree of contextualization of "foreign" content and concepts may cause loss of comprehension.
- The quality and adequacy of the materials, for example poor quality of a video or an orthography that does not cover all the necessary phonemic differentiation, may cause loss of comprehension.
- The written form of a language is often somewhat different from the spoken form, and an illiterate person may not understand the written form of the language being read.
- The accent of the reader may be difficult for the listeners.

- The person being tested may have negative attitudes towards writing or the variety of the language that has been written.
- The person being tested may be tired, distracted, or unhealthy.

Even if testing is done early, and the audio-video materials, orthography, literature, or translation gains wide acceptance, the people may still change their minds years later and want something else.

4.4.5   Participatory Methods

Procedures known as *Participatory Rural Assessment* (PRA) methods have been used by a number of development agencies worldwide for some years now. The methods and philosophy have evolved over the years and the most recent derivation is referred to as *Participatory Learning and Action* (PLA). While PRA had an emphasis on outsiders doing investigative data collection, PLA focuses more on empowering local people to do their own research to solve their own problems. This book does not advocate any one particular philosophical approach. Our primary concern here is that we learn to value the involvement of the local people, whose language we are studying and who will experience the greatest impact from research and development efforts.

4.4.5.1 *Rationale*

Recent developments in participatory methods have a lot to offer language assessment. Participatory assessment is research that involves members of the language group in the study of their own speech community. Through these methods, the people are able to provide their own input in their own way, analyze choices available to them and thus help determine the particular process necessary to achieve language development goals as they see them. There are a number of reasons why a participatory approach is beneficial. Firstly, by using this approach, we can model partnership while we carry out survey; participatory assessment cannot work without participation from all parties. Secondly, it engages the speech community to think critically about their language status and needs and, through this process, raises awareness of the latent potential for language development. The overall impact of participatory assessment is to improve the sustainability of language development.

WWW.SURVEYWIKI.INFO ▶ See Survey-Wiki for detailed guidance on participatory methods. We strongly recommend you read these details and, as you develop experience in assessment, contribute to SurveyWiki.

This is because, having contributed the input to the program, the people are more willing to take responsibility for its outcome.

Truong and Garcez (2009) emphasize the importance of dialogue to participatory methods. As dialogue is the medium used to collect data, partnership is a vital prerequisite to enable open and fluent dialogue. Through the medium of dialogue in participatory methods, we can enhance speech communities' ownership of programs and thus avoid being seen as "helicopter researchers" (Karin Lutter in Yamada 2007) who fly in, gather data, and vanish as quickly as they came, never to be seen again. This scenario is an increasing reality for local communities, and there is evidence that they are, quite rightly, beginning to resist research carried out on these terms (Yamada 2007:271). We can avoid this through a focus on partnership and the ethos of the participatory approach to language development at the Free Level as we work with the speech community on issues of specific concern to them.

4.4.5.2 Methodology

There are various tools that are used for different purposes as part of a participatory approach. When considering research of a speech community, the most important principle is to find culturally appropriate ways to meet and interact with the people. While the easiest way may be to simply arrive and start asking questions, this is probably the least effective. There are often proper social, legal, and political protocols for entering communities—a certain official may have to give permission first, followed by the agreement of a community leader. Not following these protocols may greatly impede the success of the research. Realizing the importance of partnership, we should aim to enter a speech community through existing channels of relationship, perhaps with our partners at the Negotiated Level who may already be aware of required protocols. If there is an outside agency or institution that has good relationships with the people, for example, we can carry out our research by joining that existing partnership.

There are a number of different tools used in participatory discussion to help facilitate the thinking and expression of ideas and information. Some of the general tools include Appreciative Inquiry, Cause and Effect Tree, Stakeholder Analysis, and Force Field Analysis. Some of the tools that have been adapted specifically for survey use include the Dialect

Mapping Tool, the Bilingualism tool, and the Domains of Language Use tool.

The Dialect Mapping tool will be briefly described here to give a demonstration of how a participatory method can be used in a survey. This method is used to learn what the people already know and feel about language variation in their speech community. It also helps them to start thinking about a variety that could be used for language development. In a group situation, the people are asked to write the names of individual speech communities on slips of paper. These are arranged on the ground in an approximately geographic configuration. The people are then asked to think about which villages speak the same as they, the villages that speak a little different but can still be understood, and then those who are considered part of the speech community but cannot be understood. Large loops of string are provided so that they can put a loop around all the speech communities that speak alike. They can then place a piece of paper with the number (1) by the locations they understand the best, then a number (2) on those that are understood second best, etc. Next, the people can consider what languages they speak with others. These decisions are marked by colorful geometric shapes laid next to the village names. Next they could discuss which varieties or locations would best serve as a basis for development of their language. Other questions could also be asked.

A process like this could be replicated in a number of locations. Then representatives from the different locations could be brought together to gain a wider consensus. Other tools could be used to help them think through and begin planning the next steps toward language development.

4.4.5.3 Evaluation

Participatory methods are a relatively new approach to language development. As a result, we have very little experience in applying these methods specifically to language assessment. However, this also means that the field is ripe for development of ideas and experimentation provided that we combine them with other tools that have a proven track record.

Rather than being a tool for measuring anything, participatory methods are an approach to learning. There is also an important mindset of respecting the knowledge of the people we are working with and their rights to be involved in the research. An important part of this mindset is the ability to relinquish control to the community so that assessment is carried out at times and in ways which are of maximum benefit to *them*. With time schedules often tight on survey trips, this can be very difficult to coordinate. It also means that there are fewer guarantees that the data provided by the people will be exactly the data that we would otherwise determine we need to fulfill the purpose of the survey. However, it may also prove to be just the information we really need.

One of the biggest concerns when using participatory methods is that of power relations. Often the outsider is viewed as having greater power in planning, and discussion and local people will feel they have to go along with what they think the outsider wants. Of course, historically, outsiders have forced their preferences. Sometimes the outsider is viewed as the necessary source of funding and local people do not consider their own resources. We need to work through these barriers if the local people are to be empowered and released to accomplish their own development.

4.5   Further Reading

Language Classification by Numbers **by April McMahon and Robert McMahon (2005)**

> Begins with a detailed description of the comparative method and shows how this has fared over the years. It has a good section on lexicostatistics which covers some of the pitfalls of using it as a method. Also has a good section on probability.

Historical Linguistics **by Lyle Campbell (2000)**

> This book, in its second edition, provides a thorough description of phonological, lexical, semantic, and syntactic changes that happen to a language. Linguistic classification and other topics related to historical linguistics are discussed.

Language Classification: History and Method **by Lyle Campbell and William Poser (2008)**

> This good introduction to history of comparative linguistics is a very challenging read for anyone using wordlists. Campbell and Poser highlight weaknesses with the methodology and ask us to consider alternatives.

Loanwords in the World's Languages: A Comparative Handbook **by Martin Haspelmath and Uri Tadmor (2009)**

> This is an important study into words that are more commonly borrowed and those that are less likely to be borrowed. The research for this was vast, covering hundreds of languages and years of data collection.

How New Languages Emerge **by David Lightfoot (2006)**

> A psycholinguistic approach to understanding the microscopic changes that occur to create language variation, change, and the emergence of new languages.

Participant Observation **by James Spradley (1980)**

> This classic text on observation has an excellent guide to not only carrying out observation but also analyzing the data that we collect.

Dialect Intelligibility Testing **by Eugene Casad (1974)**

> This is the foundational study on intelligibility testing including studies and detailed description of how to create recorded text tests. There is also brief information on conducting other aspects of sociolinguistic field research.

Methods for Community Participation: A Complete Guide for Practitioners **by Somesh Kumar (2002)**

> A very rich resource book with both the theory and practice of participatory rural appraisal. This is an essential text for anyone considering use of participatory methods in language assessment.

Notes on the Construction of a 'Subjective Vitality Questionnaire' for Ethnolinguistic Groups **by Richard Yvon Bourhis, Howard Giles, and Doreen Rosenthal (1981)**

> Describes important differences in assessing vitality from both an objective and subjective point of view and considers the value in having the perspective of the people involved.

***Phonostatistic Methods* by Gary Simons in *Language Variation and Survey Techniques* by Richard Loving and Gary Simons (eds.) (1977)**

This article provides a description of lexicostatistics and phonostatistics.

5 ASSESSMENT RESEARCH

In chapter 5, we expand on some of the concepts we mentioned in chapter 1. In chapters 2 to 4, we described the impact of social factors on language at the three levels: the Restricted, the Negotiated, and the Free. We also described some of the tools that we commonly use to gather data at each level and introduced specific methodologies for using tools such as RTTs or interviews. In this chapter, we talk about aspects of research that apply in all situations with all tools. We focus on an overall approach to our research that is consistent no matter what tools we are using and no matter what the purpose of the research.

We cover the following in this chapter:

- principle research **ethics,**
- the importance of the **research cycle,**
- the **ladder of abstraction** and how we use it,
- what **variables** are,
- different kinds of **data,**
- how we use **sampling** to choose participants, and
- a brief guide to some basic principles of **academic writing.**

This is only a brief introduction to the many aspects of research. We need to be familiar with other sources that cover these different aspects more thoroughly. The Further Reading section at the end of this chapter will provide some of these for you. We strongly encourage you to read as much as you can and to become more familiar with these topics at a deeper level.

CROSS-REFERENCE ► See **Section 1.2.2** on page 13 in particular.

Finally, we want to stress the importance of following correct research principles. The decision-making processes that people use to manage language development programs should be based upon trustworthy information. We achieve this level of trust by maintaining a commitment to excellence and integrity.

5.1   Ethical Considerations

These days, most academic organizations dealing with social science research have ethical principles for human subject research. Despite this, there is also debate about how appropriate these are for fieldwork such as language survey. There are few universal ethical concepts, and it is important to understand that the majority of the ethical guidelines we might follow are relative to the cultures we work in. The problem for us as surveyors is that we work in three cultures: the people we serve, the organizations we work for, and the wider academic community. Reconciling the ethical requirements of these in the same assessment project can be difficult. The wider academic community may insist that we collect written permission from participants for the use of data, but the participants in a survey may be fearful or distrustful of signing any document. This is a typical example of the kinds of dilemmas an ethical approach to field work produces.

If we are doing research in conjunction with a university or some other professional organization, they may have specific guidelines concerning ethics that must be followed. If we are collecting data that we hope to use for an advanced university degree, we need to know the policies and requirements of our institution. They may have an ethics committee that is required to review and approve our research plan before conducting the research. Even if we are not doing our research under the oversight of an ethics committee, we still need to be concerned about the ethics of our research and how we handle the information in the future. The future of the data includes:

- how data and findings are published,
- how data is archived,
- how information on each of our language helpers will be protected and preserved, and
- how permissions will be preserved.

Below, we introduce some ethical principles that are commonly held in westernized scientific institutions. We discuss each with reference to assessment and issues of cross-cultural conflict. This discussion is not meant to provide a comprehensive guide of dos and don'ts. Instead, our

QUOTE ▶ *The accountability of the social network and relationships that I formed in Ouesso are stronger and deeper than a signed piece of paper.* (Annette Harrison, SIL Central Africa Group)

NOTE ▶ We choose the term "westernized" specifically. Just because a university is in Asia, it does not mean that it follows more typically "eastern" ethical practices. Often, such universities and organizations can be at conflict with local ethics because they choose to adhere to academic practices which they believe are best because they are borrowed from a western academic context.

intention is to introduce you to issues that ethical considerations raise for research. How these principles affect our actions will depend very much on where we work, who we work with, and what purpose our work has.

5.1.1   Respect Human Dignity

Respect for human dignity implies avoiding treating people merely as data sources, shaming them or causing them to lose status. It also implies never coercing cooperation or decisions, but always recognizing freedom of choice.

We want to develop a mindset that focuses on understanding the sociolinguistic reality of the people, an understanding that will never be able to divorce the data we collect from the people who provide it. Respect for human dignity therefore means we should prioritize the people over the languages that they speak. Social concerns should therefore take priority over linguistic ones. We have to understand that issues of status and shame often accompany users of minority languages. This can cause a dilemma: we want to address these issues and improve the quality of life for people, but in order to do this, we need people to admit that there are status issues in the first place. This is further compounded if we require their agreement to then take their data and publish it officially. In effect, it may appear that we are asking them to agree to our telling the world how low their status is. This is not an easy choice for people to make.

This shows that an uncomplicated approach to "freedom of choice" may be a luxury for many we work with. As we have illustrated at each of the three levels we considered in earlier chapters, people in minority communities face huge social pressures that influence their language. At the outset of language development, when survey is often carried out, people may not actually realize they have much freedom to choose at all. One of the strengths of participatory methods is that they actively help people to realize what their range of choices is.

CROSS-REFERENCE ▶ See Section 4.4.5 on page 161 for more about participatory methods.

Also, in many cultures the ability for the *individual* to have the freedom to choose is not seen as a positive benefit to society but rather a liability. Therefore, we should guard against assumptions that individual freedom is what is considered here. Instead, many cultures consider that group cooperation, group decisions, and the freedom of the group to choose are what communicate human dignity.

5.1.2   Respect Vulnerable Persons

We should especially take care to safeguard the rights of those who may be especially vulnerable to exploitation by virtue of underprivileged economic or social status, by age, gender, mental or physical infirmity, or unfamiliarity with the larger world.

Of all the principles we consider in this section, this one is closest to becoming an impractical ideal. Most of the groups we work with are underprivileged in the way described here. Because of this, some have argued that simply by carrying out language assessment we are increasing a speech communities' vulnerability to exploitation. Certainly, we must recognize that language development is intrinsically connected to other forms of development which have the potential to cause harm to a community; for example, the economic benefits that come from employment via learning an LWC can cause dramatic and sometimes damaging social change in a community.

In practice, we can make an attempt to safeguard the vulnerable by advising on the impact of language development in our survey reports. But surveyors are not responsible for the implementation of language development, and we have to consider that we may well be opening the door to future exploitation. Taking this ethical consideration seriously should lead us to increased awareness when we visit communities and to be cautious when making recommendations. This consideration should also propel us to find ways to work more collaboratively with local communities.

5.1.3   Respect Privacy and Confidentiality

We should keep confidential any data or information given in the expectation of confidentiality, and we should respect rights to privacy.

We report in a number of ways on the assessments we do. Not all of these are formal. When presenting formal data, we should only present information freely given by participants with the understanding that it can be public information.

This respect for privacy and confidentiality includes how we talk about our survey trip to friends and colleagues, as well as informal presentations such as blogging. If someone shares something with us and asks us to keep the data confidential, they are not just referring to our survey report.

This consideration asks us to respect rights to privacy. Whether individual privacy exists at all and, if so, what forms it takes will differ from community to community as we can see from Case Study 5A.

CASE STUDY 5A
INFORMED CONSENT
EAST AFRICA

Asking individual people for informed consent can go straight against cultural practice here in East Africa.
Several times I have had the problem of needing to ask a younger person or younger woman in a household whether I can use their information as specified in our explanations. This is of course after I had already asked the head of household the same question. If he hears me asking for consent from younger people in his household after he has already given it, I have at that point seriously undermined his authority. Very tricky!!! We come, of course, from a very individualistic background wanting every single person to decide for themselves. But that is just not the culture here. If the head of household agrees, that's it.

CASE STUDY 5A SOURCE ▶ Susanne Krüger, SIL Uganda-Tanzania Branch.

CROSS-REFERENCE ▶ We discuss the issues raised in Case Study 5A more when we talk about informed consent in **Section 5.1.9** on page 175.

5.1.4   Respect Justice and Inclusiveness

We should treat individuals and communities with fairness. The results of research must not unfairly benefit, burden, or exclude some segment of the community. We should not allow the research to be used for commercial exploitation of the research participant or the community.

This consideration probably comes closest to the ethical heart of many of the speech communities we work with. It is something we need to be particularly mindful of if we are conducting assessment with a view to advising language development on the potential of grouping programs in clusters. The key here is "not unfairly." It may well be necessary to exclude certain groups from a potential cluster for very pragmatic reasons. But those reasons should be fair and clearly outlined and explained to all stakeholders.

Generally, the services of language development are not provided for profit. While we may realize this already, in many cultures we work with, reciprocity or mutual benefit is highly valued. Thus, the term "commercial exploitation" may take different forms from what we expect. In the West, it implies capitalist models of trade. Alternatively, exploitation might simply be using the data to benefit our organizations or ourselves rather than to benefit the people who have provided it. For example, spending months involved in language documentation of a community for a Ph.D. may be seen as exploitation, if the people involved see no benefit to themselves for their participation. Earlier, we mentioned that there is evidence that communities are starting to resist being treated in this way (Yamada 2007:271), and survey teams in Papua New Guinea have been told that they cannot carry out work because previous researchers took data but did not provide the community with anything as a result. Thus, if we define "commerce" in the way many minority communities do, we will be able to prevent ourselves compromising this consideration even if we do not benefit financially.

CROSS-REFERENCE ▶ See **Section 4.4.5.1** on page 161 for more about communities resisting this approach to research.

5.1.5   Minimize Harm

> *We should consider potential harm that the research might cause and seek ways to eliminate or reduce it to a minimum. This might even mean stopping the research if necessary.*

This includes, of course, harm that we might cause without realizing it. That immediately raises the question of how we are supposed to guard against actions that we are unaware of. The key to upholding this principle is taking time to understand the socio-historical and socio-political context that we are working in. For example, Araali (forthcoming) has researched indigenous cultural views of signatures in sub-Saharan Africa. From this paper, we learn that because of colonial insistence on signatures to validate unethical confessions and seizures of land rights, these people are highly suspicious of signatures as a form of agreement. In fact, rather than seeing them as a guarantee of honor, as they might be in our own cultures, they are associated with the opposite. Having learned this from our secondary research, our increased awareness puts us in a better position to uphold the ethical principle of doing no harm by not insisting on participants signing, say, a consent form. We must then look for culturally appropriate ways to demonstrate agreement.

Another area of potential problems is with questionnaires and interviews. These instruments might prompt respondents to reveal attitudes, opinions, or behaviors that could open them up to censure or even physical harm from their community or from those in the dominant society. We need to make sure that the identity of our respondents is kept confidential in order to protect them from any such eventuality.

The issue with this principle is thus trying to determine what "harm" means to the people we work with. This involves laying aside our presumptions and asking about and reflecting on the views of the local people.

5.1.6   Respect Community Context

We should recognize the role of local or higher authorities in decision making. In consultation with community leadership, we should look for ways to apply the research to give the community maximum benefit.

In assessment, we must at all times realize that we are the guests of the communities we work with and for. Our hosts range from governments and universities at the Restricted Level, NGOs and community workers at the Negotiated Level down to individual families who give us shelter at the Free Level. Because each of these is a stakeholder, each stands to derive benefit from the language development our assessments will inform, and it can be hard to balance the expectations of the different stakeholders in a program. There may be differences in local and higher authority decision making, and recognizing and respecting both of these may place us in an ethical dilemma. Different communities in a cluster may want to derive different benefits and these may be exclusive ones for various reasons.

Negotiating the tension between the different communities that stand to gain from our work is the practical outcome of applying this ethical principle. We must remember that "maximum benefit" from a language program implies a compromise between what the ideal benefit would be and what is practical given realistic limitations.

5.1.7   Value Long-Term Relations

The longer the contact, the better the chances for mutually beneficial relationships and building capacity in the local community. For multi-year programs, periodic reviews of research protocols should be conducted, with possible modification of the research.

Few assessment teams remain in contact with a community for the "multi-year" duration of a language program. So, we do not carry out "periodic reviews of research protocols" in terms of our relationship to a particular community. However, teams will need to review their protocols towards the assessment process for their context periodically. This ensures that a consistent reputation is maintained in that locale. In addition, despite working with many different speech communities, survey teams often have long-term partnerships, especially at the Restricted, and possibly Negotiated, Level, too. Our approach to these should also be reviewed periodically. Finally, individuals from teams may maintain contact with stakeholders in particular programs for years even after assessment has been completed.

If we keep this ethical principle in mind, it should help us realize that each of us has the potential for long-term mutually beneficial relationships with individuals in every community we visit on survey. The communities we visit may be more aware of this potential than ourselves are. Araali (2011:42) records how a team from the US visited a village for no more than a few hours. Years later, however, women from the village still wondered when the US team would return to continue the relationship they had started. It is highly unlikely that any members of the US team saw their visit in such a way, nor is it reasonable to expect them to. However, if the team had understood the importance that the local people attached to visiting their community, they may have been more sensitive to their hosts' expectations and left them with more realistic expectations. Araali cautions us:

> *almost every encounter in sub-Saharan Africa has a potential for producing a long-term relationship among individuals involved. When a researcher does not maintain a certain level of contact with his or her research participants after data collection, Africans are likely to conclude that they have been used as sources of data. (2011:50)*

5.1.8   Archive and Disseminate Data

> *We should provide the communities we study at least a summary of the research and its findings in a form and language they can understand. We should take care to ensure that our data is disseminated to the wider academic community in a way which respects the consent granted to us by participants.*

When we leave a community carrying data, we are taking something of the community with us. In pre-literate cultures, when we record someone's voice, story, or other oral data and then make it available for others to listen to, we are taking actions which carry a great deal more perceived risk to the participant than we might realize. We have a duty to our participants to preserve and use their data in ways which respect this. This ethical principle ensures not only that we preserve the data sensitively but also that we maximize the value of the data for our partners and the wider academic community. Not to do so would be to squander what our participants have entrusted to us.

In addition to our duty to the speech communities we work with, we also have our responsibility to our partners outside the speech community. We work with NGOs, religious bodies, health advisors, government agencies, and academic institutions all of whom can benefit from the data we collect. By collecting data and not disseminating it in a responsible and timely way, we could potentially be wasting the effort that our team and our participants have made to gather them in the first place.

All archived materials should have sufficient metadata attached to them so that other researchers have a complete understanding of the information and it can be found and referenced more easily. Metadata should include information such as the names of the researcher/s and participant/s, the agreed consent, the location of content, the date and method of data collection, and a description of the data. If audio or video was used to collect data we should also note the equipment used for recording, bit rate, and other digital information.

5.1.9   Respect for Free and Informed Consent

We should inform research participants about the methodology of our research and what risks may exist for them by participating. In terms of data, our participants should know how we or our partners will use it; this includes giving them information about potential outcomes for the participants. They should know how they can limit access to data and have full access themselves. They should be given opportunities to enter into or refuse participation at any point with no recriminations. A record of this consent, either on paper or otherwise appropriate media, should be in a form and language that the subject understands and be permanently archived.

"Free and informed consent" is probably the most hotly-debated ethical principle. Controversy centers around what various parties mean by "free" and "informed." In cultures that value the needs of the group over the individual, "free" may not be an option, or at least may be understood very differently.

Some cultures have more social structure and the consent of a leader may be sufficient for the whole community. As we saw earlier in Case Study 5A, we risk undermining status if, having gained a leader's agreement, we ask participants under their authority for their individual consent. Araali (2011:42) gives us an example to help us. In providing personal data such as name, date of birth, education details, etc., an individual in sub-Saharan Africa may have freedom to give consent. But, "for most sociolinguistic research, such as language shift, attitude, etc. which are socially and emotionally charged, the point of view of community leaders is to be sought since the interviewee's responses may be directed to facts which involve the community as a whole." Thus, the individual does not have the freedom to give consent for information which is deemed to be the property of the group the participant belongs to. In addition, freedom to discuss a topic depends not on an individual's willingness necessarily but rather on their status as a representative authority about the issue concerned. If they have not achieved this status in their community, they will not be free to consent to provide data.

The second problem lies with the word "informed." The question of how we can meaningfully inform someone in a pre-literate community of our intention to archive digital recordings on the Internet needs to be answered. We will need to find appropriate ways to explain things so that people can understand what they are giving their consent to. With the spread of cell phone technology these concepts may not be so foreign. They need to understand how the data they give will be used, whether they will be cited as the source, who will have access to it and how, and whether it will be translated into any other languages. They may also need to know whether there is any form of compensation involved either in giving data or when it is used.

While we clearly understand what we are asking them to agree to, it is often difficult for people we work with to understand the concepts involved. Often therefore, after asking for consent at the beginning of our survey activities, we also reaffirm this at the end to get confirmation. We do this because the process of participating in research may give our participants more understanding of what they have already agreed to. This understanding may lead to their feeling uncomfortable about sharing their data and wanting to change their minds about certain aspects of consent.

We need to consider the most appropriate means of documenting consent for each community involved. We could use written media or record the consent using audio or video. We also need to find out about local views of ownership of cultural knowledge as well as privacy and secrecy concerns, particularly if any of the data we collect concerns information which is taboo for certain strata of the community such as women and children. We have already mentioned that we must minimize the potential for exploitation and harm. Unless we are careful to safeguard material in the way that the community has directed us, we could be putting our participants at risk.

> QUOTE ▶ *Would it be reasonable to ask researchers, research institutions and funding agencies to learn to play by the socio-cultural norms of the researched?* (Araali, 2011:43)

Another problem is the possibility of predicting whatever "risks may exist for them by participating." Some things may be obvious, for example speaking against the government, if it is an oppressive regime, may be risking someone's life. With some common sense, we recognize that speaking ill of one's neighbor is probably not well-received in any culture. Such comments should be kept confidential. A villager may be proud to have his name published on the Internet associated with language data. However, making someone's name freely available might make them the target of some unscrupulous person.

The area of ethical principles is one that often brings up dilemmas and highlights tensions between the worldviews of the researchers and the researched. We will need to give careful consideration as to how we balance these on each of our assessment projects.

5.2   Elements of Research Methodology

Language assessment data is needed because it will inform language development decision making. Types of assessment are as diverse as the reasons they are needed. We may find ourselves asking questions about what languages people use, what varieties there are, or how specific strategies can best be implemented. But whatever the questions are, our assessment begins with the needs of whoever commissions it. These are the questions that will guide our research.

The DEPTH and SCOPE of research are two terms that are often used to describe the parameters of research, but rarely defined. In language

DEFINITIONS ► The DEPTH, or level, of research, refers to the thoroughness of the research. SCOPE, or breadth, describes what aspects will be studied and what will not be studied.

assessment, when discussing the depth of research, we are referring to the thoroughness of the research. If a wide variety of tools were used to study something, we say the research had depth. If the research did not probe for sufficient explanation of the phenomena, we say the research lacked depth. Obviously, depth of research will limit the number of things that can be studied with the resources available.

An essential foundation to any research project is the limitation of the scope of the research. This means that we must determine what we will and will not study. This also helps the researcher determine the limits of the relevance of the data that is collected. We want to be precise in the planning and execution of the survey and the reporting of the findings. If, for example, we set out to study bilingualism for a speech community, it is not possible to study all aspects of bilingualism for every person in every community. Therefore, we might limit the scope of our research to the hearing and repeating competency of a random sample of households, in select communities. We limit what we can say the data describes. From this we can attempt to describe the situation in the larger speech community, but we must be clear that this is only conjecture.

5.2.1   Returning to the Research Cycle

In the Introduction, we talked about the research cycle, the fundamental framework that underlies every type of assessment, no matter how diverse it appears on the surface.

FIGURE 8 ► The research cycle as introduced earlier. See **Section 1.2.2** on page 13 for our initial comments on its importance.

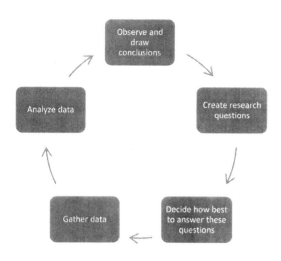

Initially, all we have are the needs and requests of those who commission the survey and any information our partners at this early stage may provide. It is observing these and drawing conclusions from them that help us to refine a purpose for the assessment. In turn, this helps us to move towards creating research questions which will guide the rest of the primary and secondary data collection and analysis.

Often, these steps are employed in an assessment project in a linear rather than cyclic process. We begin with a research question, answer it, and then move on. However, it becomes cyclic when someone takes that research and moves on to asking the next question. The research cycle is a simplistic model. Each step in the process requires multiple refined steps. For example, the three steps observe and draw conclusions, create research questions, and decide how best to answer these questions seem like simple steps. However, they require a much more systematic process. We can use another multi-step process such as *the ladder of abstraction*, as shown in Figure 9, to help us be more thorough. Processes such as this one help us to clearly think through each of the steps from defining our purpose to methodically creating each individual question to gathering information.

5.2.2   Planning and Proposals

Whether we are given a request for information from a development partnership or are planning to do research for an academic requirement, it is essential that we plan thoroughly. We may be required to present a proposal for the research. This process will help us to think through what we want to learn, how we want to gather data and analyze it, and how our research might fit in to the larger body of knowledge of both the specific situation and the science.

The planning process will require thoughtful consideration of many aspects of the research. We will need to think through everything from the theoretical foundations of our assumptions to packing lists for the survey trip. Following is a partial list of things we will need to be considered:

- The research question: what do we really want to learn?
- How are we going to answer our research question?
- How might research by others inform our research?
- How much might this research cost, and how will it be financed?
- Where will the research be conducted?

QUOTE ▶ *In my experience as a statistician, the #1 thing that makes it hard for people to analyze data is NOT their lack of knowledge of statistics. Rather it is the failure to think through their Purposes and clearly state their Research Questions BEFORE collecting any data. Thus, they end up with data but do not know what to do with it, and sometimes it ends up not even being the data they really need. (Ramzi Nahhas 2007)*

- What tools will be used to gather information, and how will it be analyzed?
- Which communities will be visited, and how will we travel there?
- How will the participants be treated ethically?
- What cultural factors may impact the research?
- What equipment will be needed on the survey trip?
- Who will be on the research team, and what roles will each person perform?
- Who will the research findings be shared with?
- How will the materials be archived?

We need to give extensive consideration to the refinement of our research questions. What is it that we really want to know? For example, we may think that we want to do bilingualism testing to find out the distribution of bilingualism proficiency in a speech community. But, we probably really want to know something like the adequacy of the L2 for meeting the needs of the speech community in certain domains.

As we consider our research we need to think through the possible findings. What are we basing our assumptions on? What do we expect the findings might be? What if the people respond another way? What value will our findings have for language development or expansion of the science of sociolinguistics? The more aspects we consider, the greater the probability that we will not be surprised by anything. We must also not allow ourselves to bias the research in any way that might skew the findings.

There may need to be different proposals written for different purposes. For example, one proposal may need to be submitted to an ethics board, another requesting funding, and another to whoever requested the research to be sure we are getting what they requested. Much of what we write in the rest of the book covers aspects of this planning process.

5.2.3   The Ladder of Abstraction

The ladder of abstraction is a model that describes a process for developing research and justifying the research that is conducted. The main strength of this model, as shown in Figure 9, is that, like a ladder, we can move either up or down. Each step represents a level in the depth of detail in the research. At the top we pose a very general question about the research we will conduct. At the bottom we define very specific investigative questions called **PROBES**. As we go down, we move between steps by asking the question "How are we going to do this?" Travelling

DEFINITION ► A **PROBE** is the specific question that will be posed to the research participant requesting a response.

upward between steps is achieved by asking the question "Why are we doing this?" The "this" is the question that is raised at the particular step of the ladder. In this way, no part of our research should be arbitrary. Each step is informed by and the result of earlier steps. Thus, we can see clearly the pattern of thought that led us from the purpose of the survey to the individual probes. We can justify each of the probes by reference all the way back to the purpose. As we develop the research moving down the ladder more questions are raised. So, the higher level research will be explored through the use of several tools using multiple probes.

The entire process starts with the **purpose.** We derive our purpose for the assessment from the strategic questions presented by whoever commissions the research. This is the starting point for further planning. In Figure 9, for an example of a possible purpose for doing research, we imagine a government agency that approaches us wanting to know if there is a need for a language development program in a particular region. This gives us a broadly defined purpose for the survey.

QUOTE ▸ *The methods used by the investigator must always be justified by his purpose.* (Simons 1977)

Next on the ladder are the **goals** of the research and we reach them by asking the question "How can we achieve our purpose?" This is stated as a more specific focus of research. While there is only one purpose, there are likely to be a number of goals. If at any stage we want to clarify that a goal is worth pursuing, we can ask the question, "Why are we pursuing this goal?" If we can answer that by referring to our purpose, our goal is worthwhile. If we cannot, we know we need to either eliminate that particular goal or reform it.

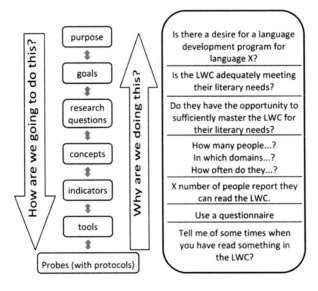

FIGURE 9 ▸ In this figure, the ladder of abstraction is on the lefthand side. The box on the right contains examples for each stage.

The next level is the **research question**. This is the heart of the research. We need to analyze each of our research questions by considering the hypotheses and assumptions underlying the purpose of the assessment. In constructing a written research question, we should consider the meaning of each word, the relationships between each element, and the assumptions being made in those relationships. As we construct research questions, we specify the **VARIABLES** and limit these to identifiable and measureable features. Going through this development process may require refining parts higher up on the ladder. In our example, a research question might ask if the people have the potential to master the LWC sufficiently for their literary needs.

At the next level are the linguistic and sociolinguistic **concepts** involved in answering each research question. These include our models of the relationships of types of information. Concepts that reflect our example could involve demography, social networks, domains of use, literacy, and multilingual proficiency. Each of these concepts has observable **indicators** which we can measure in some way, and these will fall broadly into one of two kinds of data: quantitative or qualitative. It is important to clarify exactly what these indicators are and not to allow our choice of tools to predetermine them. Tools are, by definition, subject to the indicators they measure, and we should maintain a mindset which resists the temptation to select particular tools simply because that is what we may have always done in a particular situation. Through increased experience and by improving our academic understanding of the concepts involved, we will be able to isolate indicators we may not have considered before. In turn, this may well lead to us creating new tools or improving existing ones.

DEFINITION ► A **VARIABLE** is a measurable feature or attribute of a person or thing. See **Section 5.2.4** on page 183.

FIGURE 10 ► A simplified model of the complete assessment research process.

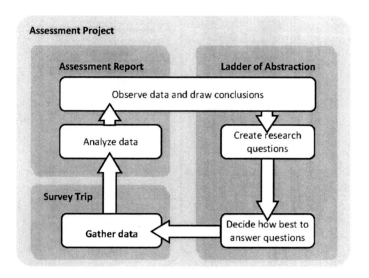

Once we have isolated these indicators and decided what type of data they show, we choose the **tools** we need to measure them. Not only do we choose the tools, we also need to develop and adapt them to the specific situation we are assessing. This includes validating and calibrating the tools so that we know they produce the data we need reliably.

CROSS-REFERENCE ► See **Section 5.4.1** on page 192 for more about validating and calibrating tools.

Finally, at the bottom of the ladder are the **probes** and **protocols**. This is the most practical level where we create probes like questions for questionnaires or tests, or schedules to guide observations. Along with the probes, we also detail the protocols or all the procedures we will follow for each of these. Although we always intend to follow protocols with precision, it is often difficult to follow the procedures completely in the field for all sorts of reasons. Therefore, it is very important that we try to be as precise as we can be with the research but also as honest as we can be when we report how we carried out the research.

CROSS-REFERENCE ► See **Section 4.4.1** on page 140 for more about observation schedules.

Figure 10 shows a simplified model of the assessment research process incorporating the ladder of abstraction into the research cycle. Of course, in reality, the process is a lot more complex. We may go through the ladder of abstraction or the whole research cycle a number of times in a spiral, digging deeper in each cycle, each time refining our approach and building on what we discover. If, for example, we include a preliminary visit to the survey area, we may have very rough primary data to reflect on, which influences how we continue with our secondary research. If we cannot make a preliminary visit, it may be possible to work with someone who has experience in that region. The important thing is to realize that the research cycle and ladder of abstraction are just models that help us to organize stages of the research process. They are tools to serve the research process, and we should never allow them to dominate and restrict what is the best practice for the particular assessment project we are working on.

CROSS-REFERENCE ► See **Section 5.2.5** on page 186 for more about types of data.

5.2.4   Variables

In language assessment, many of the things we want to know are extremely difficult to measure. It is very difficult, for example, to measure motivation. But if we know that once a month, over 80 percent of the women in a speech community visit a market in a neighboring region where an LWC is spoken, we can infer from this that they might be highly motivated to learn that LWC. Factors such as frequency of occurrence or percentages, which are measurable features or attributes of a person or thing, are known as variables. Each of these attributes varies in two ways: from person to person, or object to object, and over time.

In social science research, we are studying the relationships between variables. We ask questions like whether a person's residence, age, education, gender, etc. affect the way they use their language. We might want to know the relationship of age to the use of certain words, or the pronunciation or signing of those words? In other words, what is the relationship of one variable to another variable?

There are four kinds of relationships between variables: *independent*, *dependent*, *control*, and *intervening* (Hatch and Farhady 1982:15–16). First, we define the terms and then give you an example so that you can see them in context.

DEFINITIONS ▶ As well as being defined in the text, you can find definitions of all the variables mentioned in this section in the **Glossary** on page 239.

The **INDEPENDENT VARIABLE** is the essential thing that can be changed and we want to know about the effects of changing that variable.

- The **DEPENDENT VARIABLE** is the thing impacted or affected by changes to the independent variable.
- The **CONTROL VARIABLE** is something that limits the independent variable.
- **INTERVENING VARIABLES** are other factors which we may not be able to measure.

For example, suppose we want to study the relationship between age and the attitudes of a speech community toward their heritage language. We want to find out if knowing the age of a person will help us predict what their attitudes might be. We manipulate the independent variable (age) and observe how this affects the dependent variable (attitudes.) We choose different age groups of people and then investigate their attitudes. We may also want to see if there is a difference between those who still speak the heritage language and those who do not. The control variable is whether people say the heritage language is their dominant language or not. This acts as a filter providing data from this group to contrast with the age-related attitudes from other groups. By using control variables, we can check to see if factors that we think might have influence really do by eliminating them and observing differences this makes to data.

At all times we need to be aware of intervening variables, attributes that impact the relationship of the independent and dependent variables. In the scenario given above, there may have been events in people's lives that affect their attitudes apart from their age. However, these factors may not be measureable or they may be too numerous to measure. Because intervening variables can influence dependent variables, we need to be aware of what they are and consider how they may be influencing our data. Otherwise, our study may conclude that age does determine attitude when, in fact, it is some other variable, such as changes in the educational policy that have affected the dependent variable.

Variables can be considered by another two-way distinction labeled as **CONTINUOUS VARIABLES** and **DISCRETE VARIABLES** (Rubin and Babbie 2010:419). Continuous variables are things that can be counted and change equally from one unit to the next. For example, temperature is a continuous variable—the difference between 23° and 33° is the same as the difference between 16° and 26°. Discrete variables change from category to category; they have nominal or ordinal values. For example, the ILR bilingualism scale is an ordinal scale. We should not think that the difference between level 2+ and 3 is the same as the difference between 1 and 1+. Each of these levels simply describes a set of behaviors.

WWW.SURVEYWIKI.INFO ▶ See the **ILR** page on SurveyWiki for more on the Interagency Language Roundtable (ILR) scale of language proficiency and also **Section 3.3.1.2** on page 80.

It is particularly important for assessment research that we understand the fundamental difference between continuous and discrete variables. For example, we may travel to a village and carry out some measurements. When we analyze and present our data, we say that 487 people live there and that some have ILR proficiencies level 1 and 2+ in the LWC. One of these measurements, the population, is a continuous variable because people do not come in any other form but whole. But proficiency exists on a continuum: people become proficient in a gradual way, they do not shift from one level of proficiency to another instantly. So, when we carry out proficiency testing and reduce our measurements to a discrete level such as ILR level 2, it is extremely important that we remember that we are in fact attempting to pin down something on a continuum. Level 2 is an arbitrary and artificial level that the ILR has created to make sense of the continuum of proficiency.

CONTINUOUS VARIABLES THAT MAY BE STUDIED ON SURVEYS	DISCRETE VARIABLES THAT MAY BE STUDIED ON SURVEYS
Population	Bilingualism levels
Distance between villages	Ratings on attitudes
Birthrates	Perceptions of dialect similarity

TABLE 9 ▶Comparison of various continuous and discrete variables that are typically collected on survey trips.

Certain kinds of calculations are appropriate for continuous or discrete variables. The mode of a data set can be calculated on discrete variables, but it may not be very revealing. We can calculate medians and means of continuous variables, but usually not of discrete variables although "such technical violations are commonly found and can be useful" (Rubin and Babbie 2010:419). For example, if we asked people to rate their preferences for something on a scale of 1 to 4, we could look at the mean scores for males versus females, or young versus old. While a mean score of 1.6 for one group versus 3.8 for the other group may not have any mathematical meaning, it clearly indicates that the different groups have significantly different preferences.

Not all continuous variables require this degree of caution, because the process of reducing them to meaningful measurements does not distort them in the same way as discrete variables. Describing one person as 67 years old and another as 68 could be significant as it may determine social hierarchy, inheritance rights, prestige, etc. But if we calculate two language varieties as being 67 percent and 68 percent similar to a third, we would be very unwise to treat this as meaningful. The things that make languages similar, or dissimilar, are not practically described by an interval measurement. How can variation between noun phrase structures be combined with the semantic differences in a word to give a percentage of similarity? Thus, we should always keep in mind the qualities of the variables we measure and how these determine whether they are continuous or discrete, and we must also take into account the context of the arbitrary scales we use to measure the latter.

5.2.5   Types of Data

CROSS-REFERENCE ▶ See Section 5.4.3 on page 200 for more about how we analyze these two types of data differently.

Determining the kind of data we want is a major decision in research planning. As we plan each survey, we need to decide what kind of data will best answer our research questions; it can take some careful consideration. Generally, there are two types of data: quantitative and qualitative. Quantitative data can be measured (or quantified); qualitative data cannot be counted. For example, the age of a participant is a quantitative fact. The impact of their age on their language proficiency would be qualitative data.

DEFINITION ▶ NOMINAL DATA: information that can be grouped into categories and counted, but not put in an order.

DEFINITION ▶ ORDINAL DATA: information related to a scale that permits organization or ranking of the information, but the distances or differences between the units on the scale are not meaningful.

In language assessment, it can sometimes be helpful to classify quantitative data in various ways. When we count categories or types of things, we call these **NOMINAL DATA**. For example, there are five dogs in the village, or 15 people attended the literacy class. We can count, but not order, nominal data. When we want to order or rank things, we can create a scale to do this. We call this **ORDINAL DATA**. For example, ten people said they could speak the L2 "poorly," 15 people said they could speak the L2 "well", 20 people said they could speak the L2 "very well." We cannot, however, compare the difference between "well" and "poorly" and say that it is the same as the difference between "well and "very well." A scale with meaningful differences between values is used to collect **INTERVAL DATA**. For example, it is meaningful to say that a person spends four hours at school a day and that is twice as long as someone who is there for only two hours. Compare this with ordinal data though: It would be meaningless to say that someone who spoke "very well" was twice as good as someone who spoke "well." Finally, data that is related to a scale that has a natural zero point, such as temperature, are called **RATIO DATA**. We rarely collect ratio data on surveys but it is helpful to know what the term means.

> **DEFINITION ▸ INTERVAL DATA:** information related to a scale, which uses units that have a meaningful distance or difference between them. This permits comparison of different information at different points on the scale.

> **DEFINITION ▸ RATIO DATA:** information that can be measured on a scale that has a natural zero point.

When gathering factual data in language assessment we usually collect nominal data (*How many people live in this village?*) or interval data (*How many times a week do you use the LWC at the market?*). We collect ordinal data if what we want to know cannot be measured with precision (*How well do you speak the L2: poorly, well, very well?*).

Knowing what these different types of data are is important when it comes to drawing conclusions from data analysis. If we create an SRT and score participants' results with percentages like 55%, 65%, or 75%, it would seem, at first glance, that this is interval data. But consider this again carefully. Can we really say that the difference between bilingual ability of 55% and 65% is exactly the same as the difference between 65% and 75%? Can we really say that someone who gets 75% is 10% more bilingual than someone who gets 65%? Of course, we cannot. We have to be careful to observe the qualities of what we are collecting as data. Again, going back to our school example, we can say that a child that spends four hours at school spends twice as long as one that is only there for two hours, because measurements of time are interval data. But we cannot, therefore, conclude that their ability in the LWC as a medium of education will be twice as good because bilingual ability is not interval data, it is ordinal. Thus, it is critical to know what kinds of data we are measuring so that we can be aware of the limitations to the conclusions we draw.

> **CROSS-REFERENCE ▸** See **Section 3.4.5** on page 106 for a description of SRTs.

5.2.6   Avoiding Research Error

There are many things that can go wrong with our field research; we have mentioned many of the things we need to be cautious of throughout the book. However, there are some general errors that any researcher may

> **CROSS-REFERENCE ▸** In **Section 5.4.3** on page 200, we will share some cautions on the use of quantitative or qualitative research and findings.

encounter and should avoid. In any research, it is possible for there to be inadvertent errors. It is possible that we may impose our own bias onto the data collected, as well as the analysis and reporting. Researcher bias is the risk that comes from selecting observations and recording information that might conform to our own or others' perspectives, desires, expectations, or interpretations. We may misrepresent data as evidence based on our preconceived ideas. To avoid this bias, there are two safeguards that we should use: reflexivity and triangulation.

Reflexivity is the process of actively engaging in critical self-reflection about our own potential biases and predispositions (Ashmore 1989). It can be a good exercise for us to write out our expectations about the research and why we feel this way. We should question and evaluate these ideas.

Through the course of the research, we should carefully document incidents that demonstrate the feature we are focusing on (whether language use, certain phonetic differences, variable grammatical forms) making note of participants, locations, and topics where those variables are found. This helps us to develop a view of whether our subjective conclusions are based on one set of circumstances, participants, or topics, or whether the phenomenon noted is truly present across the community in question. We should include these documented observations at some point in our report to allow for future verification.

After the research, it is a good idea to review this information to honestly consider if our preconceived ideas have imposed a bias on our research. A related strategy we can use against researcher bias is negative case sampling. This involves intentionally looking for examples that are likely to disconfirm expectations and explanations about what we are studying. However, just because we find an exception in the data does not mean that we must doubt our research, but we do need to consider that importance of that exception.

DEFINITION ▶ PRECISION: an exact measurement that agrees with the reality of the thing being measured.

DEFINITION ▶ ACCURACY: measuring the right, complete, or real thing.

It is common to see in reports more **PRECISION** than is justified by the size of the sample or the **ACCURACY** of the measurement. For example, "twelve people were asked about where their language is spoken best; seven people preferred village X." In the report it is stated that 58.3 percent favored village X; but this degree of precision along with presentation in a percentile does not clearly communicate the limit of the sample. It would be better just to say that 7 out of 12 preferred village X. Another misrepresentation would be to say that a comparison of two 200-item wordlists shows 83.5 percent lexical similarity. In reality, such a wordlist comparison probably could not have any more accuracy than to say that there is approximately 80 to 85 percent lexical similarity.

One of the most common, and serious, errors in reports is that validity is claimed when in fact the thing measured does not really force the conclusion claimed for it. This is done when assumptions are made about the relationships of variables. This has been done most frequently when people have claimed, for example, that a high lexical similarity in a wordlist comparison shows mutual intelligibility or that a low comprehension score on an RTT shows that the two varieties are different languages.

The potential for errors in our methods and assumptions leads us to want to look at our research question from numerous angles. Triangulation is a method of working which we have discussed before. It involves cross-checking information and conclusions through the use of multiple procedures or sources. There are four main aspects of triangulation: data, methods, investigator, and theory (Denzin 2006:449).

CROSS-REFERENCE ▶ See **Section 1.2.2** on page 13 for more about triangulation.

Data triangulation involves using multiple data sources to help understand a situation. An example of data triangulation is the use of multiple wordlists of a speech variety. For example, one researcher collects a list at the library. A member of a language survey team collects a second list of the same speech variety from a speaker of the language. Another linguist not associated with the research project collects a third list. Each list serves to confirm or disconfirm the others.

Methods triangulation involves using multiple research methods to study a situation. It is possible to combine quantitative methods, qualitative methods, or both. An example of methods triangulation would be the initial use of lexicostatistics (quantitative) in combination with self-reported comprehension (qualitative). High lexicostatistical percentages (>90%) in a speech community where most people say they understand the other variety would hint that speakers of each variety belong to the same language. To further verify this finding, surveyors may want to use a Recorded Text Test (a quantitative method) to observe speakers of one group actually understanding the speech of another.

The research integrity of the previous scenarios is enhanced by **investigator triangulation** which safeguards against individual or team researcher bias by using multiple researchers (individuals or teams) in the collection and interpretation of the data. One team of researchers might carry out the phase involving lexicostatistics and the use of questionnaires whereas another team may lead the RTT trip.

Theory triangulation involves the use of multiple theories and perspectives to help interpret and explain the data. Since the field of language assessment falls within a category of applied sociolinguistics, we could consult various theories from within sociolinguistics as well as disciplines that are related to sociolinguistics, such as communications, social psychology, anthropological linguistics, and the sociology of language. One example of interdisciplinary theory development is the communication accommodation theory (CAT) by Howard Giles (1977). It has its roots in social psychology combined with sociolinguistic perspectives but has become primarily a theory of inter-group communication.

CROSS-REFERENCE ▸ See **Section 4.2.3** on page 123 for more information about language accommodation theory.

5.3   The Secondary Research Stage

Secondary research is the process of gathering information that others have already gathered to provide a background upon which to build new research. Much of science involves refining earlier findings. There may be a few places on the earth where nothing is known about the people and their languages. It would not be wise to start primary research without first knowing what data is already available. However, as we look at this information, we need to consider that it may need confirmation since other researchers probably had other aims and certainly had other perspectives. For example, early explorers may have stated that the people were bilingual simply because they found one person they could talk to. That does not mean there is bilingualism throughout the speech community, nor does it say anything about the level of bilingualism. Furthermore, theories and ideologies change over time. Early colonial explorers often had ideological perspectives which affected their interpretations of the data. We may find some of those colonialist ideologies repugnant, and we might, therefore, interpret the data quite differently. Theory also changes and grows allowing us to re-analyze data or to identify data that earlier theories might have ignored. Another major factor is that data becomes outdated and needs to be revised.

Even if we know the purpose of the research from the start of an assessment project, it is good to do secondary research that covers a reasonably wide overview. When we collect our primary research data, we may find that there are unexpected connections with other issues. For example, on a survey of language vitality in the Caribbean, we collected information from the immigration office in case we needed to identify the number of people coming from other speech communities, and it turned out to be a significant factor.

In some places, we carry out numerous assessment projects of the same type. We can use a standard outline to start collating secondary research findings. An outline like this will provide a place for information to be collected and organized, and can form the basis of the final assessment report. As we gather information, it is important to document sources, to reference citations accurately, and to build an annotated bibliography. This can help avoid plagiarism and saves time later when writing the final report.

The three main sources for secondary research data are the Internet, libraries, and knowledgeable people. Depending on where we are based, sometimes the best available information may be located in another country. Sometimes it is also possible to visit government offices to gather information or to meet knowledgeable people such as representatives of NGOs or universities. Ethically and pragmatically, it is a good policy to meet with people at the highest levels before meeting with people at lower positions of authority. In this way, we respect authority structures and do not give the impression that we are undermining them.

As we have described throughout this book, it is important to understand the sociolinguistic reality of the people that we are working with at each of the three levels we have described. For example, at the Restricted Level, this would include knowing about government policies towards minority communities. At the Negotiated Level we are concerned with issues that arise from the various social networks which people are part of. These could be regional, sociopolitical, geographic, historical, religious, or educational. Often, these concerns are more difficult to learn about than those at the Restricted Level. For example, if a regional LWC is not an official language, less may be known about it. Of course, we want to learn all we can about the situation at the Free Level, but typically there is little information available to us until we visit the speech community. Sometimes it may be possible to take a short pre-survey visit in order to clarify research questions or calibrate tools. We should also try to find knowledgeable outsiders, people who have been to the location or neighboring regions and can provide information based on their experiences there.

5.4   The Primary Research Stage

Primary research is the effort to gather new information and test new hypotheses.

5.4.1   Developing Research Tools

As we have described in several sections, there are a number of tools that we tend to use for studying various phenomena in language assessment. Generally, when we plan a survey, we are more concerned about adapting a well-proven survey tool than creating new ones. In fact, we should have a good amount of experience using the established tools and a good amount of experience in the field of study before considering any significant modification of protocols or the development of new tools. Whether we are developing new tools or preparing a proven tool for a specific survey, we need to continue to relate this work to the purpose of the survey and its research questions.

When standard tools are not suitable to implement, then, to answer the questions being asked, appropriate tools must be developed. However, that development must be based on extensive and disciplined research demonstrating the need for the new tool or protocol and equally careful research within the theoretical discipline as well as research in tool construction in order to create something that is worthwhile.

CROSS-REFERENCES ▶ See Section 5.2.6 on page 187 for more about triangulation.

We have talked about triangulation and how we can use different types of tools to collect data so that results can be confirmed through more than one data source. If the data gathered from these different tools provides similar answers to our research questions, then we can feel more confident that they have given us an accurate understanding of the situation. Another reason to use triangulation is that many of the tools that we use have their limitations and are vulnerable to problems. Tests and questionnaires are difficult to construct and may have flaws. People do not always respond as expected to a certain tool or probe. There are certain aspects of the various phenomena that we study that are difficult to perceive. We can misunderstand the observations and findings, not realizing what they are really indicating. The constraints of a survey trip and in particular the language barriers that we have to cross sometimes force us to use less than optimal procedures, and this can potentially influence the results. However, in spite of the difficulties we face, we want to plan our surveys to the best of our ability, to be as precise and exact as we can at each stage of the assessment process.

QUOTE ▶ *A surveyor's greatest fear is that someone will believe them! Once a surveyor uses a tool several times, he or she realizes how vulnerable they are to error. However, longitudinal studies that have been done on surveys that were carried out decades ago have shown a high degree of accuracy. But there is always a concern that we may not have really captured an accurate assessment of the situation. (Ken Decker, International Language Assessment Coordinator, SIL International)*

5.4.1.1 *Validation and reliability*

Protocols for tools that have been used on numerous surveys will have repeatedly proven themselves as clear, reliable, and valid. But when we develop or modify a research tool we need to assure that it provides us with accurate data. We do this before we go on a survey by giving each tool a pre-survey evaluation by testing for CLARITY, reliability, and validity. We improve clarity when we have a good translation of materials and ensure that we test descriptions and explanations for comprehension. It is helpful to compose these with complete phrases and statements using short, simple words. If the translator is confused, the result will be confusing. What we are aiming for with clarity is communication that means the same thing to each participant. To maintain reliability, we need to be consistent in the way that we administer each tool. That means we need to draw up clear and precise protocols for each surveyor to follow so that we present an identical set of stimuli to each participant. This means the same questions, in the same order, with the same materials, and the surveyor saying the same things each time. Thus, it is vital for new surveyors to be thoroughly familiar with the tools before they head out on their survey.

> DEFINITION ▸ A tool has CLARITY when people understand the intent and expectations of the tool, whether it is how to take a test or the meaning of a question.

The validity of our tools can be influenced by intervening variables depending on who we use the tools with and where we use them. It helps not to rely on our own judgment about what participants might or might not be capable of. Also, we should remember that the way we administer a questionnaire or test may affect the quality of the data collected. At the secondary research stage, we can ask knowledgeable people for information, particularly for anything that people might consider is private, embarrassing, or otherwise taboo. There are a number of issues to consider:

> CROSS-REFERENCE ▸ See Section 5.2.6 on page 187 for more on precision and accuracy.

- How will people react to the questioning or interview situation? In some cultures, direct questions may communicate anger or disapproval (or something else).
- We need to be careful about questions that ask the participant to rely too much on memory, or ask about things they would not know about.
- We need to be careful about questions that ask about concepts that participants might not be aware of.
- The educational level of the responders may influence their ability to understand and answer questions. Questions about hypothetical situations, for example, are particularly difficult in some cultures.

- It is important to understand cultural influences here because if we make our tests difficult for participants, they may feel compelled to give a "right" answer or simply not be able to respond.
- Sometimes we can help make the process easier for people by using self-administered questionnaires, assuring confidentiality and anonymity.
- Sometimes it is awkward for people to answer questions about themselves. In such a case, we may be able to ask questions in reference to other groups of people. For example, "How do other people in your community feel about...?"

CROSS-REFERENCE ► For more on choosing participants see sampling in **Section 5.4.2** on page 195.

Finally, as it is generally not possible to administer a questionnaire to everyone in a speech community, we will need to choose who participates, and this can influence the answers to questions. Recognizing and reporting these limitations (as appropriate) helps the reader to judge the character of the data subsequently reported. Do not be alarmed— these base-line data are still valuable and subsequently can be built upon.

5.4.1.2 Calibration

CROSS-REFERENCE ► For more on SRTs see **Section 3.4.5** on page 106.

Imagine that we have created an SRT to measure bilingual proficiency. We administer the test and someone passes it. What does this tell us? Does it tell us how bilingual they are? No. It simply tells us that they have passed this test. Without calibration, a score on a particular SRT has no meaning in itself. Since an SRT does not test all aspects of bilingual proficiency, it can only give us an idea of a level of bilingual proficiency. We do not know if it is a hard or easy test or if it is accurately sampling an individual's overall proficiency. The score is only relevant when shown to correlate with proficiency levels measured by a more precise method of assessing bilingual proficiency, like an oral interview. Calibration involves correlating our results with an established, empirical scale, and it is always based on the assumption that the established scale is accurate and dependable.

CROSS-REFERENCE ► The RPE was first introduced in **Section 3.4.5.2** on page 107.

NOTE ► For a complete description of the calibration of SRTs, see pages 55–70 of Radloff (1991).

When a test like an SRT is created, it needs to be calibrated against another measure, like a standard oral proficiency test. The RPE method was first developed as a method to establish a correlation for the SRT. To do this calibration, we need to test a number of people using both methods. First we test them using another established bilingualism test, and then we ask them to take the SRT. If participants who score 80 percent on the SRT consistently perform at Level 2 on the other test, we can predict that other participants from the same region getting 80 percent will have

Level 2 proficiency. In this way we can calibrate the SRT so that we know what level of proficiency each score represents in standard terms.

Calibration is also useful for refining a test. The idea here is to identify the probes that most accurately predict difference in whatever is being measured. In the example of creating an SRT, we also use calibration to identify which sentences best discriminate between different levels of bilingual proficiency. Probes that ILR level 2 participants can repeat but ILR level 2+ students cannot are helpful to discriminate between these two proficiency levels. But if ILR level 2 participants successfully repeat a sentence which ILR level 2+ students cannot, it does not help us distinguish these levels. This probe will need further refinement.

5.4.2   Sampling

It is usually not possible to study every person in a community. Conversely, we would not want to simply stand on a street corner and interview whoever passes by. That would probably provide distorted information. Therefore, we need to select certain individuals to participate in the study with the intention that they will represent the larger population. There are ways to increase the probability that those tested will be more representative of the whole community. We call this **SAMPLING**. Because the process for selecting participants will directly influence the precision of any statistical estimates, we must make sure that we carefully control the process of choosing participants.

DEFINITION ▶ SAMPLING is the process by which we collect enough of the right kind of data so that the results are the same as if we had collected all the data possible if we had had unlimited resources.

CASE STUDY 5B
SAMPLING ERROR
USA

There are numerous examples of research that has failed because proper sampling procedures were not followed. One famous case involved the predictions of political polls for the 1936 United States presidential campaign between Alf Landon and the incumbent President Franklin Roosevelt. The Literary Digest sampled ten million people whose names were chosen from telephone directories and lists of automobile owners. Two million people responded and the poll gave Alf Landon an astounding 57 percent to 43 percent victory.

CASE STUDY 5B SOURCE ▶ Rubin and Babbie (2010:191–192).

However, two weeks later Roosevelt won the election by a record 61 percent of the vote. The problem lay in the fact that in 1936 only wealthy people, who favored Landon, owned phones and automobiles. However, it was the masses of lower socioeconomic classes who favored Roosevelt's plans to rescue the nation from the Great Depression.

DEFINITION ▶ A **SAMPLE FRAME** is the total set of people we can select participants from.

The first step is to decide how well the **SAMPLE FRAME** corresponds to what we want it to represent. If we want to study attitudes across groups of people living in multiple locations but can only talk to people in one location, then our sample frame is limited to that one location. We cannot say that we have studied the entire speech community, if we are unable to sample women. For a good sample, every person in the sample frame should have an equal opportunity of being chosen. Therefore, it is important to define the sample frame. There are three basic types of sample frames, each with a strength and weakness.

DEFINITIONS ▶ As well as being defined in the text, you can find definitions of all the types of sampling mentioned in the **Glossary** on page 239.

A **COMPREHENSIVE SAMPLE FRAME** attempts to include everyone. In some cases it is possible to get lists of people, for example from a phone list. While this may include a large portion of the population, it also excludes those who do not have phones, those who choose to not list their numbers, and those who got a phone since the directory was published. If it is possible to determine the percentage of the sample frame that may not be included, this can accurately estimate the relationship of the sample to the whole population.

We can narrow the sample frame to a predictable possibility of selection by choosing a group where we can be sure of everyone's availability for selection. For example, we might select all the people who attend a workshop as the sample frame. This can guarantee the possibility for selection from all people in the sample frame, but there is no way of determining a relationship between this sample frame and the larger population.

An alternative is called **MULTI-STAGED SAMPLING**. In the first phase, we identify a set of individuals to select participants from. For example, we may select certain households, with no knowledge of who lives there. From the people we identify in those households, we select certain individuals to participate. While this includes some of the positive elements of a comprehensive sample and narrows the sample frame, we also compound the problems of the two types. In this example, homeless and people living in some kind of group housing might be excluded in the first phase. Although we have narrowed the sample frame, we still do not know how representative this sample frame is to the wider population.

Since there is not a practical way to sample everyone in a large group (over several hundred) and there are limitations to using sample frames to manage who we sample, it is important to give thorough thought to the planning, and report the realities of whom our research really represents.

Once we have identified the sample frame, we need to actually sample participants from this frame. There are many kinds of sampling methods used for different purposes. We will only describe three commonly used methods: simple random sampling, systematic sampling and stratified sampling.

SIMPLE RANDOM SAMPLING is essentially like drawing numbers from a hat. If there are 150 houses in a village and we want to sample 10 percent of the households, we could make a map and number the houses. Then, using a computer to randomly generate 15 numbers between 001 and 150, we identify the households corresponding to the numbers that the computer chose. To do this for 150 possible sample points is manageable, but if we want to sample 500 people out of a population of 10,000, the process would be quite laborious. It is also unlikely that we would be able to get a list of all the people in such a large group.

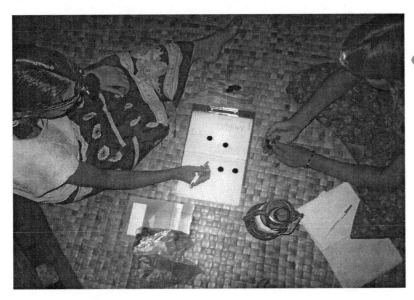

FIGURE 11 ▶ In preparation for data collection, surveyors in Papua New Guinea work by lamplight to carry out simple random sampling using counters.

A **SYSTEMATIC SAMPLE** is somewhat similar to a simple random sample. It involves identifying a systematic way to choose the sample points. If we wanted to take a systematic sample from the example above, we could divide the percentage we want to sample (10% = 0.1) by the total number available (150) to get a fraction of 1/15. We would then have a computer randomly generate a number between 1 and 150, say 37, and starting from house number 37, select every fifteenth house.

We use simple random and systematic sampling when it is unnecessary or impossible to know any of the characteristics of what is included in the sample. However, these sampling methods mean that we might end up with two samples of a group which have quite different characteristics, particularly if the group consists of diverse subjects. This potential diversity is called **SAMPLING VARIATION**. In our example above, one sampling method may choose more households with educated people than another simply because of chance.

DEFINITION ▶ SAMPLING VARIATION is the difference between two different samples of a population.

There will always be a certain amount of difference between the sample population and the whole population; this is called **SAMPLING ERROR**. There are two factors that reduce sampling error: population size and homogeneity. A larger sample size has less sampling error than a smaller sample size. There will be less sampling error with a more homogeneous population group than with a more heterogeneous group. Therefore, if we can take a larger sample or identify homogeneous sub-groups within a community, then we will decrease the sampling error. Collecting a large sample usually increases the time or cost of a survey. Therefore, we want to find ways to make it possible to sample more homogeneous groups.

DEFINITION ▶ A **SAMPLING ERROR** is a predictable difference between the attributes of our sample population and the whole population.

CASE STUDY 5C
PROVIDENTIAL SAMPLING
NIGER

CASE STUDY 5C SOURCE ▶ Annette Harrison, SIL Central Africa Branch.

During a large and involved survey in Niger, we devised a sampling strategy of several strata according to administrative divisions and tax rolls in the country. At each level, we made a random sample until we reached the people we would have listen to texts and answer questions concerning their comprehension and attitudes towards different varieties of the language we were studying. For example, we randomly selected from a list of administrative towns, and then, once there, we asked an official to draw up a list of local chiefs. Then we randomly drew names from that list, etc. When we drew up a list, we numbered each name and drew numbered bottle caps out of a bag. On one occasion, we arrived in an administrative town that we had chosen at random to discover that the president of the country would be arriving in a day or two, and so every person who could be of help to us was too busy preparing for the auspicious visit. Finally, one man, reluctantly agreed to help us draw up a list of local chiefs, of which he was one, but he said he doubted we would be able to find any of the people selected because of the upcoming official visit. As well as helping compile the list, as he was interested in our selection procedure, I asked him to be the one to pull the bottle caps out of the bag. We were beginning to wonder how we would accomplish any work in the area when, to his surprise (and ours!), the number he pulled from the bag went with his name—the only person who had demonstrated availability and willingness to help us! We were able to complete our work in the area and move on to the next before the arrival of the president.

In typical language development surveys, of the kind described in this book, we can often identify certain characteristics that differentiate groups within a community. For example, in some places men are typically more multilingual than women, educated people speak a more standardized form of the language than the uneducated, the younger tend to be more educated, etc. Our prediction is that a group that has many identifiable similarities will be similar in other ways also. Structuring our sampling by characteristics like these to reduce sampling error is called **STRATIFIED SAMPLING**.

SIMPLE RANDOM SAMPLING	• Useful when significant characteristics are unknown • Useful when there is confidence that the sample population is fairly homogeneous
SYSTEMATIC SAMPLING	• Useful when significant characteristics are unknown • Useful when there is confidence that the sample population is fairly homogeneous
STRATIFIED SAMPLING	• Preferred over the previous two methods • Decreases probable sampling error • Creates more homogeneous sub-groups

TABLE 10 ► Sampling methods and their benefits.

Having first identified the differentiating characteristics of the community, we then consider the proportional relationship of each segment to another. If half of the community men are educated but only 10 percent of the women, then half of the men and 10 percent of the women we sample should be educated. Also, if we know that 90 percent of the men under 25 years of age are educated, then we will want to split the sample group into those younger and older than 25, and 90 percent of the men we sample should be educated. From this, we are able to identify the number of people who need to be sampled.

In actual field situations there are often factors that limit the ability to follow the best research methodology. For example, in some cultures we may only be able to work with relatives of our local hosts or the people assigned to help us by the local authority figure. In such cases we need to do all we can to determine if these participants are representative of the wider population.

For some types of research, where there is no need for precision in the measurements, we are only looking for a general range of ideas or information. In such cases, it may be sufficient to simply talk to whoever volunteers. However, in most cases we want statistical evidence about a population. Table 9 shows a typical sample matrix for sampling a community.

TABLE 9 ▶ A sample matrix showing the differentiating characteristics of a community and enabling us to total what percentage of each group we want to sample. Table adapted from Blair (1990:37).

GENDER		MEN			WOMEN			TOTAL
EDUCATION		NONE	PRIMARY	SECONDARY	NONE	PRIMARY	SECONDARY	
AGE	YOUNG (15-30)							
	MIDDLE (31-45)							
	OLD (46+)							
	TOTAL							

5.4.3   Data Analysis

WWW.SURVEYWIKI.INFO ▶ See the **Data Analysis** page on SurveyWiki for tips and resources for analyzing data.

The type of data desired for analysis is shaped by what is already known of the subject. When little is known about a topic, the inquiry may start with broad questions that are refined as patterns, themes, and issues start to emerge. From the identified patterns, tentative theories might develop from which hypotheses can be deduced and eventually tested with various measurements.

Qualitative and quantitative research methods serve complementary functions. Qualitative research is used when little is known or written about a subject, whereas quantitative research is preferred once general categories are identified for measurement. Quantitative research tends to rely on some amount of previous qualitative research in order to identify the appropriate categories to be measured. Quantitative procedures, such as lexicostatistics, recorded text testing and sentence repetition tests can complement qualitative instruments such as informal interviews with members of a speech community. The overall result is a more complete understanding about languages and people in a particular context. Neither form of data or research is better; we need them for different purposes.

Methodologically, it is helpful to use spreadsheets for arranging data. For example, list the participants down one side of the spreadsheet and list the questions across the top. In this way, information on a question can be easily tabulated. For some types of data, if this is done in a computer program, it will be possible to sort the data to identify patterns.

5.4.3.1 Quantitative data analysis

Quantitative research is designed in such a way that results can be presented as numbers or statistics. Quantitative instruments can be used when we want to interview a large number of people.

We have to be careful with the use of numbers, particularly in interpreting them. People tend to believe that numbers and things that are measured are more real than when numbers are not presented. This can be misleading since numbers can be deceptive. It is frequently observed that statistics can be made to lie quite easily. Numbers are not predictive. This means that just because we can say 86 percent of the people have a certain attitude, it does not mean that 86 percent of the people will follow that attitude with a certain behavior. Furthermore, in our measurements, the difference between 87 and 85 percent should probably not be considered significant. Our tools and methods are not precise enough.

Quantitative results tend to be generalized to one or more populations. Since we generally cannot count everything, we have to use our data to estimate that the findings are representative of the larger population. However, it is possible that we have missed something important in our research, and our estimations may be inaccurate.

If we want to collect information that can be counted, the tools we use must be designed appropriately. For a questionnaire, we want a limited number of available responses to questions because this will mean similar answers can be compared. But in doing so we must be sure we include all of the important options in the choices we present as possible answers. As we have described with wordlists, recorded text tests, and sentence repetition tests, we must be careful in what we say the resultant numbers mean. Just because someone passes one of these tests, it does not mean they are fully proficient or have complete comprehension. If one wordlist is 100 percent equivalent to another, it does not mean they are exactly the same. Likewise, a 10 percent difference does not mean there is a 10 percent loss of comprehension.

Even when a quantitative approach is used to appropriately reduce some information to numbers, it may not be the exact numbers that are important. For example, if we get a comment from someone that they would like to see their heritage language written, we do not know how widespread that sentiment is in the community. We can use a well-designed questionnaire and an appropriate sampling technique to find out that 73 percent of the people feel this way. However, the precise number is not as important as the fact that it is significantly more than half but not as high as 90 percent. While the 73 percent does not tell us if the language should be written or not, it does indicate that there might be good support for language development. It also indicates that 27 percent may be resistant, and although they may be in the minority numerically, they may have the majority of influence in the community depending on who they are. In such a situation, it may be critical that we continue on to ask why more people are not more supportive, or who is not supportive of such a venture. Then we need to consider the potential impact of the dissenting segment of the population.

5.4.3.2 Qualitative data analysis

Qualitative analysis attempts to make sense out of an ongoing process. This process may be a series of discussions, dialogues, or observations. It may also take the form of products of that process. These may be tangible products such as texts or images or they may be intangible such as the learning of new skills or the change of attitudes. As this process continues, we will adapt the way that we carry out our qualitative analysis, refining it to focus in on the important aspects of our research. Initial observations may be followed by tentative and general conclusions that suggest making further observations of particular types. These, in turn, result in revised conclusions and new recommendations for yet more field research. This is an application of the research cycle with obvious applications to ongoing language assessment.

Qualitative research tends to require extended time for interviewing and observing a subject. Throughout the research, the researchers should remain open to the possibility of needing to adjust their research instrument in order to add or reformulate questions based on their subjects' previous responses. This approach is valid when qualitative researchers use purposeful sampling by carefully selecting the participants to observe or interview.

Qualitative research is designed in such a way that the results can be represented as trends or themes that can be described in words. In the report itself, individual's quotes may be cited. Results of qualitative research tend to be limited to the conclusions about the individual participants directly studied. This is in contrast to quantitative findings which may be used to make generalizations about the larger population. In this way, it is possible to misuse qualitative data too. Sometimes people will suggest that the qualitative responses of a few people are representative of the larger population. While these responses from the few may in fact represent the larger population, this cannot be proved until quantifiable data collection methods have also been used.

5.5   Participatory Process

In the previous sections, we have discussed methods of academic research for the purpose of collecting information that will be useful for decision making and strategic planning. We have also talked about the role and importance of partnerships. In this section on the participatory process, we are concerned with the mindset of the surveyor. This mindset is the belief that the speakers of the languages we study have a right to be involved in any research of their language and culture. We recognize and respect the rights of the people we work with to make their own decisions.

CROSS-REFERENCES ▶ For further discussion of participatory methods see **Section 4.4.5** on page 161. For previous discussions of partner-ships, see **Sections 2.3.3** on page 35, **3.3.4** on page 91, and **4.3.4** on page 139.

For example, if outsiders conduct research on a speech community and make decisions about the language development process, the speech community has no commitment to those decisions and may be offended by the imposition. However, if the stakeholders are cooperatively engaged in a process by which they all come to a decision together, there may be more impact. The speech community is more likely to embrace the goals and process of language development, and the goals may be more relevant for them. This is likely to be a more effective approach to development.

Engaging with the speech community and facilitating a cooperative, participatory process may take more time. It may mean that we wait for an appropriate time to do surveys and research at the request of the local community or partnership. It may also mean that we train local people to participate with or lead in the research.

This process will be implemented differently in each situation. The speech communities may not be interested but yet allow research to proceed. They may fully embrace the research and provide invaluable resources. Or they may reject the offer. We, the authors, are aware that this approach may create difficulty for outsiders doing research in some situations. However, we believe that the benefits of prioritizing participation will far outweigh the difficulties.

5.6   Academic Writing

In this section, we will present some guidelines as to what is expected when writing survey reports. Remember that most assessment is carried out by a team and that includes the writing. It is unusual for one individual to have to write a whole report. There are many reports that have been done previously that can be followed as models. Academic writing is not meant to be too creative, so deviation from standard forms is not encouraged. The most important thing to remember about academic writing is that the reader should have a clear understanding of

- the purpose and goals of the research,
- the research question(s),
- how we collected and analyzed the data, and
- the conclusions and how they relate to the purpose, goals, and research question(s).

Researchers also need to be honest about their work. We should not try to make the data say more than it really does. We need to be clear about the weaknesses of the research and data.

5.6.1   The Process

Before we begin writing, it is good to be familiar with other reports that have been written. This will give the writer an idea of the target. It is possible and important to begin writing reports from the start of the research planning. One way to help the reader of a report is by organizing the information we present. The use of an outline is very helpful for keeping information organized. There are often templates based on earlier surveys that we can follow to help us structure the report. From the beginning of the research phase it is important to keep track of where information comes from.

Drafting is a normal part of the process, so we should get used to the fact that we will need to redraft our reports a number of times. Teamwork may mean that different members of the team work on different sections of a report. Spellchecking and having someone else proofread the text are important steps to take. When editing, we need to put ourselves in the position of the reader. Things that might be clear to us may not be to the reader if we have made assumptions about what the reader might know. If we are in doubt, we should always give an explanation rather than simply hope that the reader will be able to understand. To achieve this, we should take a critical approach to writing, questioning information that we present, asking why we have included it and whether the connection to the purpose and research question will be clear for the reader.

All the information in the report should contribute to answering the research question(s). One way of ensuring this is to imagine that the reader would want to carry out exactly the same procedures and therefore needs to know each detailed step. In the conclusion, we should restate the purpose of the research and include a synopsis of how the data answers the research question(s).

There are a number of general writing principles that might be helpful to bear in mind. Unlike other forms of writing, academic writing sometimes requires the use of passive grammar. We need to consider whether it is important to mention who was actually doing the activities we describe. We may make the choice based on what is best for the reader, or whoever we are writing for may have a preference for style. The survey community is a multilingual, multicultural group of people, and it is quite likely that what we write will be read by people from a wide range of technical and language backgrounds. We should try to aim for a style that will be clear and yet simple, thus accommodating the various abilities among our readership.

Remember that there are ethical concerns for academic writing. Obviously, we should always avoid plagiarism. Sometimes research is not as successful or complete as we would like; maybe we did not test as many people as we would have liked. The best policy is to be honest. As long as readers know what the evidence is based on, they will know how much confidence to put in the research. The writer should not use any proper names or pictures of individuals unless specific permission has been obtained. We should describe people and cultures with respect. If there was any agreement to provide copies of the report to people who helped with the research, we must make sure that we follow through on that commitment.

With the rapid development of computer software it is hard to know what will be available as you read this. At the time of this writing, it is important to apply formatting styles as we write. If our text is going to be published in a journal, the journal will have preferred formatting criteria. We should mark text and headings using specific styles so we can easily create a table of contents. It is also possible to use special styles for foreign or phonetic words, but it is important to use Unicode fonts so that all the characters we write with are displayed no matter what electronic medium is used to read the text. We should compress any embedded images to minimize the size of the document. It is important to save computer files in widely available formats.

Depending on the purpose, we might produce different kinds of written reports. We should consider producing a report for the people we have studied in a form that they can understand. In some situations, we need to write a general report. This can include a wide range of information and may not have a more specific purpose other than to provide a description of the overall sociolinguistic situation. Research that is focused on a specific research question needs to be presented in a focused report. We often adapt such reports for conference presentations or publication in a journal. When we do this, we will be given fairly strict guidelines to follow. For example, papers for conferences and journals are usually relatively short. Conference presentations are generally limited to 15 or 20 minutes and journals usually have a word limit.

Journals often require their articles to be reviewed by other scholars, called peer reviews. While peer reviews criticizing our writing can be difficult to receive, we should see this as an opportunity to improve our research and writing skills. A peer review will usually address the research design and analysis. If problems are identified with these issues, it does not necessarily mean that we cannot use the research or publish the results. But problems in design, implementation, or analysis need to be acknowledged.

5.6.2   The Parts

- **Title**: The title should concisely describe the research without being too long. We need to include the authors and the date of the writing. We may want to include our academic institution or the organization that is sponsoring the research.
- **Table of Contents**: Depending on the length of the product, it may be useful to have a table of contents.
- **Abstract**: An abstract on the front page is helpful to give a quick overview of the report.
- **Headings**: Headings should be used to signpost text.
- **Text**: Paragraphs should usually begin with a topic sentence which is a sentence that contains the key idea of the paragraph. The rest of the paragraph then expands on the topic sentence. When we switch to a new idea, we need to switch to a new paragraph.
- **Tables and figures**: Where possible, maps, tables, and figures should be used to illustrate text and summarize content. These should be labeled clearly.
- **References**: The reference section of the report should only include citations referred to in the report. To help maintain bibliographical data, there are online bibliography compilers, or word processor programs may have a built in bibliography compiler. This helps with easy entry of the information and also maintains consistency. Citations should follow a standard format such as *Chicago Manual of Style*, Linguistic Society of America, APA or Harvard.
- **Appendices**: Use appendices for lengthy amounts of data, particularly for examples of questionnaires, wordlists, or full tables of results.

5.7   Technical Notes

Included in this section are introductory comments on a few technical topics. They are introductory because we can only raise these issues and cannot give the most current specifics. The standards are constantly changing and the best we can do here is point you to places where you can find something more current. We would like to encourage you to help us keep the companion website www.surveywiki.info updated on these concerns.

5.7.1 Digital technologies

There is such a wide range of new digital technologies, and the numbers and types grow daily. These offer us new tools and new ways of working. As the rate of change increases, it will take persistence to keep up with the latest technology and to know how to make the best use of it. But it will also require diligence to not be overwhelmed by the technology. Ours is a social science and we don't want to lose contact with the communities we study and the people we work with.

5.7.1.1 Recording quality

CROSS-REFERENCE ▶ See **Section 5.1** on page 168 for ethical considerations of our work, particularly **Section 5.1.9** on page 175 for information on gathering informed consent.

For many aspects of our research we make electronic recordings of data. These include still and motion pictures and audio recordings. The first concern with recordings of these types is that we gain consent from the people whose image or voice is captured. The next concern is for the recording quality. Modern digital recording equipment is capable of gathering data with unimaginable precision, and the capability increases daily. The devices are becoming smaller. Quality units are built into other devices, such as audio and video equipment built into computers, hand-held devices, and cell phones.

It is important to use the highest quality equipment available. Even if we cannot hear or see the difference between two high-quality devices, computer programs may be able to identify differences. And if they cannot today, the programs of tomorrow may be able to tell us more than what is available today.

There are three parts to recording quality to consider:

- **Capture**: this refers to the quality of our equipment—its ability to record data. The lens or microphone needs to be able to gather information as precisely as possible.
- **Output quality**: this refers to the digital formats available for doing something with the captured data, whether analysis or archiving. This relates also to the computer programs that will be used for analysis of the data. We want to record data in a format that our computer programs use.
- **Storage**: we need to consider the best form and format for storage of data. Digital media tends to degrade over time and the data may be seriously corrupted in five or ten years.

5.7.1.2 Computers, the Internet, and Cell Technologies

There are numerous computer programs available to help with various aspects of the analysis of different kinds of data. There are programs for

- analyzing wordlists,
- manipulating audio, video, and graphic data,
- for creating and analyzing questionnaires,
- managing ethnographic information,
- running statistical computations,
- managing quantities of information in a database,
- making bibliographic information readily available,
- making report writing easier,
- presenting information on the Internet, and
- storing data.

We must not underestimate the importance of the new ways of working that the Internet is providing. Minority communities have their own websites; they have a presence on social networking sites; and they are preserving their cultures through videos posted online. It is possible to communicate for free, even with video, to people all over the world. People all over the world are collaborating on projects and working together to resolve problems. There will be a continual questioning of ways that we can maximize the benefits of these technologies for improving language assessment research.

Cell phone technology has created access to communication, the Internet, and information for people in very remote locations where the traditional delivery of electricity is not available. These small, hand-held devices also make some computing capacity much more mobile. It is up to this new generation of surveyors to learn how to use these new technologies to improve our abilities to do good research and to leverage them for the benefit of the people we work with.

5.7.2   Metadata and Archiving

It is important when archiving data that it is preserved with sufficient information so that others can understand its value and context. To be comprehensive, the list of information that could be documented is quite lengthy. There can also be some differences depending on the context of the data, where it is being stored, and how its potential users may want to access it. There are four basic categories of metadata:

- **Bibliographic**: the author or contributor, title, topic, abstracts, basically information about the data which helps people to find it;
- **Administrative**: the owner and manager of the data, who has access to it and understands how the data may be used;
- **Technical**: the technical information as to how the data was collected and its qualities, things such as format, recording speed, file size, etc.; and
- **Relationships**: if the data is part of a collection, how does it relate to the other parts.

We also want to mention that there are ever-changing ways to archive and preserve data so that it will not be destroyed, lost, or corrupted. It is also important to consider how it will be made available to wider audiences, if it is to be made available.

5.8   Further Reading

The Qualitative Researcher's Companion **by Michael Huberman and Matthew Miles (2006)**

This is an extremely comprehensive guide to carrying out all aspects of qualitative research including data analysis.

The Survey Kit **edited by Arlene Fink (2002)**

This is a 9-volume set of small books that cover numerous aspects of research from developing effective survey questions to writing reports.

Survey Research Methods **by Floyd Fowler (2009)**

Now in its fourth edition, a very accessible and concise guide to the major issues involved in carrying out surveys. Good sections on survey questionnaire design. This book is not focused on *language* survey but nevertheless has much we can learn.

The Research Manual: Design and Statistics for Applied Linguistics **by Evelyn Marcussen Hatch and Anne Lazaraton (1991)**

An excellent source book for everything you need to know about how to plan a research project with a focus specifically on applied linguistics. The second part of the book has a very useful guide to statistics which they take time to explain, anticipating the struggles that the rest of us have with numbers.

Qualitative Methods in Sociolinguistics by Barbara Johnstone (2000)

Focused, as we are, on language used in society, Johnstone covers both field and analytical methods and shows how to select, collect, and analyze data. Good for those new to the field of sociolinguistic research.

Writing Academic English by Alice Oshima and Ann Hogue (2006)

The leading guide to writing academic English for high-intermediate learners of English as a foreign language. The book is full of examples and takes the learner through the process of academic writing step by step. The fourth edition was published in 2006.

6 MAKING IT HAPPEN

So far, we have talked about the importance of two things: understanding the sociolinguistic reality and the importance of scientific rigor. While the need for good understanding and research is all very well, the whole assessment process can suffer if we are not also skilled in practical management, particularly for the survey trip itself. Despite our logistical and research skills, we still must manage the factors that commonly cause stress among surveyors. It is a sobering fact that most people beginning their careers with language assessment will only last two years or so. They leave the work for many reasons, but often they discover that the stresses they face in the job are greater than they expected. If surveyors leave the role after such a short time, the assessment community loses experienced personnel before they can contribute to improving how we assess languages.

In this chapter, we present the practical side of language assessment and, in particular, the logistics and resources needed for the survey trip. This includes:

- aspects of **teamwork** including **communication** and how to resolve **conflict,**
- working in **local communities,**
- managing resources such as **finance, equipment,** and **time,** and
- dealing with **ambiguity, the unexpected,** and **stress.**

NOTE ► To calculate how many relationships you are managing use the formula n(n+1)/2 where n is the number of people on the team.

6.1   Human Resources

As we conduct research and carry out assessment, the most important resource that we will manage is people. As well as our ethical responsibilities for data collection participants, we must respect the members of the team we work with. Usually, survey teams have two to four people, but surveys with six to eight people are not unknown. The number of relationships in a team increases dramatically each time a new member is added. With two members, each of them has one relationship to manage. If we increase our team to 4 team members, we now have 10 relationships to manage, and with a team of 8, there are 36!

FIGURE 12 ► John Carter, Janell Masters and John Grummitt of SIL Papua New Guinea's survey team stand with their pilot having just landed at the start of their first survey together.

Engaging in team building activities as a group *before* any work is done together can be extremely helpful. Teams don't just happen, they must be built with conscious effort. Teambuilding or team-formation workshops can be time well invested. As new team members join an established team, some effort should also be given to helping them integrate. Newcomers can find it difficult to move into teams that already have a shared history, private jokes, and understand each other's strengths and weaknesses.

Each member of the survey team brings different personalities, skills, and abilities to our work. It is impossible to assign roles and responsibilities correctly without recognizing these differences and making the most of them. Clear understanding of these roles is based on good communication.

We must also learn the skills to resolve conflict quickly and sensitively so that we maintain this good communication.

We also need to manage the way we behave towards participants in the communities we work in. These might be people who work with us as part of the team such as knowledgeable insiders or outsiders or language helpers. They might also be our hosts, and if so, this is a special relationship we must manage with care. In addition, wherever and whomever we are with, we must remember that we are ambassadors for the organizations we represent both on duty and off. These impressions may influence the future of any development work that results from our assessment.

It is very helpful to plan a time of debriefing after a survey to review how successful the planning was and how well relationships within the team and with local people worked. This is not only to identify problems but to celebrate successes also. Yearly, or more frequent, reviews with each team member can be helpful for growth planning, discussion of expectations, and resolving problems.

6.1.1   We Surveyors

We want to outline a number of personal qualities that are helpful for the work of language assessment. It is work that can be physically and emotionally demanding, particularly on survey trips; assessment projects have suffered because surveyors have not anticipated these demands and the effects on themselves or their team. The following is a list of important qualities in a surveyor. The surveyor needs to

- enjoy learning,
- be able to follow detailed outlines and procedures,
- have a good eye for detail and be thorough,
- have a good foundation in a full range of sociolinguistic topics,
- understand research methodologies,
- have an understanding of phonology,
- be able to accurately hear and describe phonetic sounds with the use of the International Phonetic Alphabet (IPA),
- understand the central issues of anthropology,
- be willing and able to learn other languages and adapt to other cultures,
- be willing and able to write up the results of our research in the form of a coherent report,

QUOTE ▸ *Good communication not only entails unobstructed communication between team members, but also communication that is good, where those outside of the team, those we have come to serve by survey, will recognize the harmony and single purpose of the team, leaving with them a positive aroma of public relations when we depart.* (Lynn Landweer, personal communication)

- be flexible in coping with the unexpected,
- have physical resilience for work that involves travelling to remote areas, eating unusual foods, or working and staying in an uncomfortable environment,
- be self-aware of our skills and our limitations, and
- be committed to the task and the team.

This may seem like an intimidating list, but with training and a willing spirit many people do well as surveyors. Few of us will possess all of these qualities. In fact, we place a high value on teamwork because we know that we all have our strengths and weaknesses. Teams work best with members who are aware of their strengths and weaknesses, who know how these contribute to the goals of the team and are continually working to improve their abilities.

Often though, the most critical aspects of our character are so deeply a part of ourselves that we are either not aware of them or, if we are aware, we are not able to communicate them to the people around us. To help us get a better understanding of ourselves, there are a number of different tools available. One example of such a tool is the Myers-Briggs Type Indicator (MBTI). This tool uses a questionnaire to measure the differences in how we think, feel about, and interact with the world around us. Once completed, the answers to the questionnaire determine which one of 16 types of character we tend to be like. There are a number of books and other online resources that explain the types and how they interact in more detail and we have included some in the Further Reading section at the end of this chapter.

This book and classroom knowledge only go so far; ultimately we need to gain field experience and, preferably, be mentored by an experienced researcher through the whole process of planning, conducting, and writing up surveys. Furthermore, we must keep learning. We should be intentional about personal and professional development and have a growth plan and a mentor to keep us on track with learning.

6.1.2   On the Team

CROSS-REFERENCE ▶ See **Section 4.4.5** on page 161 for more about participatory methods.

We cannot overestimate the importance of teamwork for successful language assessment. It should be obvious that simply getting some people together does not mean teamwork automatically happens. Quite simply, without teamwork, we will not succeed in language assessment, even if we manage somehow to collect data and produce survey reports.

Our efforts to develop teamwork should include participation with the speech community in assessment and language development. There are skills we can learn to make teamwork a success. The participatory methods we described earlier are built on a foundation of such skills. One way to discover who we are as individuals and as a team is to take the time to get to know one another socially, or in non-survey events, so we can observe each other's interaction patterns and learn to be open enough to talk about personalities and relationships.

We need to understand who our team will include. Language assessment requires us to be trained and knowledgeable enough to carry out quality research. But as we are expected to be flexible and work in a wide variety of assessment contexts, it is best to always have someone on the team who has a significant amount of experience directly related to the purposes of the assessment. Sometimes the survey team may be accompanied by specialists who have a particular interest in what the survey is about. This might be a literacy specialist, someone who speaks one of the varieties of language we are investigating, a sociolinguistics specialist, or an anthropologist. Part of our role as surveyors is to be able to relate to different specialists and to create mutually beneficial relationships between them, the team, and the people we work with. The team may include people who are considering future language development work in the area. Be aware that the inclusion of people who have a vested interest in the outcome of the survey may affect the objectivity of the research. If our survey team has worked together for a while, we need to be sensitive as we include these people into our existing assessment team. In particular, there needs to be clarity about what their role is going to be within the team. If a survey must be done without the participation of an experienced person, the surveyors must proactively become as informed as possible.

6.1.2.1 *Roles and responsibilities*

One of the keys to a successful team is that we have clearly defined roles and responsibilities. This gives a clear organizational structure with boundaries that all team members are aware of and work within. A team is by definition a group of people who work together, typically under a team leader. It is important that a team leader is established. This is the person with responsibility for decisions within the team. When new people join the team, they need to understand the team dynamics, history, and reasons for the way the team works. Attempting to change established teams can bring more stress than working in a less than ideal environment in the first place.

A survey team may include people who perform some of the following roles:

- someone who talks to officials,
- someone who does well talking to people and inviting their participation,
- someone who is good at phonetics,
- someone who is good with the electronic equipment,
- someone who is good with documenting observations,
- someone who manages the schedule well,
- someone who manages the vehicle,
- someone who manages the supplies that will be needed,
- someone who is good at synthesis and analysis of data,
- someone who has done the secondary research,
- a helpful insider,
- someone who is good at observing the social behaviors of the host community and can alert the team to apparent social expectations,
- someone who is good at compiling and editing the report, and
- someone who is by role and skill a team leader.

Ideally, people need to feel comfortable with and be prepared for the roles and responsibilities they are assigned. However, there may be situations which require us to carry out work which we are not fully prepared to do. If a team member is unable to travel on a planned survey due to personal circumstances, other team members may have to take on his or her responsibilities at short notice. This can place great strain on us if we are not prepared to be flexible in the roles we carry out. Equally though, forcing ourselves to flex too much may be debilitating. Managing the tension between flexibility and stress is based on knowing our own limits.

Feedback from experienced surveyors indicates that teams with members who have a variety of roles and skills work much more successfully than teams where each member has only one role. Without variety, boredom can be a very real stress factor, particularly if team members have to wait for others to complete their tasks. Variety also enables the team to be flexible on the field. Often situations we encounter determine exactly who on the team would be best to carry out a certain task at a particular time. Often it is hard to know who this is in advance because we cannot predict many situations.

6.1.2.2 Communication

Knowing ourselves well is of little use if we cannot communicate what we know to our teammates. Equally, if we are unhappy with how someone else on the team is behaving or unhappy with our situations, we need to be able to discuss this with the others. Not discussing this is only going to make the situation worse. Underlying irritations when we are preparing to go on a survey trip may be easy to ignore when we are working at our base. We can always go home and switch off. But on a survey trip, there is nowhere to go without the team going with us. Often, teams "live in each other's pockets" for a week to a month, and there may be nowhere private we can discuss things if they come up.

Consideration of all of these factors means that good communication is vital from the start of a team, or when new members join the team. Below, we have listed some dos and don'ts that are particularly important for successful teamwork.

> **DON'T** assume that just because someone shares our language, they have the same communication values. Varying values exist the world over, despite shared languages.

> **DO** assume that cultural differences will change people's understanding of how communication takes place. We should learn as much as we can about different cultural communication values. We need to be proactive and ask people from different cultures about their communication styles as well as what good communication means to them. We should make a point of sharing communication values that are important to us.

> **DON'T** forget that we need to vary our communication to suit the medium of communication and the skill levels of the person we are communicating with. Telephone conversations and email can be particularly problematic for example, particularly for non-native speakers who may have less experience and do not have the language skills to manage conversations in their L2.

> **DO** be aware of factors that might make communication difficult: time of day, stresses on us or the other person, distractions, and the topic. We should use our awareness of these factors to plan when it might be best to communicate.

> **DON'T** blame others for not understanding something we communicated. Instead, we need to accept responsibility for the breakdown, apologize,

and try to resolve the situation. And, importantly, we need to ask them to provide feedback on how we can improve our communication in the future.

DO remember that people are more important than tasks.

6.1.2.3 Conflict resolution

Despite our best efforts, communication breaks down at times, and we end up in a conflict situation. It is important to realize that conflict is going to happen and to be prepared for dealing with it. It is simply not realistic to presume that we can manage an assessment project without encountering interpersonal conflict at some point with someone. It is helpful to understand that conflict does not need to be a negative thing. Certainly, there can be negative outcomes from conflict, but that is more about how conflict is managed than about conflict itself. We avoid conflict because we have not learned how to deal with it when it comes along. Unless we are prepared for conflict, we will probably spend most of our time dealing with the effects of it rather than with its source. This results in a vicious cycle of unresolved and repetitious conflict.

Cross-Reference ▸ See **Section 6.4** on page 238 for more resources.

Conflict can be positive because it gives us opportunities to learn more about ourselves and others. If we start with this attitude, we will not be so stressed when conflict happens. Again, as with communication, there are plenty of resources to help us manage conflict, and we should refer to them in our professional development. Here, we have included a simple checklist to help with resolution when conflict occurs.

1. First of all, we should check that everyone involved accepts that there is a conflict. For people from some cultures, this may be difficult if conflict is personalized. For them, accepting that conflict exists may risk causing someone embarrassment. What may be a conflict for us may not seem so for others. At this stage, letting people know that we think there may be a problem might surprise some people. We need to be prepared for that. In mixed cultural teams, be sure to find out what signals conflict. For example, "blunt communication" for one person may signal that that there is a problem but for another person it may just be an expression of an opinion. And there may not be any conflict at all.

2. Each person involved needs time to state their own view of the situation. Again, we need to avoid the risk of causing someone to lose face. We can do that by encouraging everyone not to make statements about others but about themselves instead. While each person states their viewpoint,

no one else should comment or interrupt.

3. We should attempt to find common ground by asking questions that are exploratory (Are you saying…? So, if we did that, what would happen? Are there any other solutions?).

4. People need to have their hurts or frustrations acknowledged as being reasonable and understandable, and we should not expect people to deny or suppress feelings like these. Thus, there should be a focus on requesting changes in behavior, not changes in attitudes or feelings, and we should be prepared to suggest how these changes could be possible so that everyone will feel satisfied. However, there can be some attitudes, such as insubordination, that are unacceptable.

5. It can be helpful to agree what we plan to do in the future in order to prevent the likelihood of the conflict recurring.

6. If the conflict is serious or previous attempts to resolve it have not worked, we should try to find someone to act as a mediator who can help manage the process above. This should be someone neutral who everyone involved is happy to accept in their role as mediator.

7. Throughout the conflict-resolution process, it is very important to realize that the slightest hint of criticism or hostility may cause the problem to get worse. Minimizing this by managing our body language, tone of voice, and temptation to blame can be very important.

CASE STUDY 6A
ON THE PHONE
PAPUA NEW GUINEA

This telephone conversation took place between a surveyor who was planning a survey trip and someone who ran a boat company:

CASE STUDY 6A SOURCE ▶ Juliann Spencer, Language Surveyor, SIL Papua New Guinea.

Surveyor: *Yes, hello, I was wondering how much it would cost to take a boat from G to A.*

Boat Guy: *Well, it will take 15 gallons of fuel.*

Surveyor:	*OK, but we don't have a boat. We want to hire a boat.*
Boat Guy:	*OK, well it will take 15 gallons of fuel.*
Surveyor:	*OK, but how much will it cost?*
Boat Guy:	*From G to A? Yeah, that will take 15 gallons of fuel.*
Surveyor:	*But if four people just want to hire a boat, how much will they need to pay to hire the boat?*
Boat Guy:	*Ohhhhh... you can't fit in one boat. You will need at least two or three, probably four. Yes, four boats should be fine.*
Surveyor:	*Oh... how many people can fit on one boat?*
Boat Guy:	*About ten people.*
Surveyor:	*OK...well...there are only four of us.*
Boat Guy:	*Yes, so you will need four boats.*
Surveyor:	*But we want to go in one boat. There are only four of us.*
Boat Guy:	*Oh! There are four of you! I thought you said there were forty! Oh, yes, you can easily go in one boat.*
Surveyor:	*[back at square one] OK, so how much will it cost for four people to go in one boat from G to A?*

6.1.3 In the Community

Managing roles, responsibilities, communication, and conflict on our teams is one thing. Managing these things in the community adds another significant dimension. As we interact and live with the communities we work in, the risk of misunderstandings and difficulties with communication is much greater. We, therefore, need to take great care in how we work with people in the communities we visit. When we sense that there has been a misunderstanding or public relations blunder, we should remember that what we have done may be less important than what we do after we have done it. There is a way in every culture to apologize, and getting help to make up for what we have done goes a long way toward reconciliation and leaving a good public relations impression behind.

6.1.3.1 *Working with local helpers*

In the community, one of the main types of people survey teams work with is people who help us with the local language. Often survey teams use an LWC to communicate with them and, in such a case, both the surveyor and the language helper will be working in an L2 while thinking in their L1s. It is easy to see how misunderstandings could occur.

In addition to this, cultural differences will surface in attitudes to work, time, ethics, roles, and a host of other factors. There are also areas that we will be aware of because of our training but which our national helpers are unlikely to know. We will need to allow for this. Local people who volunteer to help us on a survey will do so from a variety of motives, not all of which will be the same as ours but, to them, just as valid. The more aware we are of the potential for these things to cause a problem, the less likely any conflict that arises will be serious and the less likely we are to be frustrated by differences in cultural attitudes.

In order to help us effectively, these volunteers will need to know what we expect of them. We should be as clear as possible about who we represent, what we want, and why, so that they can help us. When they give us what we want, we need to encourage them and ask for more of the same. If they do not provide us with what we expected, it is better to remain silent than to say something negative or critical. This may also be an indication of our misunderstanding, and we can pursue a better understanding. A good survey will never rely on one data source in any case, so if there are difficulties working with one person in one community, these should not put the primary research at risk.

Thus, it is vital that we do sufficient research on the community before we begin the survey in such things as appropriate payment for hospitality, services, guidance along the way, expectations concerning food, sharing, and so forth. Once we arrive, we should then raise our awareness, proactively observing and emulating the behavior of our hosts: how they sit, where they sit, how loudly they speak, gender divisions, what eye contact is made. In other words, whatever is defined as courteous adult behavior in the communities we work in should be our model.

If we are working in a participatory way with people in the community, we also need to know what they expect of us. This may be much more difficult to learn. As much as we may want to work at an egalitarian level, they may perceive a power difference. They may not feel comfortable expressing any expectations of us. This emphasizes the need to develop a relationship and partnership with people in the community.

6.1.3.2 Host–guest considerations

Sometimes, survey teams are the first point of contact between a speech community and development organizations. Because of this, we have a unique opportunity to open doors for mutually beneficial relationships that may last decades. However, creating such enduring relationships means being able to make a positive impression in the communities we visit, and to do that, we need to manage the host–guest relationship well.

Our expectations of what a guest should do may not match those of our hosts, and while this is unlikely to result in conflict, it will not help the relationship building that we are aiming to achieve with the community. While we cannot presume to be an expert on a speech community that we have never met before, we should make it a priority in our secondary research to find out as much as we can about the cultural background of our hosts. Others may have travelled in the area before us; we can learn a lot from their accounts. We should talk with local helpers or knowledgeable outsiders and ask them directly about host–guest expectations whenever possible. Again, this emphasizes the importance of developing relationships and partnerships with people in the community.

CASE STUDY 6B
HEADPHONE ENVY
NIGER

CASE STUDY 6B SOURCE ▶ Annette Harrison, SIL Central Africa Branch.

I was doing recorded text tests with some women and working with a local man who was interpreting in Zarma and French for me. The whole operation was very interesting to the women, and they were all anxious to try on the headset we were using. One woman really struggled with the hometown test, however. She couldn't answer the questions, though the interpreter assured me that she insisted that she was a native speaker from that same village. I had to replay sections for her, and she was still unable to answer. Yet she insisted on continuing the frustrating process until the end of the recording. The interpreter kept assuring me that she understood, but it really didn't look like it. At the end, the woman removed the headset, smiling, and the interpreter turned to me and said something like, "Don't worry about her test scores. She's deaf." I guess she just wanted to wear the fancy headset!

We may want to consider what resources we bring into the communities we visit. The latest technology can make the survey trip easier or more comfortable, but we might not be comfortable with the impression we give about the importance of that technology and the need for the community we visit to have it. As Case Study 6B shows, our technology can sometimes have a quite unexpected impact on the local people.

Gift giving is an essential part of visiting someone in some cultures, and so gifts will be expected as in Case Study 6C. In some regions it is appropriate to pay guides in cash, but it is equally important not to overpay them because of the burden it places on them for reciprocal gifting. In other places money is nearly worthless, instead salt, knives, or matches are valued. Some survey teams take food with them so that they won't be a burden on their hosts who may struggle to provide for their own families. Others take food to share with the community as the community shares with them. We cannot describe a universal list that every team needs to take with them for each survey trip, but we do want to emphasize the need to research ahead of time and be aware that what we pack and what the communities see us bringing with us will communicate very clearly about what is important for us and the team on our survey trips.

CASE STUDY 6C
GIFTS GALORE
TANZANIA

We were in the Malila area doing survey when we went to a small village to do some in-depth research. We did a group interview, took a wordlist and did individual interviews. We didn't really give much to anyone apart from some sugar and tea to the village as a whole and sodas to the people who helped with wordlists, since they worked longer than anybody else. One old lady was very intrigued by the pen of the surveyor interviewing her. She asked repeatedly during the interview if she could have the pen. The surveyor said, "Yes but I still need it to finish the interview." In the end she gave the old lady the pen. We continued with the work. A couple of hours later the old lady came back and presented her interviewer with a live chicken. She was so happy about getting a gift that she had to give one back. A little later, the village leader apologized as he hadn't been able to give us any food to eat. He was feeling so bad about it

CASE STUDY 6C SOURCE ▶ Susanne Krüger, SIL Tanzania-Uganda Branch.

that he gave 1000 Tanzanian Shillings (about 75¢ at the time) to buy tea and something to eat in the next town. In the culture here, it is impossible to refuse a gift. It would be refusing hospitality. So, we took the money and the chicken and left with a bit of a funny feeling about taking things after people had given us so much of their time.

Non-verbal communication contributes significantly to the overall amount of communication we send and receive. But when we have no shared language, it can almost equal 100 percent of our message. Because of this, it means that even when we are not talking, we are being watched and we are communicating something. When we take a break in our data gathering, and we are using the time to sleep, read, or enter data into our computer, we will be communicating something by doing this. We need to consider what this might be and whether it will be interpreted positively or not.

CASE STUDY 6D
INTERVIEW IMPROVISATION
TANZANIA

CASE STUDY 6D SOURCE ▶ Susanne Krüger, SIL Tanzania-Uganda Branch.

During the Pangwa survey in southwestern Tanzania we went to a village to do individual interviews. We had already randomly chosen the participants a couple of days early with the help of the village leader and now came to actually talk to these individuals. When we arrived we were told there was a funeral. Actually, it turned out not to be a funeral but the celebration of putting down a stone on the grave one year after the actual funeral. Everybody was there eating and celebrating. So we were invited and got plates of food and with our food walked around finding our individuals and interviewing them in a much more social setting than usual.

Finally, as the flexible attitude demonstrated in Case Study 6D shows, every opportunity we have to interact with people in different cultures will give us a deeper understanding of them. This is particularly important in survey where findings from data as impersonal as lexicostatistics can be informed by more personal data. Observations and impressions we may get from interacting informally with people outside our typical data collection activities can be especially valuable to balance impressions we get from less personal data. Often, when people think they are not being observed or studied, they will behave more naturally and reveal data that is more accurate than under test conditions. Surveyors may find that this occurs naturally before their eyes while they happen to be relaxing or resting. Playing with children, hanging out around the fire, sharing a meal, helping with some work, and doing as many of the natural day-to-day activities as possible can still mean we are collecting valuable data.

6.2   Other Resources

We have spent time talking about people because they are the greatest resource that we will have to manage on survey. After all, people are the very motivation for assessment work in the first place. There are also other resources that we need to manage on a survey trip including money, equipment, and time.

6.2.1   Finance

Every survey trip needs money to make it happen. It needs to be managed well and usually there needs to be an accurate accounting of its use. Money also has a way of causing problems that other resources do not, so being wise in how we handle it can minimize these risks.

We need to prepare budgets as part of our survey proposals. These budgets should include everything we think we will need to spend money on. Budgets typically include:

- **food and drink**: not only for the team but possibly for our hosts and helpers too. Will we be able to find places to buy food on the way? Can we get clean drinking water or do we have to take it, filter it, or otherwise purify it? Do we have any dietary requirements on our team which must be met?
- **transport**: will we take our own vehicle, public transportation, or do we hire someone? Can we buy fuel or do we need to purchase it in advance? Some transport we might take will require us to pay for both passage and fuel and may also charge for baggage if we have a lot. We need to find out if this is the case in advance if we can and take extra finance to allow for this if we cannot. Remember to carry the denominations that will be most useful since we may not be able to get change. Do we have enough contingency money for emergency evacuation transport if it is needed? Will we

need to hire a vehicle? If we do hire one, what happens if it breaks down? Do we know how to get to where we are going? Alternatively, will we be walking and need to employ guides or porters?

- **gifts**: in many cultures where reciprocity is valued, gifts will be expected in exchange for information. In most cases, this should never be money but rather some material goods appropriate to the culture of the community we work in.
- **data collection**: we may need to buy equipment, make photocopies, make extra trips to libraries to collect secondary data, buy batteries, and purchase the equipment to backup data. As with gifts for hospitality, we may be expected to give gifts to participants in exchange for data.
- **accommodation**: where will we sleep and will we need to pay for it? Do we have to pay per room or per person? Will cultural taboos forbid everyone sharing one room if the team is mixed gender? How much extra might it cost to allow for this?
- **personnel**: we may have to employ language helpers or advisors for our project or at least cover their costs as they provide us with help.

To find out what we need to spend money on and how much, it is helpful to talk to people who are either experienced with survey in our areas or have experience travelling there and can help estimate costs for us. However, these estimates may not be accurate, and we should always take more than we need to allow for contingencies. Some costs will occur when we are at our base, but most of our spending will take place on the survey trip itself. Whenever money is spent, one person should be responsible for keeping a record of this. Receipts and a duplicate record of expenses should be kept whenever possible.

There are, in many countries, real risks with taking large amounts of money into remote areas that we might survey. Earning cash may not be possible for many communities we might visit if they practice subsistence lifestyles. They may either have little to sell or no access to markets. The sudden appearance of a group of seemingly wealthy individuals, each of whom seems to have an amazing supply of equipment and expensive technology, presents a temptation that might be hard to resist. Likewise, in urban areas there are similar risks. On crowded public transport or in crowded marketplaces, there are thieves who actively target individuals who might seem to be carrying cash.

There are a number of things we can do to manage risk in this area. Firstly, we should only take as much cash as we need. If possible, we should get cash on the trip from banks or other sources so that we are only carrying a minimal amount at any point on the trip. If we have to take all the cash we need for the entire trip, it is wise to split up the amount between members of the team. It is helpful if team members can use money belts to carry this cash rather than leaving it in bags because, if a bag gets stolen or lost, we lose our money too. Displaying large amounts of money in public, for example when paying for something, will draw unwanted attention to us and the team and so should be avoided. Instead, we can carry only a small amount of money in a wallet, but then hide the rest somewhere else.

Money and our attitudes towards it have the potential to cause more conflict than most things. To avoid this, some survey teams split money between members and in addition, some teams split the responsibility for different areas of spending with one member responsible for travel costs while another is responsible for food. While many teams divide their money between members in this way, some do not share this responsibility with team members who are local people. While this may seem discriminatory and difficult to accept, the reasoning behind it is that local people often have different ideas about the use of money and material resources than do expatriate workers.

CASE STUDY 6E
HELPING THE NEEDY
SOUTHEAST ASIA

CASE STUDY 6E SOURCE ▶ SIL's Mainland Southeast Asia Group survey team.

Preparing for a survey, the team split all the money needed between all the team members. Some were expatriates and some were local people. The survey trip went well and, financially, things weren't as expensive as the team had thought. When they returned to base, there was some money left over. At the same time as they returned, a local team member received news that a relative was sick and needed some money urgently to pay for hospital treatment. The local team member gave some of their survey trip money to help his relative. A few days later, the team members were settling accounts for the trip and found out about the sick relative and that survey trip money had been given to him. It turned out that the relatives could not repay the money and the local team member could not afford to repay it either. While the local team member understood that the money was not his to give, he said that helping the sick was a priority. An expatriate was very upset with this saying that as the money was not his to give, maintaining his responsibility to the team was a priority. In their own cultures, both team members were "right" and this conflict took several weeks to resolve.

In Case Study 6E, different ideas about stewardship and responsibility caused conflict. In sharing money between team members, it is important therefore to know how we should keep it and account for it.

6.2.2 Equipment

There is a great variation in the types of equipment needed depending on where in the world the survey team works. While the following list implies rugged, backpacking-type travel, most surveys are done in places where we can take some form of vehicular transportation, and there are places to stay that do not require carrying a tent. There may even be stores where some supplies can be purchased. Some surveys are done in places where we are able to stay in hotels, eat in restaurants, and stores are plentiful.

One of the most crucial things about equipment for our survey trips is that once we leave the base, we may not be able to get anything we have forgotten. To avoid this, we need to create detailed checklists of what we need and check and re-check that we have everything before the trip. In a similar way to money, equipment needs to be determined before the trip, distributed between team members, and properly maintained. The same guidelines for security apply: if we have to take expensive items of equipment with us, such as cameras, recording equipment, and computers, we must be discrete with these.

Some common items we may need include:

> **Data collection**: more copies than anticipated of every questionnaire, wordlist, recording, etc. that we plan to use; plenty of pens; recording devices, and spare batteries/chargers and, if using removable media, plenty of spares of these; notebooks for journaling, and entries for observation and reflection. GPS devices are becoming increasingly common to navigate by and to provide reference points to map data. Smaller, hand-held computing devices can be used for administration of some kinds of tests e.g., RTTs,

and for data collection. If travelling by car, using lighter socket chargers can provide essential power for devices we might take if we have the right adaptors. It is helpful not to rely only on electronic sources for data storage unless we have reliable backup. The environment of a survey trip is unkind to electronic media. Heat, moisture, dust, and constant jostling and jarring can damage equipment. If we take a computer and backup everything on a separate device, we should be careful not to store these together. If we do, losing one means losing the other. Have one team member carry the backup and another one the original. Flash drives are cheap and small and having a number of them allows the team to keep multiple copies of data backed up and in different locations. While they are also easy to keep out of sight be aware that they are also easier to lose sight of. We may want to consider passing on copies of our data to local communities and, if so, need to decide what media we are going to use for these.

Clothing: enough clothing for every environment we will be experiencing; protective clothing for extremes e.g., mosquito nets, waterproof clothing, hats; good footwear (do not attempt to break in a new pair of shoes on a survey trip or go barefoot if you have never done this before!). Will we need to wash any of our clothing ourselves? If so, take the necessary resources for this including something to wash clothes in. If not, some people like to bring an extra bag for soiled clothes.

Comfort: sleeping bag, sleeping mat, ear plugs, eye mask, toiletries to help feel fresh. Going without shaving gear may save space on a survey trip, but maintaining the routine of shaving may also help to keep some sense of continuity. We may have an audience when bathing, thus, a bathing garment would be recommended. Each individual has different needs and knows the levels of comfort they need to help them lessen stress.

Emergency: each team will need certain items to help them in an emergency situation including basic first aid equipment, possibly even items such as clean syringes. Before the trip begins the team should have contingency plans for which everyone knows their part. A satellite phone or some other way of making contact with base may be necessary in the some remote areas. Before we go, we may need to establish a plan for evacuation if it becomes necessary. It is also important to leave a complete description of the survey plans so that others can find us if necessary.

Survey type: the equipment needs of a team may differ considerably depending on what the purpose of the assessment process is. For example, in assessing signed languages, a video camera is a necessity whereas on other types of survey, it would be a luxury item.

All of the equipment we take should be useful to us or the people we are going to meet. It is useless taking along a data recorder if team members do not know how it functions. Similarly, if we are going to need to drive a Land Rover with manual transmission, we need to practice that before we leave if we have only driven an automatic. On one infamous survey, the team decided to use mountain bikes for transport. When these turned out to be useless because of the terrain, it became something of a nightmare having to carry them. Thus, in our preparation for survey make use of any available topographical maps available, and seek advice from those who have lived in the region. Similarly, all our equipment should be useful to us for the entire duration of the trip. If we run out of batteries, our equipment will be useless. Taking along a solar charger may sound like creative resource management until we encounter weeks of cloudy weather. If we take our own transport, we will probably need both spare parts and the expertise to replace parts ourselves. Practicing new skills before leaving on a trip will help to lower stress levels when the inevitable breakdown-in-the-rain-at-night-miles-from-anywhere scenario happens.

While it is important to take the necessities for our trips, we need to remember that getting enough down time and relaxation is important to maintain stress levels. Escaping from the survey routine and making the most of our leisure opportunities will help to make survey trips more enjoyable. Also remember that any number of factors might prevent us from doing survey work: we may experience travel delays, may arrive in a community and find no one willing or able to help, or be prevented from working by weather. Whatever our circumstances, we need to make the most of it, whether for information, conversation, or personal rest and recreation.

Case Study 6G shows that, in the end, knowing what to take with us means knowing both our team and the reality of the situation we will be visiting in as much detail as we   can.

CASE STUDY 6F
FURNITURE DELIVERY
CHAD

Particularly on surveys in the Northern and Central areas of Chad, survey teams found that they often needed to include a rather unexpected item on their packing lists. In rural areas, it is quite common for people to sit on mats because furniture made out of wood

*is rare. Culturally, it is not appropriate for men and women
to share the same mats and, if the community has few*

> *resources, there may not be enough mats to share with visitors.
> Survey teams learned to take their own mats with them when
> visiting these areas, making sure that they had enough for both
> the male and female members of their team to sit separately.*

6.2.3   Time

Being good time managers in language assessment is less about getting things done within a set timeframe and more about making sure that enough time is allocated to the right things and people. In a culture where time spent building relationships is far more important than time allocated to completing tasks, a survey team under the pressure of their itinerary risks conveying the wrong message. By passing through briefly and apparently only for the purpose of collecting data from people, it is easy to give the impression that the team does not value people because they devote no time to building relationships. This will likely lead to future problems in spite of the team's best intentions.

Managing time on survey is complicated by the ambiguity and unexpected nature of much that happens in the assessment process. So, the important thing is to build flexibility for this into our plans. Scheduling contingency time will allow us to relax when things take longer than we expect. In addition, having more time than we anticipate will allow us to fit in more with the culture of many of the communities we survey. It is likely that events, rather than time, will be the focus of the speech communities we work with. Knowing and accepting this can relieve many of our frustrations.

Some of the issues relating to managing time in the assessment process are:

> **Transport**: if we are reliant on public transport of any kind, we may have little or no control over when or if it leaves and how long or whether it gets to its destination. Even private transport can be delayed by weather, an accident, or a breakdown.

> **People**: each of us has different ideas about punctuality. We might arrange to interview a knowledgeable outsider at 1 p.m. knowing that we should be finished by 3 and can make the team meeting at 3:30. We might be frustrated then when they turn up at 2:30.

Pace: different people work at different speeds. Writing up the report of a language assessment can be frustrating if writers are writing in an L2 or in a style they are unused to. Analysis can take much longer than expected due to ambiguity in the data. If a survey requires hiking, we need to remember that people walk at very different paces depending on terrain, climate, and even the time of day.

Routine: we may make our plans but find ourselves unable to carry them out because local routine places greater priority on other events. These include national holidays, local festivals, harvests, school term dates, and daily routines. In Papua New Guinea, most data collection is carried out in the late afternoons and evenings because during the day local people work in their gardens, which can be a lengthy trek from the village.

Climate: in some areas, survey is completely impractical at certain seasons when weather makes roads and rivers impassable. Back-to-back survey trips are therefore planned for the dry season with all secondary research and report writing being done during the rainy season.

CASE STUDY 6G
SLEEPWALKING IN THE SAHARA
NIGER

CASE STUDY 6G SOURCE ▶ Annette Harrison, SIL Central Africa Branch.

While working in Niger, we carried out an extensive survey of a large language group, divided by clans and life-styles. One of the important questions involved whether sedentary members of the group would accept literature that was already being developed in the linguistic variety of the nomadic clans. This involved several months of fieldwork, using two vehicles and a team of seven.

Because we were using a sampling system based on lists of residents of an area, sometimes we had to go and find the people who had been chosen to listen to recordings and respond to questions. At one point, Byron, our team leader, had to find someone who was herding out in the bush. There was only one person available to guide him to the correct location, a man with whom he had no language in common. That didn't bother Byron too much, as he had learned common hand signals used in Niger to direct drivers.

So he started out through the bush, watching the hand of his passenger guide. The hand continued to indicate that Byron should continue straight ahead, and he drove for some time

through the trackless area. He kept looking at his guide's hand, and the hand continued to indicate straight ahead. When Byron finally looked up at the man's face to verify that he really should continue driving straight, he saw that the man had fallen asleep! And how long had he been asleep? The guide was as startled and lost as Byron was. They eventually figured out where they were and found the person they were looking for, but there were a few tense moments when both the guide and Byron realized they were lost on the edge of the Sahara desert!

6.3   Stress Factors

6.3.1   Managing the Unexpected

Despite all the best preparations we can make, language assessment is so prone to unexpected events that many surveyors say, "The unexpected is the expected." So, rather than aim to eliminate unpredictability from our assessment projects, it is wiser to be ready for it in spite of all we do.

CASE STUDY 6H
DISTURBED BY DEATH
PAPUA NEW GUINEA

When I was studying linguistics, I went with another student to work with a translator in a village in New Ireland, a large island in Papua New Guinea. We had planned to be there about three or four weeks, depending on when we could arrange to get a boat to take us to and from this remote location. During this time we had planned to run a Translation Awareness Workshop over a few days, so the community could be better informed about what was involved in the Bible translation process. Just before the workshop was to be held, someone in the village died, and there was no

CASE STUDY 6H SOURCE ▶ Rebekah Drew, ethnomusicologist, SIL Papua New Guinea.

way that the workshop could go ahead as we had planned. We rescheduled it for two weeks later, when we knew the mourning, funeral, exchanges, and feasting would be over. But it was all in vain, as someone else died the following week! We never did get to run our workshop.

Obviously, not everything is as unpredictable as death. No amount of

FIGURE 13 ▶ At the survey office in Ukarumpa, Papua New Guinea, surveyors Alison Kassell and Margaret Potter look over maps for a forthcoming survey trip with Bonnie MacKenzie, SIL Papua New Guinea Survey Department Team Leader.

planning could have helped the literacy team in Case Study 6H. But being aware of the likelihood of something so unexpected is good preparation for when it happens. One useful way to manage this is to develop our ability to see everything that comes along as an opportunity to achieve things we had not expected. By doing this, the team relieves stresses and turns the unexpected into a positive experience for both the team and the community they visited.

6.3.2   Managing Ambiguity

Just as we can experience the unexpected in the logistical side of our work, it can also arise in our data. Language assessment is carried out to answer specific research questions and achieve specific purposes for those that request them. When these questions cannot be answered clearly, it is often difficult to achieve the aims of the survey and this can mean months of work seem to amount to very little. Ambiguity in data is common in language assessment. It can exist right at the very start if those who request the survey do not give clear indications of their intentions. It exists both in secondary and primary research, and it also exists at the data collection and analysis stage. This is why it is important to pilot test tools before using them on surveys.

Although, ideally, we should attempt to eliminate ambiguity from each stage of the process, this is often an ideal which is unattainable in many assessment situations for many reasons. Being able to live with ambiguity and draw conclusions from it is an attitude which could therefore save us considerable stress when working as a surveyor. Some people simply cannot bring themselves to accept that what they have spent months working on does not actually provide them with any concrete conclusions. This can be frustrating and lead to disillusionment.

Again, being prepared to expect this is the first thing we can do. But we can also be honest with ourselves about when this is the case and learn not to force data to demonstrate trends we would like to see. When confronted with ambiguity, we may need to take a step back from the data, to try another approach to analysis or let someone else with a different outlook analyze it. We might also want to assess why it is that ambiguity exists. Case Study 6J presents an example of the kind of ambiguity that is extremely common. In India, one surveyor was puzzled by simply trying to find out something as basic as the name of the language she was working on.

CASE STUDY 6J
WHAT'S IN A NAME?
INDIA

CASE STUDY 6J SOURCE ▶ Sue Hasselbring.

It was certainly something unexpected for me on my early surveys, but after a few, I realized that name confusion was more to be expected than not. One person gives you the name of their ethnolinguistic group (ethnonym), another gives the name of the village, district, region, state and adds a language suffix, another gives the name that outsiders call them, another gives a clan name and adds a language suffix, another gives the caste name, another gives the caste name in the regional language and adds a different language suffix...and on and on....

Clearly, the ability to manage ambiguity will go a long way to ensuring we manage the stress that comes from the language assessment task.

6.4   Further Reading

Knowing Me, Knowing You: Exploring Personality Type and Temperament by Malcolm Goldsmith and Martin Wharton (2004)

> Explanations of personality types as described by the Myers Briggs Type Indicators with very useful sections detailing how each of the types needs to adapt communication in relating to others.

Teamwork: How to Build Relationships by Gordon Jones and Rosemary Jones (2002)

> Covers the essentials of team management including some good sections on conflict resolution.

Building Credible Multicultural Teams by Lianne Roembke (2000)

> With a particular focus on the mission community and integration with local team-members, this book is valuable for the original focus it has. She deals with decision making, lifestyles, finances, and even living together.

GLOSSARY

ACCOMMODATION THEORY

explains why it is that people change their language to become more or less like that of the person they are with.

ACCURACY

measuring the right, complete, or real thing.

ACROLECT

in a **CREOLE** continuum, the variety of language most similar to the **SUPERSTRATE**. Compare with **BASILECT** and **MESOLECT**.

ASSESSMENT

see **LANGUAGE ASSESSMENT**.

ATTITUDE

see **INSTRUMENTAL ATTITUDE** and **SENTIMENTAL ATTITUDE**.

ATTRIBUTION THEORY

first proposed by Fritz Heider in 1958 and based on the idea that we do not want to see behavior as random but as the result of what we believe about behavior. These beliefs are so strong that we even have them in situations where they can be proved to be invalid.

BASILECT

in a **CREOLE** continuum, the variety of language least similar to the superstrate. Compare with **ACROLECT** and **MESOLECT**.

BIDIALECTALISM

the learned ability to use two different **DIALECTS**.

BILINGUALISM

the learned ability by an individual to use two different languages. See also **COMMUNITY BILINGUALISM**.

BORROWING

the practice of taking words from another language and incorporating them into one's vocabulary.

CHUNKING

the process whereby the human mind pre-assembles strings of language together based on common patterns of vocabulary and grammar.

CLARITY

a tool has clarity when people understand the intent and expectations of the tool, whether it is how to take a test or the meaning of a question.

CLOSED QUESTIONS

require the participant to choose from a number of options when they answer. Compare with OPEN QUESTIONS.

CODE-SWITCHING

when people mix two or more languages for certain words, phrases, or sentences while communicating with another member of their own language group, code-switching happens. When one language forms the basis for syntax and another language is used to vary vocabulary or other non-structural features, you have the makings of pidginization (see PIDGIN) and eventually creolization (see CREOLE).

COGNATES

words which are descended from the same root word. We can also say a word is cognate with another.

COMMUNICATIVE COMPETENCE

the awareness of the appropriate situational use of the language. Compare with LINGUISTIC COMPETENCE.

COMMUNITY BILINGUALISM

the distribution of differing bilingual proficiencies throughout a SPEECH COMMUNITY.

COMPREHENSION

what is understood when communication takes place.

COMPREHENSIVE SAMPLE FRAME

a SAMPLE FRAME that attempts to collect data from everyone who can be included.

CONTINUOUS VARIABLE

Continuous variables are things that can be counted and change equally from one unit to the next. Temperature is a continuous variable. Compare with DISCRETE VARIABLE.

CONTROL VARIABLE

something that limits the INDEPENDENT VARIABLE. For example, if we want to know how age affects language ability, we might sample different ages of people. However, if we know that no women in a particular community have access to the opportunity to learn the language, gender would be a controlling variable. Compare with INDEPENDENT VARIABLE, DEPENDENT VARIABLE, and INTERVENING VARIABLE, and see also DISCRETE VARIABLE and CONTINUOUS VARIABLE.

CREOLE

a language that was once a PIDGIN but now is the HERITAGE LANGUAGE of a people. It is typified by a process by which it has expanded the grammatical structures and lexical choices that are considered part of the new language.

CRITICAL PERIOD HYPOTHESIS

the theory which states that there is an age at which language acquisition moves from being a subconscious to a conscious activity. Scientists still have very little insight into exactly when this occurs or why.

DATA

see **INTERVAL DATA**, **NOMINAL DATA**, **ORDINAL DATA**, **QUALITATIVE DATA**, **QUANTITATIVE DATA**, and **RATIO DATA**.

DEPENDENT VARIABLE

the thing impacted or affected by changes to the **INDEPENDENT VARIABLE**. For example, if we want to know how age affects language ability, as we vary the age of our participants their language ability will change. Language ability in our research is therefore dependent on the age of our subjects. See also **INDEPENDENT VARIABLE**, **CONTROL VARIABLE**, and **INTERVENING VARIABLE**, and see also **DISCRETE VARIABLE** and **CONTINUOUS VARIABLE**.

DEPTH

or level of research refers to the thoroughness of the research. See also **SCOPE**.

DIALECT

a regionally or socially distinctive variety of a **LANGUAGE**.

DIGLOSSIA

a social situation in which two or more languages, or language varieties, co-occur in a **SPEECH COMMUNITY**, each with a distinct social function.

DISCRETE VARIABLE

Discrete variables jump from category to category; they have nominal or ordinal values. A scale such as the **ILR SCALE**. Compare with **CONTINUOUS VARIABLE**.

DOMAIN

a cluster of language features including: speakers, location, topic, and a language form associated with these other features. The location component is understood more often as a location in social space more than a location in geographic space. Thus, wherever fishmongers meet to talk with other fishmongers about fish using their unique in-group language forms, this describes a domain of language use

DOMINANT LANGUAGE

the language that a person has their best competency in. It may or may not be their **HERITAGE LANGUAGE**.

DOUBLETS

words which are distinct in meaning in one language but not in another. Leg and foot are distinct in English, for example, but in Japanese the word *ashi* is used for both.

ETHNOGRAPHY

a branch of anthropology that studies human cultures and their behavior.

EXOGAMY

the practice of marrying outside the community. Traditionally, for example, the Jewish community does not allow exogamy.

FORMAL LEARNING

refers to learning a language through a structured program of learning. Compare with **INFORMAL LEARNING**.

GRADUATED SCALE

When a question asks the participant to rate their feelings about something on a scale of one to five, this is a Graduated Scale.

HERITAGE LANGUAGE

a language that has been used in the home for multiple generations.

HOMETOWN TEST

when carrying out Recorded Text Tests, a test in which people are tested on a language sample that is meant to represent their own language variety. This serves as a screening device to verify that a person is competent in this language variety and capable of passing the test.

IDIOLECT

the unique speech variety of an individual.

ILR SCALE

The Interagency Language Roundtable scale is used to measure oral proficiency in a language. It was previously known as the FSI (Foreign Service Institute) scale.

INDEPENDENT VARIABLE

the essential thing that can be changed when doing research. For example, we want to know about the effects of changing it. In other words, if we want to know how age affects language ability, we will vary the age of our participants and see how it affects the data we collect. See also **DEPENDENT VARIABLE, CONTROL VARIABLE,** and **INTERVENING VARIABLE,** and see also **DISCRETE VARIABLE** and **CONTINUOUS VARIABLE.**

INDICATOR

a linguistic **VARIABLE** that has no social value attached to it. Although, it does have different forms linguistically, these do not have any social significance. Contrast this to a **MARKER.**

INFORMAL LEARNING

a typical, natural way of gaining a more native-like proficiency in another language through social contact with users of that language. Compare with **FORMAL LEARNING.**

INHERENT BILINGUALISM

the ability to use another language that is due to similarity between the speaker's **HERITAGE LANGUAGE** and the **L2.** It is not a commonly used term. Compare with **LEARNED BILINGUALISM** and also **INHERENT INTELLIGIBILITY.**

INHERENT INTELLIGIBILITY

is the natural, unlearned comprehension of another language that is possible without any exposure to the other variety. This understanding is possible because of linguistic similarities. For example, American English speakers understand Australian English simply because it shares features of their speech. This is because both are descended from British English. Compare with **INHERENT BILINGUALISM.**

INSTRUMENTAL ATTITUDE

considers language as a tool which enables people to achieve their aims.

INSTRUMENTAL MOTIVATION

happens when someone wants to learn new skills for some other aim such as getting work. Compare with **INTEGRATIVE MOTIVATION**.

INTEGRATIVE MOTIVATION

a focus on the social benefits of learning; the learner wants to integrate into a new **SPEECH COMMUNITY**, for example. Compare with **INSTRUMENTAL MOTIVATION**.

INTERVAL DATA

are values on a scale that has some sort of meaningful differences between values. For example, it is meaningful to say that someone spends four hours at school a day and that is twice as long as someone who is there for only two hours. See also **QUALITATIVE DATA**, **QUANTITATIVE DATA**, **NOMINAL DATA**, **ORDINAL DATA**, and **RATIO DATA**.

INTERVENING VARIABLE

other factors for which we may not be able to measure while we carry out our research. For example, if we want to know how age affects language ability, it may be that due to a recent festival, all young men have spent the last three days without sleep. As we collect data from them, we have no way of measuring how much this affects their language ability although we are aware of it. See also **INDEPENDENT VARIABLE**, **DEPENDENT VARIABLE**, and **CONTROL VARIABLE**, and see also **DISCRETE VARIABLE** and **CONTINUOUS VARIABLE**.

INTELLIGIBILITY

the quality of being able to be understood in communication. It differs from **COMPREHENSION**, which is what is understood in communication.

L1

commonly understood to be the first language that a child acquires. In this book, we define L1 as the **HERITAGE LANGUAGE** or the language of the home **DOMAIN**. See also **L2**.

L2 (L3, ETC.)

is an additional language acquired or learned after the **L1**.

LANGUAGE

the sum total of all the linguistic varieties that are used by a group of people who consider that they all use the same language.

LANGUAGE ASSESSMENT

the process of regularly monitoring and studying language use.

LANGUAGE CHAIN

a sequence of **DIALECTS** that gradually change from one to another.

LANGUAGE DEATH

the result of language shift, when people stop using a language for social communication. This may be because the people who use the language have themselves become extinct, or it may be because they have decided to use other languages to replace it.

LANGUAGE DEVELOPMENT

a result of a series of on-going, planned actions that a community takes to ensure that their **LANGUAGE REPERTOIRE** continues to serve their changing social, cultural, political, economic, and spiritual needs and goals.

LANGUAGE MAINTENANCE

refers to behaviors in a **SPEECH COMMUNITY** that tend to preserve the use of a language.

LANGUAGE OF WIDER COMMUNICATION

a language that is used by a speech communities to communicate with each other on a regular basis but which is not a **HERITAGE LANGUAGE** for any group.

LANGUAGE PLANNING

the process of a governing body choosing specific languages for specific purposes and implementing those choices.

LANGUAGE REPERTOIRE

the range of languages or varieties of a language that are available to an individual or **SPEECH COMMUNITY** to meet their needs and goals.

LANGUAGE SHIFT

occurs when, because of **SPEECH COMMUNITIES** coming into contact, people decide to move from one language to another language as a preferred medium of communication.

LANGUAGE SURVEY

the activity of doing **SECONDARY RESEARCH** and **PRIMARY RESEARCH**, data collection, analysis, and reporting activities for **LANGUAGE ASSESSMENT**. A language survey may refer to the data collection trip.

LANGUAGE SURVEYORS

people who do the **SECONDARY RESEARCH** and **PRIMARY RESEARCH**, data collection, analysis, and reporting activities for **LANGUAGE ASSESSMENT**.

LEARNED BILINGUALISM

results from a learner choosing and making an effort to learn a second language. Compare this with **INHERENT BILINGUALISM.**

LEXEME

the minimal unit of meaning that a word can be reduced to. So, while English has *walked, walks,* and *walking,* the underlying lexeme is *walk.*

LEXICOSTATISTICS

computational methods used to determine the historical linguistic relationship between wordlists.

LINGUISTIC COMPETENCE

the ability to control the formal linguistic patterns of a language. Compare with **COMMUNICATIVE COMPETENCE.**

LINGUISTIC SWAMPING

occurs when the **HERITAGE LANGUAGE** is overwhelmed by speakers of another language or **DIALECT** moving into the territory of the heritage language speakers.

LWC

see **LANGUAGE OF WIDER COMMUNICATION**.

MARKER

a linguistic variable that has social value attached to it such as the way different people pronounce certain words. Compare this to an **INDICATOR**.

MESOLECT

in a **CREOLE** continuum, a variety of the language that is neither the furthest from the **SUPERSTRATE** nor the most closely related to it. Compare with **BASILECT** and **ACROLECT**.

METADATA

the information that is collected about data and data collection; the *who, what, when, where*, and *how* about data.

MIXED LANGUAGE

a language that forms as a person combines features from two or more input languages.

MOTIVATION

see **INSTRUMENTAL MOTIVATION** and **INTEGRATIVE MOTIVATION**.

MULTILINGUAL EDUCATION

attempts to help children first learn reading, writing, and other subjects in their **L1**, then at some later stage they shift to an **L2** as either the medium of instruction or as a subject.

MULTILINGUALISM

the ability of a person to use more than one language. Use of the term makes no claim as to how proficient the person may be in any of the languages, nor, when referring to a community, does it imply that everyone has equal proficiency. See **COMMUNITY BILINGUALISM**.

MULTI-STAGE SAMPLING

a subset of individuals from a **SAMPLE FRAME** is identified and then, within this, a further type of individual is chosen to provide data. Any errors in sampling with this method are likely to be compounded therefore. See also **SIMPLE RANDOM SAMPLING**, **STRATIFIED SAMPLING,** and **SYSTEMATIC SAMPLING**.

MUTUAL INTELLIGIBILITY

the ability of users of two different varieties to understand each other's language. Although the term mutual is used, we should not assume that they understand one another equally. **INTELLIGIBILITY** is generally asymmetric or directional, which means that, for example, group A understands group B better than B understands A.

NATIONAL LANGUAGE

a type of **LWC** that has gained prominence for communication between ethnolinguistic groups throughout a country.

NGO

a non-governmental organization. UNICEF is an NGO.

NOMINAL DATA

When we count categories or types of things, we call this nominal data. For example, there are five dogs in the village, or 15 people attended the literacy class. You can count, but not order, nominal data. See also **QUALITATIVE DATA**, **QUANTITATIVE DATA**, **ORDINAL DATA**, **INTERVAL DATA**, and **RATIO DATA**.

OFFICIAL LANGUAGE

a language that is given official status and support by a government.

OPEN QUESTIONS

allow the participant to answer freely in whatever way they want. Compare with **CLOSED QUESTIONS.**

ORALITY

expression through non-written speech.

ORDINAL DATA

When we want to order or rank things, we can create a scale to do this. We call this ordinal data. For example, ten people said they could speak the L2 "poorly," 15 people said they could speak the L2 "well," 20 people said they could speak the L2 "very well." We cannot however compare the difference between "well" and "poorly" and say that it is the same as the difference between "well and "very well." See also **QUALITATIVE DATA**, **QUANTITATIVE DATA**, **NOMINAL DATA**, **INTERVAL DATA,** and **RATIO DATA**.

ORTHOGRAPHY

a standardized writing system. It consists of the rules of using the script and also describes the script itself. The script alone is not an orthography. A language can have more than one orthography. Serbian, for example, is digraphic and uses both Latin and Cyrillic orthographies.

PARTICIPATORY METHODS

research methods that harness the power of a local community to solve their own problems and make their own decisions. They also serve to restrain the power of the researcher.

PARTNER AGENCIES

the organizations, institutions, or agencies who are working together with a local **SPEECH COMMUNITY** for language and community development.

PARTNERSHIP

a relationship where parties commit to share complementary resources to achieve mutually agreeable goals, working together at each stage of planning, implementation, and evaluation.

PHONE

the smallest unit of sound in speech.

PHONOSTATISTICS

any of several computational methods to determine the linguistic distance or percentage of linguistic similarity between wordlists.

Pidgin

a language that no one speaks as their **heritage language**. It has formed by a process of reducing grammatical structures and the number of lexical choices from the selection of languages available to the speakers of the pidgin.

Precision

an exact measurement that agrees with the reality of the thing being measured.

Primary Research

involves collecting new, previously unknown information.

Probe

the specific question that will be posed to the research participant requesting a response.

Qualitative Data

information that describes a subjective quality such as someone's attitude. See also **Quantitative Data, Nominal Data, Ordinal Data, Interval Data,** and **Ratio Data.**

Quantitative Data

information that describes an amount or quantity of something such as someone's age. See also **Qualitative Data, Nominal Data, Ordinal Data, Interval Data,** and **Ratio Data.**

Ratio Data

these have a natural zero point, such as temperature. We rarely collect ratio data for language assessment. See also **Qualitative Data, Quantitative Data, Nominal Data, Ordinal Data,** and **Interval Data.**

Reference Dialect

language varieties which are standardized for formal purposes, such as literature and education.

Regional Language

a type of **LWC** that has gained regional acceptance due to its usefulness for communication between ethnolinguistic groups.

Register

a particular style of language such as formal or informal, technical or simple.

Reliability

if a test or **tool** produces consistent results no matter who administers it and each time it is used, it is reliable. See also **Validity.**

RTT

a Recorded Text Test is designed to help assess someone's comprehension of another language variety.

Sample Frame

the total set of people we can select participants from. A comprehensive sample frame attempts to gather data from every single person in the sample frame. This is extremely rare in language assessment. A narrow sample frame attempts to identify a group within the sample frame where everyone will be available to provide data, such as all the participants in a workshop. See also **Sampling.**

SAMPLING

the process by which we collect enough of the right kind of data so that the results are the same as if we had collected all the data possible if we had unlimited resources. If we sample well, we will be able to say that our results reflect the entire **SPEECH COMMUNITY** we are working with. See also **SAMPLE FRAME**, **MULTI-STAGE SAMPLING**, **SIMPLE RANDOM SAMPLING**, **STRATIFIED SAMPLING**, and **SYSTEMATIC SAMPLING**.

SAMPLING ERROR

a predictable difference between the attributes of our sample population and the whole population.

SAMPLE FRAME

the total set of people we can select participants from.

SAMPLING VARIATION

the difference between two different samples of a population

SCOPE

or breadth, describes what aspects will be studied and what will not be studied.

SECONDARY RESEARCH

involves collecting information from research which has already been carried out.

SEMANTIC FIELD

a set of **LEXEMES** that are connected in meaning or type. In English, *head, arm,* and *tongue* are all part of the semantic field of body parts. Alternatively, *blue, broken,* and *big* are in the semantic field of adjectives.

SENTIMENTAL ATTITUDE

views language as a symbol of the identity of a people.

SIL INTERNATIONAL

a faith-based, not-for-profit **LANGUAGE DEVELOPMENT** organization, formerly known as *The Summer Institute of Linguistics*.

SIMPLE RANDOM SAMPLING

using some method to randomly identify data sources within a **SAMPLE FRAME**. We could number all the participants at a workshop, for example, and then use a computer to generate random numbers to select those who will do a questionnaire we have prepared. See also **MULTI-STAGE SAMPLING**, **STRATIFIED SAMPLING**, and **SYSTEMATIC SAMPLING**.

SOCIAL NETWORK

a pattern of social associations or relationships.

SOCIOLINGUISTICS

the study of how languages are used in different social situations and how social and cultural factors affect linguistic interaction.

SPEECH COMMUNITY

a hypothetical group of people who do not necessarily share the same **HERITAGE LANGUAGE**, but they do share common normative socio-behavioral rules concerning when different speech forms are used with one another. This can include multilingual, diglossic (see **DIGLOSSIA**), and monolingual communities. People are members of many speech communities at the same time, and a speech community may include a number of different languages. The term includes forms of language that are not spoken such as literature and also communities that do not use speech such as the Deaf.

STAKEHOLDER

an individual or group that is affected by and/or influences the outcomes of a development program.

STRATIFIED SAMPLING

In order to reduce **SAMPLING ERROR**, we may want to sub-divide our **SAMPLE FRAME** so that we sample within recognized sub-groups within the community. For example, if most young men have attended a school where an **LWC** is spoken and only around half of the young women have, we will want to make sure that 50 percent of the women we sample are educated and most of the men are. See also **MULTI-STAGE SAMPLING**, **SIMPLE RANDOM SAMPLING**, and **SYSTEMATIC SAMPLING**.

SUPERSTRATE

a language that has had the most significant influence on the creation of a **PIDGIN** or **CREOLE**.

SURVEY

see **LANGUAGE SURVEY**.

SURVEYORS

see **LANGUAGE SURVEYORS**.

SYSTEMATIC SAMPLING

similar to **SIMPLE RANDOM SAMPLING**. It involves identifying a systematic way to choose the sample points from our **SAMPLE FRAME**. If we wanted to take a systematic sample from 150 households, we could divide the percentage we want to sample (10% = 0.1) by the total number available (150) to get a fraction of 1/15. We would then have a computer randomly generate a number between 1 and 150, say 37, and starting from house number 37, select every 15th house. See also **MULTI-STAGE SAMPLING** and **STRATIFIED SAMPLING**.

TRIANGULATION

involves using more than one methodology and more than one **TOOL** to collect data so that results can be confirmed through more than one data source.

TOOLS

instruments for collecting information that involve established procedures, for example, a questionnaire or a language proficiency test.

VALIDITY

a **TOOL** or test has validity if it actually measures what we design it to measure and not something else unexpectedly. See also **RELIABILITY**.

VARIABLE (DATA)

See **CONTINUOUS VARIABLE**, **CONTROL VARIABLE**, **DEPENDENT VARIABLE**, **DISCRETE VARIABLE**, **INDEPENDENT VARIABLE**, and **INTERVENING VARIABLE**.

VARIABLE (SOCIOLINGUISTIC)

parts of language which vary depending on the social context. Variables are influenced by social factors such as whether or not certain phonemes are pronounced such as the [h] at the start of the word *hotel*.

VITALITY

the commitment and availability of resources to the users of a **HERITAGE LANGUAGE** to maintain their language.

REFERENCES

Araali, B. B. 2011. Perceptions of Reaearch assistants on how their research participants view informed consent and its documentation in Africa. *Research Ethics* June 7:39–50.

Aronin, L., and D. Singleton. 2008. Multingualism as a new lingusitic dispensation. *International Journal of Multilingualism* 5(1):1-16.

Ashmore, M. 1989. *The reflexive thesis.* Chicago: University of Chicago Press.

Babajide, A. 2001. Language attitude patterns of Nigerians. In H. Igboanusi and I. Ohia (eds.), 1–13.

Backstrom, P. C. 1992. Balti. In P. C. Backstrom and C. F. Radloff (eds.), *Languages of northern areas*, Volume 2, 3–30. Islamabad: National Institute of Pakistan Studies and Summer Institute of Linguistics.

Baker, C. 1985. *Aspects of bilingualism in Wales.* Clevedon: Multilingual Matters.

Baker, C. 1988. *Key issues in bilingualism and bilingual education.* Clevedon: Multilingual Matters.

Baker, C. 1992. *Attitudes and language.* Clevedon: Multilingual Matters.

Beacco, J.-C. 2005. *Languages and language repertoires: Plurilingualism as a way of life in Europe.* Strasbourg: Council of Europe.

Bergman, T., ed. 1989. *Survey reference manual.* Dallas: Summer Institute of Linguistics.

Bergman, T. G. 2001. To test comprehension of a translation by those of a different speech. *Notes on Sociolinguistics* 6(3):89–92.

Betancourt, H., and B. Weiner. 1982. Attributions for achievement-related events, expectancy, and sentiments: A study of success and failure in Chile and the United States. *Journal of Cross-Cultural Psychology* 13(3):362–374.

Blackledge, A. 2004. Constructions of identity in political discourse in multilingual Britain. In A. Pavelenko and A. Blackledge (eds.), *Negotiation of identities in multilingual contexts,* 68–92. Clevedon: Multilingual Matters.

Blair, F. 1990. *Survey on a shoestring: A manual for small-scale language surveys.* Dallas: Summer Institute of Linguistics and University of Texas at Arlington.

Bourhis, R. Y., H. Giles, and D. Rosenthal. 1981. Notes on the construction of a "Subjective Vitality Questionnaire" for ethnolinguistic groups. *Journal of Multilingual and Multicultural Development* 2(2):145–155.

Briggs, C. 1986. *Learning how to ask: A sociolinguistic appraisal of the role of the interview in social science research.* Cambridge: Cambridge University Press.

Brown, H. D. 2000. *Principles of language learning and teaching.* White Plains, N.Y.: Addison Wesley Longman.

Campbell, L. 2000. *Historical linguistics* , Second edition. Cambridge, Mass.: The MIT Press.

Campbell, L., and W. Poser. 2008. *Language classification: History and method.* Cambridge: Cambridge University Press.

Canut, C. 2002. Perceptions of language in the Mandingo Region of Mali. In D. R. Preston (ed.), *Handbook of perceptual dialectology,* 31–39. Amsterdam: Benjamins.

Casad, E. 1974. *Dialect intelligibility testing.* Norman: Summer Institute of Linguistics of the University of Oklahoma.

Chambers, R. 1997. *Whose reality counts?: Putting the first last.* London: Intermediate Technology Publications.

Chomsky, N. 2002. *Syntactic structures*, Second edition. Berlin: Mouton de Gruyter.

Clyne, M. 1997. Multilingualism. In F. Coulmas (ed.), *The handbook of sociolinguistic*, 301–315. Oxford: Blackwell.

Coste, D., and D.-L. Simon. 2009. The plurilingual social actor: Language, citizenship, and education. *International Journal of Multilingualis* 6(2):168–185.

Coulmas, F. 2005. *Sociolinguistics: The study of speaker's choices.* Cambridge: Cambridge University Press.

Crystal, D. 1985. *A dictionary of linguistics and phonetics.* New York: Basil Blackwell.

Crystal, D. 2002. *Language death.* Cambridge: Cambridge University Press.

Decker, K. 1992. *Sociolinguistic survey of Northern Pakistan.* Accessed 2009, from SIL Sociolinguistics Publications: http://www.sil.org/sociolx/pubs/abstract.asp?id=32850.

Denzin, N. K. 2006. *Sociological methods : A sourcebook*, Fifth edition. New Brunswick: Transaction Publishers.

Dorian, N. 1981. *Language death: The life cycle of a Scottish Gaelic dialect.* Philadephia: University of Pennsylvania Press.

Dörnyei, Z. 2005. *The psychology of the language learner.* London: Routledge.

Duranti, A. 1997. *Linguistic anthropology.* Cambridge: Cambridge University Press.

Edwards, J. 1985. *Language, society, and identity.* Oxford: Basil Blackwell.

Edwards, J. 1994. *Multilingualism.* London: Routledge.

Edwards, J. 2002. Forlorn hope? In L. Wei, J.-M. Dewaele, and A. Housen (eds.), *Opportunities and challenges of bilingualism*, 25–44. Berlin: Mouton de Gruyter.

Fasold, R. 1984. *The sociolinguistics of society.* Oxford: Blackwell.

Ferguson, C. 1959. Diglossia. *Word* 15:325–340.

Fink, A. 2002. *The survey kit*, Second edition. Thousand Oaks, Calif.: Sage Publications.

Fishman, J. 1967. Bilingualism with and without diglossia; diglossia with and without bilingualism. *Journal of Social Issues* 32(2):29–38.

Fishman, J. 1991. *Reversing language shift.* Clevedon: Multilingual Matters.

Fishman, J. 1999. Sociolinguistics. In J. A. Fishman (ed.), *Language and ethnic identity*, 152–163. Oxford: Oxford University Press.

Fishman, J. 2001. Who speaks what language to whom and when? In L. Wei (ed.), *The bilingualism reader*, 89–110. New York: Routledge.

Foley, W. A. 1997. *Anthroplogical linguistics: An introduction.* Chichester: Wiley-Blackwell.

Fowler, F. J., Jr. 2009. *Survey research methods*, Fourth edition. Beverly Hills: Sage Publications.

Gallois, C., B. Watson, and M. Brabant. 2009. Attitudes to language and communication. In M. Hellinger, and A. Pauwels (eds.), *Handbook of language and communication*, 595–618. Berlin: Mouton de Gruyter.

Gardiner, R. C. 2001. Integrative motivation and second language acquisition. In Z. Dörnyei , and R. Schmidt (eds.), *Motivation and second language acquisition*, 1–20. Honolulu: University of Hawaii Press.

Garett, P., N. Coupland, and A. Williams. 2003. *Investigating language attitudes: Social meanings of dialect, ethnicity, and performance.* Cardiff: University of Wales Press.

Giles, H. 1977. *Language, ethnicity, and intergroup relations.* London: Academic Press.

Goldsmith, M., and M. Wharton. 2004. *Knowing me, knowing you: Exploring personality type and temperament.* London: SPCK Publishing.

Gooskens, C. 2007. The contribution of linguistic factors to intelligibility of closely related languages. *Journal of Multilingual and Multicultural Development* 28(6):445–467.

Grimes, B. 1992. Notes on oral proficiency testing (SLOPE). In E. Casad (ed.), *Windows on bilingualism*, 53–60. Dallas: Summer Institute of Linguistics and the University of Texas at Arlington.

Grimes, B. F. 1985. Language attitudes: Identity, distinctiveness, survival in the Vaupés. *Journal of Multilingual and Multicultural Development* 6:389–401.

Grimes, B. F. 1987. The SIL second language oral proficiency evaluation. *Notes on Linguistics* 40.

Grimes, J. E. 1995. *Language survey reference guide.* Dallas: Summer Institute of Linguistics.

Grin, F. 1999. Economics. In J. A. Fishman (ed.), *Handbook of language and ethnic identity*, 9–24. Oxford: Oxford University Press.

Grosjean, F. 2008. *Studying bilinguals.* Oxford: Oxford University Press.

Haspelmath, M., and U. Tadmor. 2009. *Loanwords in the world's languages: A comparative handbook.* The Hague: Mouton De Gruyter.

Hatch, E. M., and A. Lazaraton. 1991. *The research manual: Design and statistics for applied linguistics.* New York: Newbury House.

Hatch, E., and H. Farhady. 1982. *Research design and statistics.* Rowley: Newbury House Publishers.

Headland, T. 2004. Basketballs for bows and arrows: Deforestatioin and Agta culture change. *Cultural Survival Quarterly* 28(2):41–44.

Heller, M. 2006. Code switching and the politics of language. In L. Wei (ed.), *The bilingualism reader*, Second edition, 163–176. London: Routledge.

Himmelmann, N. P. 2006. Language documentation: What is it and what is it good for? In J. Gippert, N. P. Himmelmann, and U. Mosel (eds.), *Essentials of language documentation*, 1–30. Berlin: Mouton de Gruyter.

Hinnenkamp, V. 2005. Semilingualism, double monolingualism, and blurred genres—on (not) speaking a legitimate language. *Journal of Social Science Education* 1.

Holmes, J. 2008. *An introduction to sociolinguistics*, Third edition. London: Longman.

Huberman, A. M., and M. G. Miles. 2006. *The qualitative researcher's companion.* Thousand Oaks: Sage Publications.

Hymes, D. 1968. The ethnography of speaking. In J. Fishman (ed.), *Readings in the sociology of language*, 99–138. The Hague: Mouton.

Hymes, D., M. Swadesh, and J. Sherzer. 1971. *The origin and diversification of language.* Chicago: Atheron Aldine.

Igboanusi, H., and I. Ohia. 2001. Language conflict in Nigeria: The perspective of ethnic minorities. In H. Igboanusi (ed.), *Language attitude and language conflict in West Africa*, 125–142. Ibadan: Enicrownfit Publishers.

Ihemere, K. U. 2006. An integrated approach to the study of language attitudes and change in Nigeria: The case of the Ikwerre of Port Harcourt City. *Selected Proceedings of the 36th Annual Conference on African Proceedings Project.*

Johnstone, B. 2000. *Qualitative methods in sociolinguistics.* Oxford: Oxford University Press.

Jones, G., and R. Jones. 2002. *Teamwork: How to build relationships*, Second edition. London: Scripture Union.

Joseph, B. D., J. Stephano, N. G. Jacobs, and I. Lehiste, eds. 2003. *When languages collide: Perspectives on language conflict, competition, and language coexistence.* Columbus: Ohio State University.

Karan, M. E., and J. Stalder. 2000. Assessing motivations: Techniques for researching the motivations behind language choice. In G. Kindell, and M. P. Lewis (eds.), *Assessing ethnolinguistic vitality: Theory and practice.* Dallas: SIL International.

Kindell, G. E. 1991. *Proceedings of the Summer Institute of Linguistics International Language Assessment Conference.* Dallas: Summer Institute of Linguistics.

Kloss, H., and G. D. McConnell. 1974. *Composition linguistique des nations du monde.* Laval: Centre International de Recherché sur le Bilinguisme.

Kosonen, K. 2005. The role of language in learning: What does international research say? In *First Language First: Community-based Literacy Programmers for Minority Language Contexts in Asia.* Bangkok: UNESCO.

Kosonen, K., C. Young, and S. Malone. 2007. *Promoting literacy in multilingual settings.* Bangkok: UNESCO Bangkok.

Kulick, D. 1992. *Language shift and cultural reproduction: Socialisation, self, and syncretism in a Papua New Guinean village.* Cambridge: Cambridge University Press.

Kumar, S. 2002. *Methods for community participation: A complete guide for practitioners.* London: ITDG.

Labov, W. 2001. *Language in society 29: Principles of linguistic change*, Volume 2: Social factors. Malden, Mass.: Blackwell Publishers.

Landweer, M. L. 2009. *Use of the Recorded Text Test in Papua New Guinea: Some initial thoughts.* unpublished paper.

Landweer, M. L. 2010. Land-language link. In K. A. McElhanon, and G. Reesink (eds.), *A mosaic of languages and cultures: Studies celebrating the career of Karl J Franklin*, 351–380. Dallas: SIL International.

Larson, M. 1984. *Meaning-based translation: A guide to cross-language equivalence.* Lanham: University Press of America.

Le Page, R. B. 1997. *The evolution of a sociolinguistic theory of language,* F. Coulmas, ed. Oxford: Blackwell.

Lewis, M. P. 2009. *Ethnologue: Languages of the world,* Sixteenth edition. Dallas: SIL International.

Lewis, M. P., and G. F. Simons. 2010. Assessing endangerment: Expanding Fishman's GIDS. *Romanian Review of Linguistics* 55(2):103–120.

Lightbown, P. M., and N. Spada. 1999. *How languages are learned,* Second edition. Oxford: Oxford University Press.

Lightfoot, D. 2006. *How new languages emerge.* Cambridge: Cambridge University Press.

Lockwood, W. B. 1972. *A panorama of Indo-European languages.* London: Hutchinson.

Loving, R., and G. F. Simons, eds. 1977. Language variation and survey techniques. *Workpapers in Papua New Guinean Languages 21.* Ukarumpa: Summer Institute of Linguistics.

Luycx, A. 2003. Weaving languages together: Family language policy and gender socialization in bilingual Aymara households. In R. Bayley, and S. R. Schecter (eds.), *Language socialization in bilingual and multilingual societies,* 25–43. Clevedon: Multilingual Matters.

Makoni, S., and A. Pennycook. 2006. *Disinventing and reconstituting languages.* Clevedon: Multilingual Matters.

Marshall, J. 2004. *Language change and sociolinguistics: Rethinking social networks.* Basingstoke: Palgrave Macmillan.

McMahon, A., and R. McMahon. 2005. *Language classification by numbers.* Oxford: Oxford University Press.

Milroy, L. 1987. *Observing and analysing natural language: A critical account of sociolinguistic method,* Second edition. Oxford: Basil Blackwell.

Mishler, E. G. 1986. *Research interviewing: Context and narrative.* Cambridge, Mass.: Harvard University Press.

Mohsin, A. 2003. Language, Identity, and the State in Bangladesh. In S. Ganguly, and M. E. Brown (eds.), *Fighting words: Language policy and ethnic relations in Asia,* 81–104. Cambridge, Mass.: MIT Press.

Moore, M. 2010. *Air passengers 'more trusting of pilots who sound posh'.* Accessed March 29, 2010, http://www.telegraph.co.uk/travel/travelnews/7532922/Air-passengers-more-trusting-of-pilots-who-sound-posh.html.

Myers-Scotton, C. 2002. *Contact linguistics: Bilingual encounters and grammatical outcomes.* Oxford: Oxford University Press.

Nahhas, R. 2007. *The steps of language survey: An outline of practical methods.* Chiang Mai.

Nash, J. E. 1987. Policy and practice in the American Sign Language community. *IJSL* 68:7–22.

Norman, D. A. 1976. *Memory and attention: An introduction to human information processing.* Second edition. New York: John Wiley & Sons.

O'Leary, C. F. 1994. The role of Recorded Text Tests in intelligibility assessment and language program decisions. *Notes on Literature in Use and Language Programs* 48–72.

Ochs, E. 2002. Becoming a speaker of culture. In C. J. Kramsch (ed.), *Language acquisition and language socialization: Ecological perspectives,* 99–121. London: Continuum Press.

Ochs, E., and B. B. Schieffelin. 2009. Language acquisition and socialization: Three developmental stories and their implications. In A. Duranti (ed.), *Linguistic anthropology: A reader,* 296–328. Chichester: Wiley-Blackwell.

Ogunsiji, Y. 2001. A sociolinguistic study of the language attitude in market transaction. In H. Igboanusi (ed.), *Language attitude and language conflict in West Africa,* 68–95. Ibadan: Enicrownfit Publishers.

ÓLaoire, M. 2008. The language planning situation in Ireland: An update 2005–2007. In R. B. Kaplan, and R. B. Baldau (eds.), *Language planning and policy in Europe: The Baltic States, Ireland, and Italy,* 256–261. Clevedon: Multilingual Matters.

Orlich, D. C. 1978. *Designing sensible surveys.* Pleasantville, N.Y.: Redgrave Publishing Company.

Oshima, A., and A. Hogue. 2006. *Writing academic English,* Fourth edition. White Plains, N.Y.: Pearson/Longman.

Padilla, A. M. 1999. Psychology. In J. A. Fishman (ed.), *Handbook of language and ethnic identity,* 109–121. Oxford: Oxford University Press.

Pavelenko, A., and A. Blackledge. 2004. *Negotiation of identities in multilingual contexts.* Clevedon: Multilingual Matters.

Pease-Alvarez, L. 2003. Transforming perspectives on bilingual language socialization. In R. Bayley, and S. R. Schecter (eds.), *Language socialization in bilingual and multilingual societies,* 9–24. Clevedon: Multilingual Matters.

Peter, L., and H.-G. Wolf. 2001. Aku in the Gambia: Terminological problems, functional distrubution, and popular attitude. In H. Igboanusi (ed.), *Language attitude and language conflict in West Africa,* 96–104. Ibadan: Enicrownfit Publishers.

Radloff, C. 1991. *Sentence repetition method for studies in community bilingualism.* Dallas: Summer Institute of Linguistics and the University of Texas at Arlington.

Roembke, L. 2000. *Building credible multicultural teams.* Pasadena, Calif.: William Carey Library.

Romaine, S. 2000. *Language in society: An introduction to sociolinguistics,* Second edition. Oxford: Oxford University Press.

Rubin, A., and E. R. Babbie. 2010. *Research methods for social work,* Seventh edition. Pacific Grove: Brooks Cole.

Sadembouo, E. 1989. Constitution and function of a language committee and the choice of a reference dialect. In T. Bergman (ed.), *Proceedings of the Roundtable on Assuring the Feasibility of Standardization within Dialect Chains,* 10–33. Nairobi: Summer Institute of Linguistics.

Sanders, J. 1977. On defining the center of a linguistic group. *Workpapers in Papua New Guinea Languages* 21:263–294.

Saville-Troike, M. 1982. *The ethnography of communication.* Oxford: Blackwell.

Scheiffelin, B. B. 1990. *The give and take of everyday life: Language socialization of Kaluli children.* Cambridge: Cambridge University Press.

Schmidt, C. D. 2006. *My church—my language? Language attitudes and language policy in a South African church.* Leipzig: Institut fur Afrikanistik, Universitat Leipzig.

Showalter, C. J. 1991. Getting what you asked for: A study of sociolinguistic survey questionnaires. In G. E. Kindell (ed.), *Proceedings of the Summer Institute of Linguistics International Language Assessment Conference,* 302–325.

Showalter, S. 2001. *The same but different: Language use and attitudes in four communities of Burkina Faso.* Dallas: SIL International.

Simons, G. F. 1977. The role of purpose and perspective in planning a language survey. In R. E. Loving and G. F. Simons (eds.), *Workpapers in Papua New Guinea Languages 21.*

Spradley, J. 1980. *Participant observation.* New York: Holt, Rinehart and Winston.

Truong, C. L., and L. Garcez. 2009. Participatory methods for language documentation and conservation: Building community awareness and engagement. *1st International Conference on Language Documentation and Conservation.* Manoa: University of Hawaii.

UNESCO Ad Hoc Expert Group on Endangered Languages. 2003. *Language vitality and endangerment.* Paris: UNESCO.

Wandruszka, M. 1979. *Die mehrsprachigkeit des menschen.* Munich: Piper.

Wardhaugh, R. 2009. *An introduction to sociolinguistics,* Sixth edition. Oxford: John Wiley & Sons.

Wolfram, W., and N. Schilling-Estes. 2006. *American English: Dialects and variation,* Second edition. Oxford: Basil Blackwell.

Wurm, S. 2001. *Atlas of the world's languages in danger of disappearing.* UNESCO Publishing.

Yamada, R.-M. 2007. Collaborative linguistic fieldwork: Practical application of the empowerment model. *Language Documentation and Conservation,* 257–282.

INDEX